Artificial Intelligence and Machine Learning for Real-World Applications

This book introduces foundational and advanced concepts in artificial intelligence (AI) and machine learning (ML), focusing on their real-world applications and societal implications. Covering topics from knowledge representation and model interpretability to deep learning and generative AI, *Artificial Intelligence and Machine Learning for Real-World Applications: A Beginner's Guide with Case Studies* includes practical Python implementations and case studies from healthcare, agriculture, and education. Beginning with core concepts such as AI fundamentals, knowledge representation, and statistical techniques, the text gradually advances to cover ML algorithms, deep learning architectures, and the basics of generative AI. Detailed discussions of data preprocessing, model training, evaluation metrics, and Python-based implementation make this book both practical and accessible.

- Offers real-world examples and case studies illustrating the societal impact and practical applications of AI and ML technologies
- Discusses data preprocessing techniques, model selection, and evaluation metrics with practical implementation in Python and in detail
- Explores AI problem-solving processes, knowledge representation, and model training strategies, catering to readers with varying levels of technical expertise
- Covers AI and ML principles spanning statistical techniques, ML algorithms, deep learning structures, and generative AI basics
- Focuses on societal applications in healthcare, agriculture, and education, addressing challenges faced by the elderly and special needs individuals

This book is for professionals, researchers, and scholars interested in the applications of AI and ML.

Artificial Intelligence and Machine Learning for Real-World Applications

A Beginner's Guide with Case Studies

Latesh Malik, Sandhya Arora, and Urmila Shrawankar

CRC Press
Taylor & Francis Group
Boca Raton London New York

CRC Press is an imprint of the
Taylor & Francis Group, an **informa** business

A CHAPMAN & HALL BOOK

First edition published 2026
by CRC Press
2385 NW Executive Center Drive, Suite 320, Boca Raton FL 33431

and by CRC Press
4 Park Square, Milton Park, Abingdon, Oxon, OX14 4RN

CRC Press is an imprint of Taylor & Francis Group, LLC

© 2026 Latesh Malik, Sandhya Arora, Urmila Shrawankar

ISBN: 978-1-032-87346-6 (hbk)
ISBN: 978-1-032-87345-9 (pbk)
ISBN: 978-1-003-53217-0 (ebk)

DOI: 10.1201/9781003532170

Typeset in Times
by Apex CoVantage, LLC

Contents

Preface

Artificial intelligence (AI) and machine learning (ML) are revolutionizing the way we interact with technology, solve complex problems, and make decisions across various domains. These technologies are not only shaping industries but also transforming our daily lives. From automating tasks and enhancing decision-making to advancing healthcare and education, AI and ML have far-reaching societal applications.

This book, *Artificial Intelligence and Machine Learning for Real-World Applications: A Beginner's Guide with Case Studies*, is designed to provide readers with a structured and in-depth understanding of AI and ML, covering both theoretical foundations and practical applications. The book is divided into twelve chapters, each focusing on the critical aspects of AI and its role in various sectors.

Chapter 1 begins with an overview of AI and ML, discussing their historical development, fundamental concepts, and key differences. This chapter explores the evolution of AI from rule-based systems to modern deep learning models. It also introduces various AI paradigms, including symbolic AI, statistical AI, and connectionist AI, along with an overview of major AI applications in today's world.

Chapter 2 is the core of AI. This chapter delves into various search algorithms and strategies used in AI to solve complex problems efficiently. It covers uninformed search techniques such as breadth-first search and depth-first search, as well as informed search techniques like A* and heuristic-based searches. Additionally, the chapter discusses constraint satisfaction problems and optimization methods used in AI-driven solutions.

Chapter 3 discusses structured knowledge representation for reasoning and decision-making. It explores different representation techniques, including semantic networks, frames, ontologies, and first-order logic. It also discusses expert systems and their applications, shedding light on how AI models store and retrieve information effectively.

Chapter 4 introduces ML, different types of data, and their importance in training ML models. Preprocessing of data, removal of noise, missing data handling, data transformation, feature engineering, and dimensionality reduction of data are covered in this chapter. Preprocessing techniques are explained with snippets of code for real-life application.

Chapter 5 covers key supervised learning algorithms, including linear regression, logistic regression, decision trees, support vector machines (SVMs), naive Bayes classifier, cross validation, and hyperparameter tuning. All techniques are explained with snippets of code for practical applications such as spam detection, fraud detection, and medical diagnosis, which are discussed to illustrate real-world use cases. Code snippets of algorithms are also given at relevant places.

Chapter 6 explains clustering, k-means, and hierarchical and DBSCAN clustering. It also discusses the association rule mining concept, the a priori algorithm and its example, and Python code snippets.

Chapter 7 discusses neural networks and convolutional neural networks and its variants. Activation, loss, and regularization functions used in deep learning are covered here, along with some case studies that demonstrate how to program these functions in Python.

Chapter 8 introduces generative AI. It starts with the basic architecture of large language models (LLMs), basic LLMs, and its components. It explains the functionality of generative adversarial networks. Retrieval augmentation generation is discussed using a flowchart of activities. The use of transfer learning is also discussed.

Chapter 9 presents AI, which has many useful applications that ease human life. Everyone's health is an essential and highest priority concern. Therefore, the help of technology in such an important part of life is very important. AI does it. It provides many tools for the healthcare domain with the highest speed, accuracy, and comfort. These tools are not only helping everyday people, but they are also assisting physicians and medical professionals in a true sense.

Chapter 10 explains that nowadays agriculture is not only for farming and growing grains, fruits, and vegetables, but also for much more. It starts from checking the quality of soil, source of water, prediction, growth of plants, marketing of products, and finding distributors, to getting global recognition, and much more. Agriculture is not just a farmer's job, and technology is especially essential in helping farmers do these tasks and make some profit. AI plays a very important role in this sector. The inclusion of such AI technologies in agriculture will create a sustainable future and growth in the economy for farmers, especially in rural areas with many challenges.

Chapter 11 elaborates how AI helps in transforming the education system. Nowadays learning in only a physical environment has totally changed. AI has helped enhance facilities and made these facilities available to everyone. This chapter provides a complete knowledge of AI-driven approaches for learning in a different environment.

Chapter 12 provides complete details of how to create a quality life at any age or with any physical disability. AI provides new opportunities and solutions, which may help users perform everyday tasks with more ease and independence.

Acknowledgments

This book is the outcome of curiosity, queries from students, our lecture notes, our lab work, and our lab material. We have been associated with this subject matter for more than 7 years through our research work, lectures, workshops, and seminars.

Many professionals have helped write this book. We take this opportunity to thank the mentors, teachers, and friends for motivating us throughout this journey.

The authors thank all the students who motivated them by asking them the right questions at the appropriate time. Without their help with queries and curiosity, the idea of writing this book would never have occurred.

The authors also thank the principal at and colleagues in the Department of Computer Science and Engineering, MKSSS's Cummins College of Engineering for Women, Pune; Government College of Engineering, Nagpur; and Ramdeobaba University, Nagpur for supporting them and molding this work. The authors acknowledge the support of the reviewers who helped them through their critical comments and creative suggestions, which eventually helped them improve the content of the book. Many of the ideas in this book come from statistics and related courses like data science and machine learning. The authors thank all the professors who helped and taught them the basic concepts of subjects. Thanks to the editorial team at CRC Press for their support and bringing the book to reality.

Finally, we would like to thank our family members for their support, good wishes, encouragement, and understanding while we wrote this book.

About the Authors

Latesh Malik is an associate professor and head of the Department of Computer Science and Engineering, Government College of Engineering, Nagpur, and chairman of the Board of Studies, Computer Engineering Related Branch Board, RTM Nagpur University (2022–2027). She earned her PhD (computer science and engineering) at Visvesvaraya National Institute of Technology in 2010; MTech (computer science and engineering) at Banasthali Vidyapith, Rajasthan; and BE (computer engineering) at the University of Rajasthan. Dr. Malik is a gold medalist in BE and MTech. She has more than 27 years of teaching experience. She is a life member of ISTE, CSI, and ACM and has published more than 160 papers in international journals and conferences. Dr. Malik is the recipient of two RPS and one MODROB by AICTE. She has guided 30+ PG projects, and 12 students have earned their PhDs under her guidance. She is the author of seven books published by University Press, India, and CRC Press, USA.

Sandhya Arora is a full professor in the Department of Computer Engineering, Cummins College of Engineering for Women, Pune. She earned her PhD (computer science and engineering) from Jadavpur University, Kolkata, in 2012; MTech (computer science and engineering) from Banasthali Vidyapith, Rajasthan; and BE (computer engineering) from the University of Rajasthan, India. She has 27+ years of teaching experience. She is a life member of ISTE, CSI, and ACM. She has contributed more than 60 research publications and authored seven books with University Press, India, and CRC Press, USA.

Urmila Shrawankar, PhD, is a professor and director, School of Computer Science and Engineering, Ramdeobaba University, Nagpur (MS), India. She is a recipient of many awards and grants. She is the author of 2 books, editor of 4 books and 25 book chapters, and has published approximately 200 research papers in international journals and conferences of high repute. Also, Dr. Shrawankar has 8 granted and 10 published patents as well as 20 registered copyrights. She is the editor-in-chief, an editorial board member and a member, and is on the international advisory board of many journals. Moreover, she serves as a reviewer for many refereed journals and reputed conferences. Dr. Shrawankar participated in many international conferences worldwide as a core organizing committee member, technical program committee member, special session chair, and session chair. She is a member of IEEE (SM), ACM (SM), CSI (LM), ISTE (LM), IE (LM), and IAENG. She was published in the Marquis Who's Who.

1 Introduction to Artificial Intelligence and Machine Learning

1.1 INTRODUCTION

Artificial intelligence (AI) is a multidisciplinary field of computer science that aims to create intelligent machines capable of mimicking human cognitive functions. These functions encompass a wide range of capabilities, including the following:

1. **Learning:** The ability to acquire knowledge and skills from experience.
2. **Reasoning:** Using logic to draw inferences and make decisions.
3. **Problem-solving:** Finding solutions to complex issues.
4. **Perception:** Interpreting and understanding sensory inputs (visual, auditory, etc.).
5. **Natural language processing (NLP):** Understanding, interpreting, and generating human language.
6. **Planning:** Devising strategies to achieve goals.
7. **Creativity:** Generating novel ideas or artifacts.
8. **Emotional intelligence:** Recognizing and responding to human emotions.

AI can be categorized into two main types:

Narrow or Weak AI is designed to perform specific tasks within a limited domain. Examples include voice assistants such as Siri, Alexa, and Google Assistant, recommendation systems, and spam filters.

General or Strong AI/Artificial General Intelligence (AGI) is a hypothetical AI with human-like cognitive abilities across various domains. No examples are known yet as it is a theoretical concept that is still mainly in research.

Machine learning (ML), a subset of AI, focuses on the development of algorithms and statistical models that enable computer systems to improve their performance on a specific task through experience. Unlike traditional programming where rules are explicitly coded, ML algorithms learn patterns from data to make predictions or decisions without being explicitly programmed. ML can be broadly classified into three categories:

1. Supervised Learning: The algorithm learns from labeled data to make predictions or decisions.
2. Unsupervised Learning: The algorithm identifies patterns in unlabeled data.
3. Reinforcement Learning: The algorithm learns through interaction with an environment, receiving feedback in the form of rewards or penalties.

DOI: 10.1201/9781003532170-1

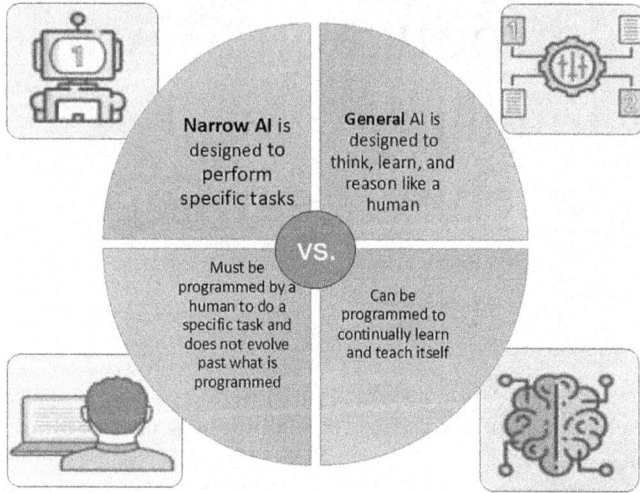

FIGURE 1.1   Narrow AI versus General AI.

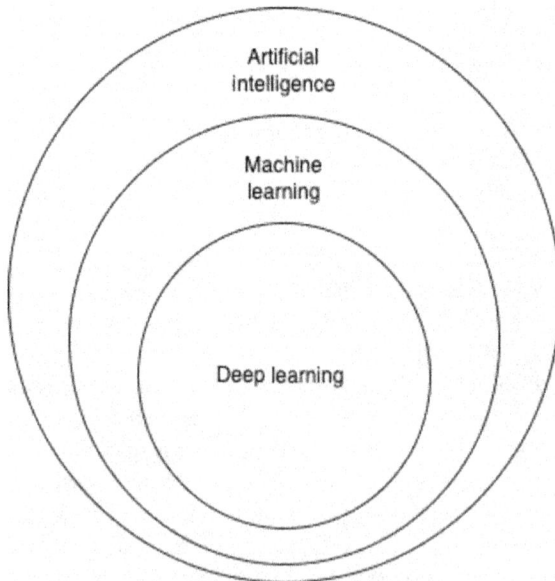

FIGURE 1.2   AI, ML, and Deep Learning Subsets.

Deep learning (DL) is a subset of ML that uses artificial neural networks with multiple layers to learn and represent complex patterns in data. It excels at tasks like image recognition, speech processing, and natural language understanding. DL models can automatically learn hierarchical features from raw data, often outperforming traditional ML techniques on complex tasks.

Natural language processing (NLP) focuses on the interaction between computers and human language. It combines computational linguistics, ML, and DL to enable computers to understand, interpret, and generate human language. NLP powers applications like machine translation, sentiment analysis, chatbots, and text summarization.

Large language models (LLMs) are a recent advancement in AI, positioned at the intersection between DL and NLP. These are massive neural networks trained on vast amounts of text data, capable of understanding and generating human-like text. LLMs like generative pre-trained transformer (GPT) models have shown remarkable capabilities in tasks ranging from text completion to answering questions and even basic reasoning.

Conversational AI (Conv. AI) refers to technologies that allow machines to engage in human-like dialog. It typically combines ML and NLP and may incorporate DL and LLMs. Conv. AI systems can understand context, maintain coherent conversations, and perform tasks based on user input. Applications include virtual assistants, customer service chatbots, and interactive voice response systems.

1.1.1 KEY COMPONENTS OF AI

The key components of AI include ML, NLP, computer vision, robotics, and expert systems. These components work together to enable machines to perform complex tasks.

1.1.2 BRANCHES OF AI

- **ML:** Algorithms that enable computers to learn from data.
- **NLP:** Techniques for understanding and generating human language.
- **Computer Vision:** Enabling machines to interpret and process visual information.
- **Robotics:** Designing intelligent robots that interact with the environment.
- **Expert Systems:** Systems that mimic the decision-making abilities of human experts.

1.1.3 FUNDAMENTAL PRINCIPLES OF ML

ML is a subset of AI focused on creating algorithms that allow machines to learn from and make decisions based on data.

1.1.4 TYPES OF ML

- **Supervised Learning:** Learning from labeled data (e.g., classification and regression).
- **Unsupervised Learning:** Finding patterns in unlabeled data (e.g., clustering and association).
- **Semi-supervised Learning:** Combines labeled and unlabeled data for training.
- **Reinforcement Learning:** Learning optimal actions through trial and error.

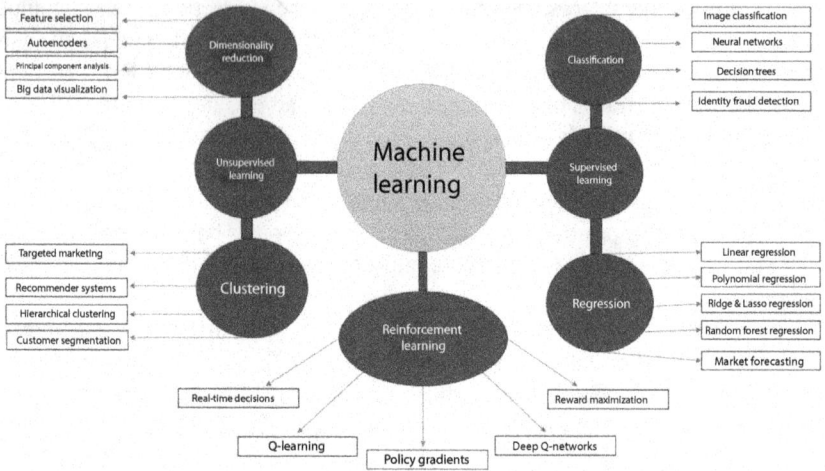

FIGURE 1.3   Different Tasks in ML.

Key Concepts in ML

- **Data:** The backbone of ML; quality and quantity of data impact model performance.
- **Model:** A mathematical representation of a process or system.
- **Training and Testing:** Training involves teaching the model using a dataset; testing evaluates its performance.
- **Overfitting and Underfitting:** Challenges related to model generalization.
- **Evaluation Metrics**: Common evaluation metrics include accuracy, precision, recall, F1 score, and confusion matrix.

1.1.5   KEY ALGORITHMS AND TECHNIQUES

1.1.5.1   Supervised Learning Algorithms

- **Linear Regression:** Predicting numerical values using a linear approach.
- **Logistic Regression:** Used for binary classification of problems.
- **Decision Trees:** Splitting data into branches to reach decisions.
- **Support Vector Machines (SVMs):** Finding the best boundary that separates classes.

1.1.5.2   Unsupervised Learning Algorithms

- **K-Means Clustering:** Partitioning data into clusters based on similarity.
- **Hierarchical Clustering:** Building a hierarchy of clusters.
- **Principal Component Analysis (PCA):** Reducing the dimensionality of data.

1.1.5.3   Reinforcement Learning Algorithms
- **Q-Learning:** Learning a policy for optimal actions.
- **Deep Q-Networks (DQNs):** Combining Q-learning with DL.

1.1.5.4   DL Techniques
- **Neural Networks:** Models inspired by the human brain.
- **Convolutional Neural Networks (CNNs):** Specialized for image processing.
- **Recurrent Neural Networks (RNNs):** Used for sequential data.

1.2   UNDERSTANDING AI: DEFINITION AND GOALS

1.2.1   WHAT IS AI?

Artificial intelligence, i.e., AI, sometimes also called machine intelligence, is the intelligence demonstrated by machines. AI is the science of making machines or systems that act like humans and think like humans. It can do things that are considered "smart."

AI is the wide-ranging branch of computer science that refers to the creation of computer systems, concerned with building smart machines capable of performing tasks that typically require human intelligence such as reasoning, decision-making, leaning, understanding and problem-solving.

AI is like teaching computers to think, behave, and make decisions like humans but with the help of algorithms and data. It is all about making machines smarter so they can do tasks that usually require human intelligence, such as understanding language, recognizing images, processing data, and solving problems. AI has a deep impact on human lives and the economy.

Example: In 2017, Hurricane Harvey devastated the seacoast of Texas. The storm caused wide flooding and damage, and it displaced thousands of people. In the wake of the storm, a platoon of experimenters from Google AI used AI to help with the relief efforts. They developed an AI-powered system that could dissect satellite imagery to identify areas that had been swamped. The system was suitable to identify swamped areas much more snappily and directly than traditional methods. The experimenters shared their system with the Federal Emergency Management Agency (FEMA), and FEMA used it to coordinate relief efforts. The system helped FEMA identify people who wanted to be saved and to deliver food and water to affected areas. This story shows how AI can be used to break real-world problems. AI can be used to dissect data snappily and directly, and it can be used to develop results to complex problems.

1.2.2   UNDERSTANDING AI

AI systems can perform tasks commonly associated with human cognitive functions or skills such as learning, self-correction, creativity, interpreting speech, and identifying patterns. Understanding AI involves grabbing the fundamental concepts, application, and implications of this most revolutionary and rapidly advancing field. AI systems typically learn how to do the tasks by processing the massive amount of data, identifying the patterns, etc. Understanding the capabilities of AI gives the means to capitalize on its potential, fueling progress and achieving breakthrough in various fields. AI is a dynamic and evolving field, and staying informed and engaged is essential to understanding its current state and future developments.

1.2.3 WEAK AND STRONG AI

There are two main approaches to AI: weak AI and strong AI. Strong AI is a more ambitious concept that suggests machines could achieve human-level intelligence and problem-solving abilities. Proponents of strong AI believe that computers, when properly programmed, could surpass human experts in certain tasks and even possess a form of consciousness. This view contrasts with the idea of AI as simply a tool for studying the human mind. John Searle is credited with coining the term "strong AI" to represent this hypothesis about the potential for machines to exhibit genuine reasoning and problem-solving skills.

Weak AI takes a more limited approach to AI. Unlike strong AI, it focuses on developing machines that excel at specific tasks rather than achieving human-level intelligence. Proponents of weak AI believe that while computers can be programmed to mimic some aspects of human thought processes, they are unlikely to ever truly replicate the full range of human cognitive abilities. Weak AI systems are valuable tools for solving specific problems, but they lack the general intelligence and adaptability found in humans. An illustrative example of weak AI is a chess program, which can make strategic moves based on complex algorithms but cannot understand the nuances of the game in the same way a human player can.

Strong AI delves into the philosophical question of whether machines can achieve true intelligence, indistinguishable from human thought. This school of thought proposes the possibility of building machines that replicate the full spectrum of human cognitive abilities, not just mimic them. However, achieving this level of AI poses significant challenges.

- **Experiential Gap:** A machine, unlike a human, wouldn't possess the vast repertoire of life experiences that shape human thought and decision-making. It wouldn't have encountered the complexities of emotions, values, and moral dilemmas that inform human cognition.
- **Embodied Intelligence:** Even if a machine's brain functioned similarly to that of a human, its physical embodiment could significantly differ. A robotic body with wheels instead of legs and sensors instead of eyes would perceive and interact with the world in fundamentally different ways, impacting its understanding.

These are just some of the hurdles that strong AI needs to overcome in its quest to create machines with human-level intelligence.

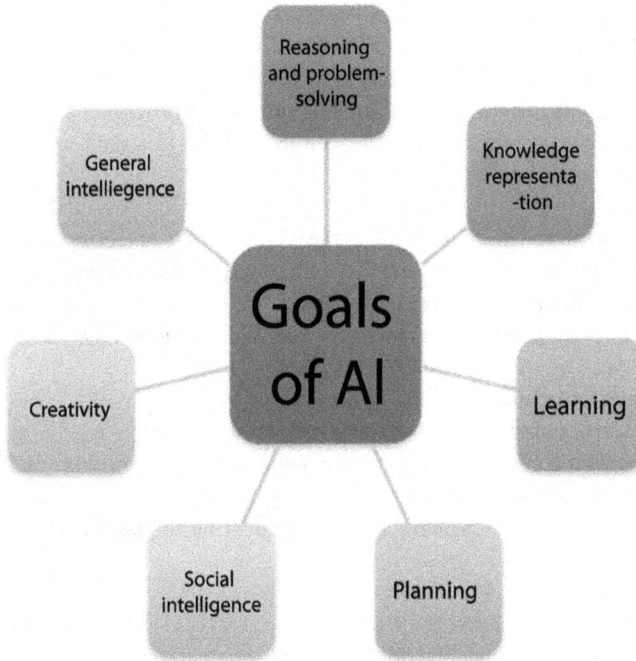

FIGURE 1.4 Goals of AI.

1.2.4 Goals of AI

As we know, AI is a field of innovation and technical advancement; therefore, it also has a vast area of application. The ultimate goal is to develop systems that can understand, learn, and adapt to diverse tasks and challenges, contributing to advancements in technology and transforming various industries.

The aim of AI is to develop technology that enables computers and machines to work intelligently and independently. Following are some essential goals of AI.

- **Reasoning and Problem-Solving**
  AI research places a strong focus on creating effective problem-solving algorithms capable of logical reasoning and simulating human thinking when dealing with complex puzzles. AI systems employ methods that handle uncertain situations and address the challenge of incomplete information.
- **Knowledge Representation**
  The primary goal of knowledge representation and engineering in AI is to facilitate the ability of machines to solve complex real-world problems. This can include tasks like medical diagnosis, natural language interaction, recommendation systems, and more.

- **Learning**

  Learning is a core element of AI solutions, involving the ability of computer algorithms to enhance an AI system's knowledge based on observations and past experiences. In practical terms, AI programs process sets of input–output pairs for specific functions and use this data to predict outcomes for new, unseen inputs.

- **Planning**

  Intelligent agents must possess the ability to set objectives and achieve them effectively. To do this, they need to envision future scenarios, creating a representation of the world's state, and predict the consequences of their actions. They should be capable of making decisions that maximize the utility or value of the available choices.

- **Social Intelligence**

  Affective computing, sometimes known as "emotion AI," constitutes a specific branch of AI that is concerned with the recognition, understanding, and emulation of human experiences, feelings, and emotions. Ongoing research efforts are oriented toward augmenting the social intelligence of machines.

- **Creativity**

  AI plays a crucial role in promoting creativity and improving human problem-solving. It has the ability to analyze vast amounts of data, explore multiple options, and come up with creative solutions that enhance our ability to perform tasks more effectively. For example, AI can offer a wide range of interior design possibilities for a 3D-rendered apartment layout, igniting creativity and enhancing the overall design experience.

- **General Intelligence**

  AI researchers are dedicated to the development of machines possessing general AI capabilities. The ultimate goal is to significantly enhance overall productivity, leading to more efficient task execution. Moreover, this progress can alleviate humans from participating in hazardous activities, such as bomb defusal, where AI systems can take on these tasks with lower risk.

1.3 HISTORY OF AI

The history of AI is a story of an integrated, challenging path full of breakthroughs. AI learns from experience, adjusts its processes based on what it learns, and uses the knowledge to achieve specific goals. Over time, it has gathered a vast amount of data and made a stronger impact on numerous fields, from marketing to space research, analyzing the important factors and providing better solutions. AI began to grow as an independent field of study in the 1940s and 1950s, when computers were gaining shape and structure in the commercial market for the first time.

The 1940s and 1950s mark the birth of AI. The origins of AI date back to the mid-20th century, when the foundations of the field were laid. In 1943, Warren McCulloch and Walter Pitts introduced a simple computational neuron model that could be recognized early for artificial neural networks. In 1950, Alan Turing published "The Turing Test," one of the first correspondences regarding the possibility of machine intelligence.

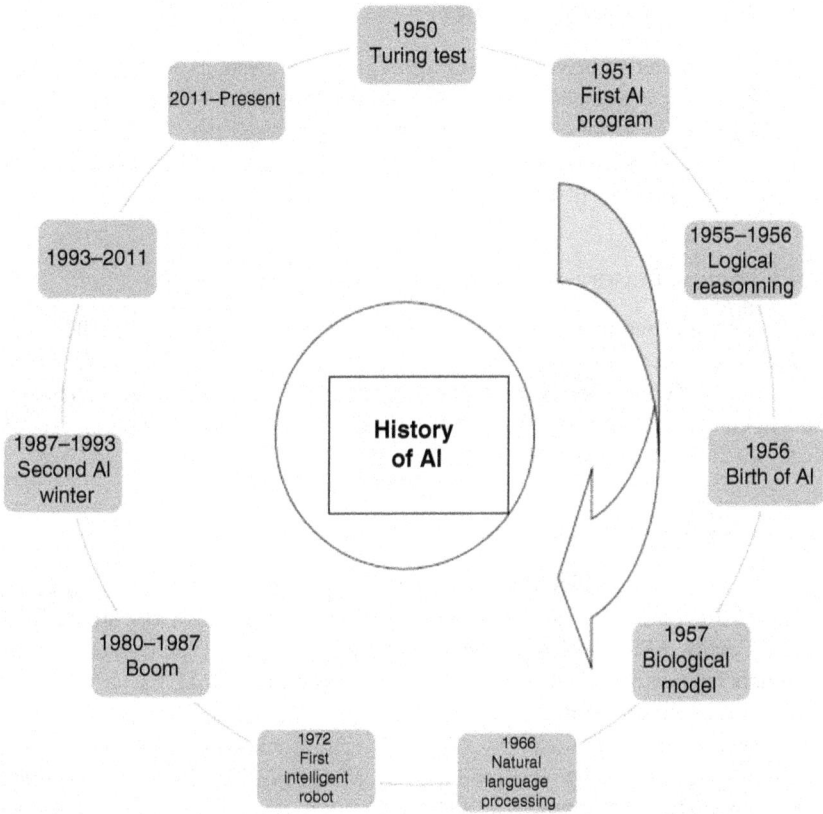

FIGURE 1.5 History of AI.

1.3.1 BIRTH OF AI (1950–1956)

During the 1940s and 1950s, scientists across various disciplines, including mathematics, psychology, engineering, economics, and political science, began exploring the concept of AI.

1.3.2 TURING TEST (1950)

A computer scientist and a British mathematician, Alan Turing developed the Turing test in 1950. The Turing test is a common method to test a machine's ability to exhibit human-like intelligence.

The basic idea of the Turing test is simple: a human judge has a case-based conversation with a human and a machine and then decides which of the two is considered human. The Turing test is widely used as a measure of progress in AI and has inspired much research and experimentation aimed at developing machines that can pass the test.

1.3.3   The First AI Program (1951)

In 1951, Christopher Strachey, a future director of the Systems Research Group at Oxford University, developed the first successful AI program. This program, known as Strachey Checkers, ran on a Ferranti Mark I computer at the University of Manchester and demonstrated the ability to play a complete game of checkers at a reasonable pace by the summer of 1952.

1.3.4   Logical Reasoning and Problem-Fixing (1955–1956)

Logical reasoning has been the cornerstone of AI research. A significant milestone in this area was the development of the Logic Theorist, a theorem-proving program created in 1955–1956 by Allen Newell, J. Clifford Shaw, and Herbert Simon. This program aimed to prove theorems from *Principia Mathematica*, a three-volume work by Alfred North Whitehead and Bertrand Russell.

1.3.5   Birth of AI (1956)

The term "artificial intelligence" was coined in the 1956 Dartmouth Conference, considered a pivotal event in the history of AI. The conference was organized by John McCarthy, Marvin Minsky, Nathaniel Rochester, and Claude Shannon, and researchers from various fields spoke about the possibilities of AI. Early AI research in this era focused on symbolic processes and problem-solving. One of the earliest AI frameworks in this era was the Logic Theorist framework developed by Allen Newell and J.C. McCarthy, and produced by McCarthy. The logician was able to prove mathematical hypotheses, and the framework is considered one of the first models of AI designs. The 1956 convention laid the groundwork for AI, but progress was slower than initially expected due to limitations in computing power and the difficulty in building intelligent machines. However, these limitations allowed for further research and development over the next decades.

1.3.6   1974

The programs developed in the years after the Dartmouth Conference were mere "miracles": for most people, computers solved algebraic word problems, expressed concepts in geometry, and learned English. At the time, few believed that machines performed such "intelligent" actions and these were at all possible. The researchers expressed great hope in the fields of privacy and publishing, predicting the development of intelligent machines completely in less than 20 years.

1.3.7   Biological Model (1957)

A landmark in the history of AI was the invention of perceptron by Frank Rosenblatt in 1957. Perceptron was the first artificial neuron triggered by biological processes in the human brain. It was designed to mimic the way the human brain processes sight and sound.

The perceptron was a simple algorithm capable of recognizing visual objects. It was used to process visual features and make decisions based on the information obtained. While the perceptron showed promise for solving simple problems, it was limited by the technology and computing power available at the time.

Systematics of the 1960s: The 1960s saw the development of computers that could emulate the decision-making abilities of experts around the world in specialized work. Dendral (pharmacological analysis) and MYCIN (medical opinion) are currently undergoing expert development.

1.3.8 NATURAL LANGUAGE PROCESSING (1966)

NLP dates back to the early days of AI research, i.e., the 1950s and 1960s. Early work in NLP focused on developing systems that could understand human speech and acquire it. One of the first influential programs was Newell and Simon's 1956 creation of the "logician," which could prove mathematical hypotheses. In the late 1950s and early 1960s, researchers began to investigate language translation and original text analysis. But great strides were made in NLP in the 1970s and 1980s when researchers began to develop more sophisticated algorithms for speech understanding and generation.

A notable achievement in this period is the first chatbot ELIZA developed by Joseph Weizenbaum in 1966, which can engage in simple natural language conversations.

1970s—Knowledge Representation*: In the 1970s, cognitive science focused on knowledge representation to clarify the knowledge and understanding of experts. High-level knowledge representation was also developed in management and semantic communication.

1.3.9 FIRST INTELLIGENT ROBOT (1972)

In Japan, Waseda University initiated the WABOT project in 1967 and in 1972 completed WABOT-1, the world's first "intelligent" humanoid robot, or an android that moves limbs using its hand and limb control system and can grab and move objects using its touch-sensitive hands. Its vision system was capable of measuring distance and direction using external receivers and artificial eyes and ears. Its dialog system was capable of communicating in Japanese, with facial expressions.

1.3.10 FIRST AI WINTER (1974–1980)

The term "AI summer" refers to a period of declining investment and interest in AI as R&D effort stagnates or declines. The first AI winter occurred in the 1970s and 1980s after an initial period of great anticipation and optimism about the prospects of AI in the 1950s and 1960s. During AI winter, progress in AI research was slower than expected, and some of the limitations of the existing technology became increasingly apparent. Many early AI programs failed to live up to the high expectations set by early AI pioneers. This has led to a decline in funding for AI research and public and commercial interest in the project.

The AI winter was a time of reflection and reassessment for the AI research community, resulting in a shift in focus to practical and achievable goals.

1.3.11   BOOM (1980–1987)

During the 1980s, the expert system framework gained widespread adoption by companies globally, and knowledge engineering became a central focus of AI research. Concurrently, the Japanese government significantly invested in AI through the Fifth Generation Computer Systems project. Another promising development of the era was the resurgence of neural network research, led by John Hopfield and David Rumelhart.

1.3.12   SECOND AI WINTER (1987–1993)

The financial crisis of the 1980s led to a decline in business interest in AI, as numerous companies encountered difficulties. However, despite the setbacks, the field of AI continued to advance. Researchers such as robotics pioneers Rodney Brooks and Hans Moravec advocated for a new approach to AI.

1990s—Reinvention and Machine Learning: In the 1990s, AI experienced a renaissance driven by advances in ML, neural networks, and NLP. The development of experts and expert shells enables the real work of AI in many practical ways.

1.3.13   AI (1993–2011)

Despite its long history of over half a century, the field of AI has recently made significant strides in achieving its original goals. However, within the business world, the reputation of AI is still perceived as less than perfect. This divide is evident within the field itself, where there is no consensus on why the initial ambition of creating human-level intelligence has yet to be fully realized. As a result, AI has splintered into various subfields, each focused on tackling specific problems or utilizing different approaches.

Deep Blue made history on May 11, 1997, when it defeated world chess champion Garry Kasparov, marking the first time a computer program had achieved such a feat. Developed by IBM, this specialized version of the framework was able to process a staggering 200 million moves per second, twice as many as it had in its initial loss against Kasparov. In another impressive display of technological advancement, a Stanford robot emerged victorious in the 2005 DARPA Grand Challenge by navigating a 131-mile uncharted desert trail without any human intervention.

2000s—Big Data and DL: The lack of big data and powerful computing gave rise to DL, leading to major advances in imaging, AI speech, and NLP.

2010s—AI Is Integrated into Daily Life: AI-powered tasks and machines, including virtual assistants, recommendations, and autonomous cars, became part of daily life. DL, driven by advances in neural networks and graphics processing units (GPUs), has revolutionized the field.

MAJOR EVENTS IN HISTORY OF AI

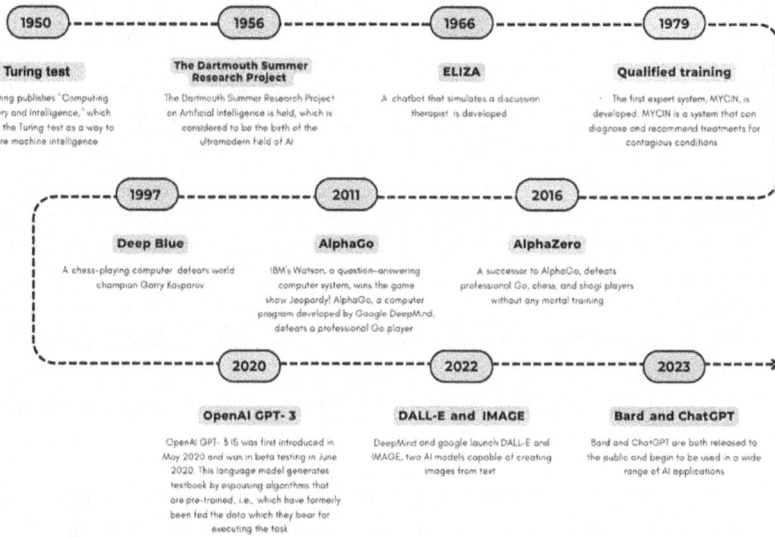

1950 - - - - - - - - - - - - - **1956** - - - - - - - - - - - - - **1966** - - - - - - - - - - - - - **1979** - - - - - - →

Turing test

Alan Turing publishes "Computing Machinery and Intelligence," which proposes the Turing test as a way to measure machine intelligence

The Dartmouth Summer Research Project

The Dartmouth Summer Research Project on Artificial Intelligence is held, which is considered to be the birth of the ultramodern field of AI

ELIZA

A chatbot that simulates a discussion therapist is developed

Qualified training

The first expert system, MYCIN, is developed. MYCIN is a system that can diagnose and recommend treatments for contagious conditions

1997 - - - - - - - - - - - - - **2011** - - - - - - - - - - - - - **2016** - - - - - - - - - - - - - →

Deep Blue

A chess-playing computer defeats world champion Garry Kasparov

AlphaGo

IBM's Watson, a question-answering computer system, wins the game show Jeopardy! AlphaGo, a computer program developed by Google DeepMind, defeats a professional Go player

AlphaZero

A successor to AlphaGo, defeats professional Go, chess, and shogi players without any mortal training

2020 - - - - - - - - - - - - - **2022** - - - - - - - - - - - - - **2023** - - - - - - →

OpenAI GPT- 3

OpenAI GPT- 3 is was first introduced in May 2020 and was in beta testing in June 2020. This language model generates textbook by espousing algorithms that are pre-trained, i.e., which have formerly been fed the data which they bear for executing the task

DALL-E and IMAGE

DeepMind and google launch DALL-E and IMAGE, two AI models capable of creating images from text

Bard and ChatGPT

Bard and ChatGPT are both released to the public and begin to be used in a wide range of AI applications

FIGURE 1.6   Major Events in History.

1.3.14   AI (2011–PRESENT)

During the early years of the 21st century, a significant breakthrough was made with the widespread availability of vast amount of data, commonly referred to as "big data." Coupled with increasingly affordable and efficient computers, as well as advancements in ML technology, this development proved to be highly effective in tackling various challenges across all sectors of the economy. In fact, as discussed in the renowned paper "Big data: The next frontier for innovation, competition, and productivity," as the demand for AI-related products, hardware, and software continued to grow, it reached a whopping 8 billion dollars in 2016, as reported by the New York Times, with the media even dubbing it a "frenzy."

2020s—Ethics and Business Governance: The 2020s will see increased communication on AI ethics, including AI algorithms and disruptive technologies and business injustice. Countries and organizations develop policies and procedures for the development and use of intelligence.

1.4   PROBLEMS AND TECHNIQUES IN AI

Problem-solving techniques in AI refer to the approaches and strategies used to address and solve complex problems or challenges in AI systems. These techniques are fundamental to AI's goal of simulating human-like problem-solving and decision-making abilities. Here's a definition of problem-solving techniques in AI:

> Problem-solving techniques in AI encompass a diverse set of methodologies and algorithms that enable AI systems to analyze, evaluate, and generate solutions for a wide range of problems. These techniques often involve the application of logical reasoning, optimization, search algorithms, and learning mechanisms to find efficient and effective solutions, ultimately contributing to the development of intelligent systems capable of tackling complex real-world challenges.

These techniques include methods like search algorithms (e.g., depth-first search and breadth-first search), knowledge representation and reasoning (e.g., expert systems), ML (e.g., supervised learning and reinforcement learning), and heuristic-based approaches.

AI focuses on specific types of problem and particular techniques to be used to obtain a solution.

To derive a solution, one must follow four steps, which are mentioned below and characterized in the figure.

1. Define and fix problem statements such that it can target the problem objective more effectively. The problem statement should also include the pre-conditions and post-conditions to obtain an acceptable solution.
2. Analyze the problem and select features that can majorly contribute in deciding the success of the system.
3. Bifurcate tasks into atomic subtasks, i.e., into tasks that cannot be decomposed further. Represent the role of each task and required knowledge necessary to solve the problem.
4. Analyze the tradeoff between available solving techniques and choose the best problem-solving strategy to apply to the targeted problem for achieving a viable solution.

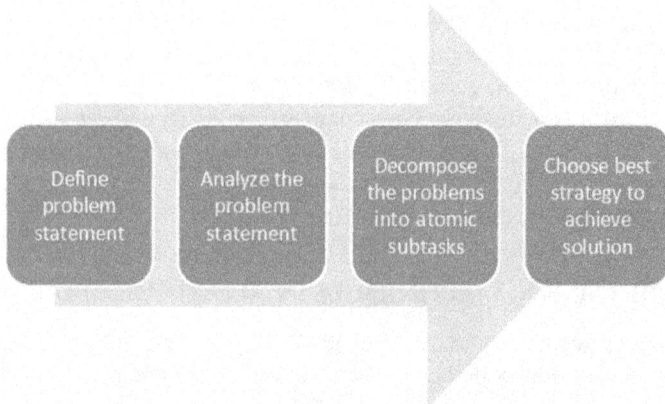

FIGURE 1.7   Key Steps in AI to Deriving a Solution.

Intelligence requires knowledge to be voluminous. If knowledge is hard to accurately characterize, constantly changing, and organized differently from the way it will be used, then AI methods are useful.

Problem-Solving Agents: A problem-solving agent is a goal-based agent that decides what to do by finding a sequence of actions that leads to desirable states.

1.4.1 GOAL FORMULATION

Goal formulation outlines a process for choosing and developing a single goal from a list of options. Problem formulation is defined as follows:

This stage defines the relevant actions and states needed to achieve a previously formulated goal. Following this comes the search phase, where the system identifies the best sequence of actions to reach the goal. A search algorithm analyzes the problem and proposes a solution as a series of actions. Finally, the execution phase implements the recommended actions.

1.4.2 WELL-DEFINED PROBLEMS AND SOLUTIONS

A formal problem definition typically consists of four key elements:

1. **Initial State:** This describes the starting point for the agent, where it begins its journey toward the goal.
2. **Actions:** These are the available options the agent can take in each state it encounters. The initial state, actions, and transition model (implicit in actions) collectively define the **state space**, encompassing all possible states reachable from the starting point through a sequence of actions.
3. **Goal Test:** This is a mechanism to determine if the agent has reached a successful or desired state.
4. **Path Cost Function:** This function assigns a cost value to each action taken, reflecting the overall performance measure. It's typically denoted as c(s, a, s'), where s represents the current state, a is the action performed, and s' is the resulting state.

1) Water Jug Problem:

The water jug problem involves two water jugs of different capacities to measure a specific amount of water. The primary goal is to figure out how to use the jugs to measure the exact amount of water required. The problem typically requires logical thinking and can be presented in various scenarios with different jug sizes and target amounts.

Example:

Problem:

You have two water jugs:
Jug A with a capacity of 3 liters.

Jug B with a capacity of 5 liters.

The goal is to measure exactly 4 liters of water using these jugs.

Solution:

- Fill Jug B to its full capacity, which is 5 liters.
- Pour the water from Jug B into Jug A. After this step, Jug A has 3 liters of water, and Jug B has 2 liters remaining.
- Empty Jug A completely.
- Pour the remaining 2 liters of water from Jug B into Jug A.
- Fill Jug B to its full capacity again, which is 5 liters.
- Carefully pour water from Jug B into Jug A. Stop pouring when Jug A is full. At this point, you will have filled Jug A to its maximum capacity of 3 liters, leaving 4 liters of water in Jug B.

Now, you've successfully measured 4 liters of water using the 3-liter and 5-liter jugs.

This solution uses a combination of filling, emptying, and pouring between the two jugs to achieve the desired measurement of 4 liters without the need for any additional equipment.

Implementation of the water jug problem in Python is given below. Data structures used to solve this problem is queue.

INPUT:

```
from collections import deque

def water_jug_problem(jug_a_capacity, jug_b_capacity,
target):
    # INITIALIZE BFS VARIABLES
    visited = set()
    queue = deque([[(0, 0, [])]])

    while queue:
        jug_a, jug_b, path = queue.popleft()

        # CHECK FOR SOLUTION
        if jug_a == target:
            return path + [(jug_a, jug_b)]

        if (jug_a, jug_b) in visited:
            continue

        visited.add((jug_a, jug_b))

        # GENERATE POSSIBLE NEXT STATES

        # Fill Jug-A
```

```python
        if jug_a < jug_a_capacity:
            queue.append((jug_a_capacity, jug_b, path +
[(jug_a_capacity, jug_b)]))

        # Fill Jug-B
        if jug_b < jug_b_capacity:
            queue.append((jug_a, jug_b_capacity, path +
[(jug_a, jug_b_capacity)]))

        # Empty Jug-A
        if jug_a > 0:
            queue.append((0, jug_b, path + [(0, jug_b)]))

        # Empty Jug-B
        if jug_b > 0:
            queue.append((jug_a, 0, path + [(jug_a, 0)]))

        # Pour from Jug-B to Jug-A
        pour = min(jug_b, jug_a_capacity - jug_a)
        if pour > 0:
            queue.append((jug_a + pour, jug_b - pour,
path + [(jug_a + pour, jug_b - pour)]))

        # Pour from Jug-A to Jug-B
        pour = min(jug_a, jug_b_capacity - jug_b)
        if pour > 0:
            queue.append((jug_a - pour, jug_b + pour,
path + [(jug_a - pour, jug_b + pour)]))

    return None # No solution found

# PROBLEM PARAMETERS
jug_a_capacity, jug_b_capacity, target = 4, 3, 2
solution = water_jug_problem(jug_a_capacity, jug_b_
capacity, target)

# PRINT SOLUTION
if solution:
    print(f"Solution to measure {target} gallons using
{jug_a_capacity}-gallon and {jug_b_capacity}-gallon
jugs:")
    for step, (a, b) in enumerate(solution):
        print(f"Step {step}: Jug-A = {a} gallons, Jug-B =
{b} gallons")
else:
    print("No solution found.")
```

OUTPUT:

Solution to measure 2 gallons using 4-gallon and 3-gallon jugs:

Step 0:Jug-A = 4	gallons, Jug-B = 0 gallons
Step 1:Jug-A = 1	gallons, Jug-B = 3 gallons
Step 2:Jug-A = 1	gallons, Jug-B = 0 gallons
Step 3:Jug-A = 0	gallons, Jug-B = 1 gallons
Step 4:Jug-A = 4	gallons, Jug-B = 1 gallons
Step 5:Jug-A = 2	gallons, Jug-B = 3 gallons
Step 6:Jug-A = 2	gallons, Jug-B = 3 gallons

=== Code Execution Successful ===|

2) Chess Problem:

In a chess problem, the start is the initial configuration of a chessboard. The final state is the any board configuration, which is a winning position for any player. We can have multiple final positions, and each board configuration can be thought of as representing a state of the game. Whenever the player tries to move any piece, it leads to another state of game.

State: Each legal arrangement of pieces on the chessboard is considered a state. This includes the position of all pieces (pawns, rooks, knights, bishops, queen, and king) for both white and black, along with whose turn it is to move.

Size: The number of possible states in chess is massive, estimated to be around 10^{120}. It's practically impossible to explore every single one.

Operators: The legal moves available to the player whose turn it is define the operators. Each move transforms the current state into a new state.

3) Eight-Puzzle Problem:

Problem: The eight-puzzle problem, also known as the sliding puzzle, is a classic problem-solving task in AI.

Description:

The eight-puzzle consists of a 3x3 grid with eight numbered tiles and one empty space, often represented in numbers from 1 to 8 and an empty slot. The goal of the puzzle is to rearrange the tiles from an initial configuration to a goal configuration by sliding the tiles into the empty space. Each tile can be moved vertically or horizontally into the adjacent empty slot.

State: Each unique arrangement of the numbered tiles on the 3x3 board is considered a state. This includes the position of the blank space as well.

Size: The number of possible states in the eight-puzzle is significantly smaller than that in chess, at 9!/2 (around 362,880). This allows for more exhaustive search techniques compared to those used in chess.

Operators: The legal moves available define the operators. In this case, a move involves sliding the blank space into an adjacent tile's position, creating a new state.

4) Traveling Salesman Problem:

Problem:

The traveling salesman problem (TSP) is a classic combinatorial optimization problem in the field of AI.

Description:

In the TSP, a salesman is given a list of cities and the distances between each pair of cities. The goal is to find the shortest possible route that the player visits each city exactly once and returns to the starting city. This problem is NP-hard, meaning that as the number of cities increases, the number of possible routes grows factorially, making it computationally challenging to find the optimal solution for large instances.

State: While there's no single agreed-upon definition, a state in the TSP can represent different stages of the salesman's journey. Here are two common approaches:

Partial Tour: The current set of cities visited, potentially including the starting city and not necessarily complete.

Remaining Cities: The set of cities yet to be visited by the salesman.

Size: The number of states depends on the chosen representation and the number of cities (n). With n cities, the number of partial tours can grow exponentially (roughly $(n-1)!$), making exhaustive search impractical.

Operators: An operator represents visiting a new city that hasn't been visited before.

1.5   AREAS OF AI

Each subfield within the field of AI holds its own unique significance and contributes to the overall advancement of AI in various ways. The introduction to AI is like opening the door to a world where computers can think and learn like humans. It involves various technologies, such as ML and robots, and has the power to change how we work and live. But we need to be careful about how we use AI because it can raise important ethical and social questions. Understanding AI is becoming more and more important as it becomes a big part of our future.

1.5.1   AI Subfields

The importance of a specific subfield can vary depending on its applications and research objectives. Here are some key subfields within AI that hold considerable importance.

1.5.1.1   Robotics

One of the most well-known subfields of AI is robotics. AI plays an important role in robotics that enables machines to comprehend their surroundings, make decisions, and carry out actions. Manufacturing and medical industries both use robots.

Robotics combines AI with mechanical design and engineering and bridges the gap between the digital and physical worlds. Robots are capable of perceiving their surroundings, processing data, and carrying out actions determined by AI.

Robotics in AI is an innovative fusion of machines with AI that has resulted in the creation of intelligent, adaptable, and autonomous robotic systems. The importance of this integration is seen in its numerous applications across industries, where it contributes to enhanced efficiency, precision, and robots' capacity to operate in complex and dynamic problems.

Significance:

Autonomous Operation: Robots with AI are able to perform tasks independently, making decisions based on current knowledge without constant human supervision. Applications in the manufacturing, logistics, and healthcare sectors all depend on this.

Adaptability: AI-enabled robotic systems can adapt to dynamic environments and deal with unexpected scenarios. This adaptability is advantageous in circumstances where responsibilities could change or differ over time.

Reliable and Efficient: AI-enhanced robots are capable of carrying out jobs more effectively and precisely. This is especially useful in manufacturing operations where robots may optimize workflows and increase product quality.

Human–Robot Collaboration: AI makes it possible for robots to comprehend and react to human gestures, orders, and natural language, enabling a safer and more effective human–robot collaboration.

Learning Experience: ML helps robots learn from the environments and from experiences so that they can improve their performance. This is required especially for operations where robotic grasping and object manipulation are used.

Applications of Robotics:

Robotics is a common practice around the world, as we all know. Therefore, they are used in multiple sectors, and a few of them are listed below:

- Manufacturing and industry
- Logistics and warehousing
- Medical field and argo industry
- Education and research
- Space exploration

1.5.1.2 Expert System

Expert systems are computer programs designed to mimic human experts in solving complex problems. They utilize a structured knowledge base and rules to provide recommendations and decisions. These systems have applications in fields such as medicine, finance, engineering, customer support, and education, aiding in tasks that require specialized human expertise. Examples of expert systems include DENDRAL, MYCIN, PXDES, and CaDeT.

Basic Elements of Expert Systems:

1. **Knowledge Base:** Knowledge base is a repository that stores information, facts, and rules related to a specific domain. It contains the expertise of human specialists and is the foundation for the decision-making process of the expert system.
2. **User Interface:** The user interface provides a platform where users can interact with the system. Users can input information, ask questions, and receive recommendations or solutions. The interface can be text-based or graphical, depending on the complexity of the system and the user's preferences.
3. **Rule Base:** Expert systems operate based on a set of rules that define the relationships between different pieces of information and guide the decision-making process. These rules are typically represented in the form of "if-then" statements, where the "if" part contains conditions or premises, and the "then" part contains conclusions or actions.
4. **Inference Engine:** Because it is the core processing unit of the system, the inference engine is referred to as the expert system's brain. It uses the knowledge base and inference rules to draw conclusions or infer new information. It assists in the generation of error-free answers to the user's queries. The system retrieves knowledge from a knowledge repository using an inference engine. It employs various reasoning methods, such as forward chaining (starting with known facts and deriving conclusions) or backward chaining (starting with a goal and working backward to find supporting evidence).

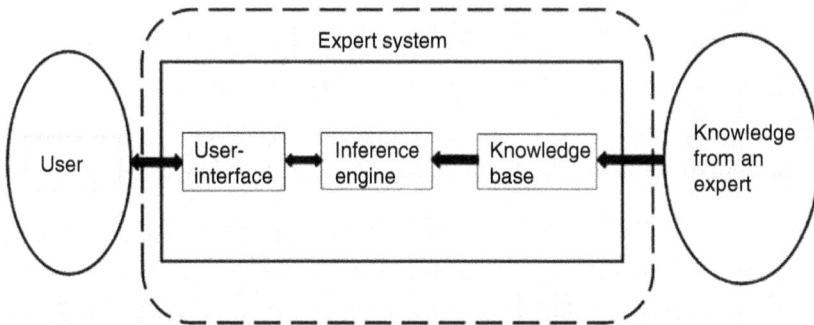

FIGURE 1.8 Inference Engine in an Expert System.

Significance:

The significance of expert systems lies in their ability to tackle complex problems and provide solutions that would typically require human expertise. Expert systems are more significant in knowledge representation and in decision-making processes. Due to their consistency and availability, they are mostly used in various areas. Some expert systems have the ability to learn from experience, refining their knowledge base over time. This adaptability allows them to improve their performance and accuracy.

Application of Expert System:

As we know, expert systems are capable of making their own decisions; therefore, they are applied in various fields, such as the following:

- Medical diagnosis
- Financial analysis
- Troubleshooting technical problems
- Manufacturing processes
- Customer support.

1.5.1.3   Machine Learning

ML is a major branch of AI. In ML, we use data and algorithms, which are also used to imitate the way we humans reply and learn, adding the delicacy and the effectiveness.

The term "machine learning" was actually developed in 1959 by Arthur Samuel, an IBM hand who was a colonist in computer gaming and AI.

ML, a core component of AI, enables computers to learn from data and make predictions. It encompasses various methods, including supervised learning (using labeled data), unsupervised learning (identifying patterns in unlabeled data), and reinforcement learning (decision-making based on rewards). ML has broad applications in NLP, computer vision, recommendation systems, and healthcare. Recent advancements in ML and technology have led to innovations such as self-driving cars and Netflix's recommendation system. There are four primary ML modes: unsupervised, semi-supervised, supervised, and reinforcement learning.

Significance:

Data-Driven Opinions: ML helps the colorful different associations use large quantities of data to make meaningful perceptivity and to take data-driven opinions.

Robotization and Effectiveness: So, with the help of colorful ML algorithms, we can automate complex tasks and processes, which automatically reduces the time and sweat needed to do them manually. This also automatically leads to increased effectiveness in colorful different diligence.

Scientific Exploration and Disquisition: In the fields of scientific exploration and disquisition, machine literacy is being increasingly used to dissect complex datasets, pretend the models, and make prognostications. It's helping scientists gain new perceptivity and accelerate new discoveries by having colorful different operations in the fields of astronomy, climate modeling, medicine discovery, etc.

Autonomous Vehicles and Robotics: So, ML algorithms play a veritably important part in independent vehicles and robotics, as they enable these systems to perceive and interpret their terrain, make the right opinions in the real-time terrain, and acclimatize to the changing circumstances, which ultimately lead to the advancements in robotic sidekicks, tone-driving buses, drones, etc.

Healthcare Advancements: ML helps in diagnosing the complaint, planning treatment, medicine discovery, and developing substantiated drugs.

Speech Recognition: The search machine Google allows users to search anything with the help of the "search by voice" feature.

Traffic Prediction: The Google Maps used by numerous people at the moment helps us find the shortest paths to take to reach our destination.

Spam Email Filtering: The machine learning algorithms help in filtering spam emails and important emails.

1.5.1.4   Deep Learning

DL is one of the most used field in AI. It solely focuses on the development and operation of artificial neural networks, which are called deep neural networks or deep neural models, with multiple layers to autonomously learn and extract intricate patterns from data. These models are said to be veritably important and inspired from the structure and functioning of the mortal brain.

The algorithms for DL are designed in such a special way that enables them to automatically learn and represent complex patterns, as well as connections among the data by organizing multiple layers of connected artificial neurons.

DL drives numerous AI operations and services that ameliorate robotization, performing logical and physical tasks without mortal intervention. DL technology lies behind everyday products and services (similar to digital sidekicks, voice-enabled television remotes, and credit card fraud discovery) and arising technologies (similar to self-driving cars).

Significance:

Handling Complex Data: DL excels at processing and understanding complex and high-dimensional data, similar to images, videos, audio, and textbooks. It can automatically learn intricate patterns and representations from raw data, enabling it to perform grueling tasks that were preliminarily delicate or insolvable using traditional ML techniques.

Improved Performance: DL has achieved remarkable performance advancements in several areas, including computer vision, NLP, speech recognition, and recommendation systems. Deep neural networks can learn hierarchical representations that capture both low-position and high-position features, leading to more accurate and robust prognostications or opinions.

End-to-End Learning: DL enables end-to-end learning, where models can directly learn from raw input data and induce meaningful labor without the need for homemade point engineering. This simplifies the development process and reduces the dependence on sphere-specific knowledge, making applying DL to new problems and disciplines easier.

Robotization and Effectiveness: DL allows for robotization and effectiveness in colorful diligence. It can automate complex tasks, such as image and speech recognition, data analysis, and decision-making processes. By automating these tasks, DL reduces mortal trouble, increases productivity, and enables real-time processing and decision-making capabilities.

Advancements in Computer Vision: DL has revolutionized computer vision by enabling accurate object discovery, image bracket, segmentation, and image generation. Operations range from tone-driving buses and surveillance systems to medical imaging and stoked/virtual reality.

Natural Language Processing: DL has made significant advancements in NLP tasks, including machine restatement, sentiment analysis, textbook generation, and question–answering systems. It has enabled more accurate language understanding and generation, easing better mortal-computer commerce and communication.

Scientific Research and Healthcare: DL has made significant benefactions to scientific exploration and healthcare. It has been used to dissect large-scale genomic data, help in medicine discovery, prognosticate complaints, and support medical image analysis. DL models have the eventuality to accelerate scientific discoveries and facilitate patient care.

Real-World Applications: DL has set up operations across colorful diligence, including finance, retail, manufacturing, entertainment, and cybersecurity. It has been used for fraud discovery, demand soothsaying, substantiated marketing, quality control, content recommendations, and more, leading to better effectiveness, client experience, and business issues.

Applications of DL:

- NLP
- Computer vision
- Healthcare
- Robotics
- Gaming

1.5.1.5 Computer Vision

A branch of AI, computer vision enables computers and systems to extract useful data from images, videos, and other visual inputs.

This extracted information can then be used to make decisions or provide suggestions. Just as AI empowers computers to think, computer vision allows them to perceive, examine, and comprehend the visual world.

Human vision operates in a similar manner to computer vision but with one key advantage: humans have extensive experience gained over a lifetime. This enables us to distinguish objects, estimate their distance, detect motion, and identify anomalies within an image.

Significance:

Autonomous Vehicles: Autonomous vehicles can comprehend their surroundings by using computer vision. In order to find road borders, understand signposts, and recognize other vehicles, obstructions, and people, computer vision algorithms assess the scene around the vehicle as it is being recorded by several cameras. The autonomous vehicle can then drive itself on roads and highways, avoid obstacles, and securely transport its occupants to their destination.

Facial Identification: Programs that utilize computer vision to identify people in photos, such as facial recognition software, heavily rely on this area of research. Computer vision algorithms are used to recognize facial characteristics in pictures, and they then compare those characteristics to recorded face profiles. Facial recognition is becoming more common in consumer gadgets to confirm the identification of the users. Social networking programs employ facial recognition to identify users and tag them. Law enforcement utilizes facial recognition software to identify criminals in surveillance films for the same reason.

Mixed and Augmented Reality: Computer vision plays a crucial role in augmented reality, enabling the integration of digital content into real-world environments via devices like smartphones and wearables. Augmented reality applications utilize computer vision algorithms to identify surfaces such as tabletops, ceilings, and floors, accurately determining depth and scale, and positioning virtual objects within the real-world context.

Healthcare: The growth of health technology has been profoundly influenced by computer vision. One of the many uses for computer vision algorithms is automating the process of searching for cancerous moles on a person's skin or finding signs in an X-ray or MRI image.

Applications of Computer Vision:

- Lane Monitoring: An autonomous vehicle must have lane tracking in order to determine which lane it should stay in and avoid idly moving about the road.
- Detection of Traffic Signs: An important task accomplished with computer vision and DL is the detection of traffic signs. Consider a driverless car that doesn't stop at a stop sign or speeds through a school zone. Thus, it is crucial to recognize these signs and take appropriate action.
- Pathfinder: This is a self-driving car's brain, which instructs the vehicle where it can travel and how to safely plan its future route. Different algorithms, like the PathNet algorithm, can be used to accomplish this.

1.5.1.6   Natural Language Processing

NLP is a branch of AI that focuses on the interaction between computers and human language.

To enable machines to understand, interpret, and generate human language, algorithms and models are developed. NLP has diverse applications, including machine translation, chatbots, sentiment analysis, and text summarization. It plays a crucial role in enhancing the efficiency and intuitiveness of human–computer interaction.

  I. NLU or Natural Language Understanding
 II. NLG or Natural Language Generation

There are specifically five main steps in NLP: lexical analysis, syntactic analysis, semantic analysis, disclosure integration, and pragmatic analysis.

Significance:

Human–Computer Interaction: NLP enables more intuitive and natural human–computer communication. This is evident in the growing prevalence of voice assistants, chatbots, and virtual agents in our daily lives.

Language Translation: NLP technology has enabled people to interact and access information globally by bridging language barriers. This is vital for business, education, diplomacy, and cross-cultural exchange.

Healthcare: NLP facilitates the development of drugs, epidemiological research, record analysis, and effective patient care. In addition, it might assist with the identification and treatment of disease prescriptions.

Data Analysis and Processing: Unstructured textual data can be investigated using NLP to gather useful knowledge. It is necessary for social media analysis, market research, and business intelligence because it may be employed for sentiment analysis, content analysis, and categorization.

Customer Service: Through the use of NLP for processing requests from customers, chatbots and virtual assistants may improve the efficient functioning of support and customer service operations.

Applications of NLP:

The wide range of NLP relies on its applications. Here are some of the crucial fields where NLP is utilized:

- Speech recognition
- Automatic voice input
- Chatbots and virtual assistants
- Text classification
- Machine translation

1.5.1.7   Automation

AI automation offers the potential to improve productivity, decrease errors, and handle jobs that might be too repetitive or data-intensive for people to handle. But it also calls into question the necessity for ethical and secure AI systems, its effect on employment, and other issues. AI automation optimizes business processes by integrating AI technologies with additional tools. Automation can take place via hardware, such as robotic process automation (RPA) in the real world, or software, wherein AI systems look into data, learn from it, and make options in the future.

Significance:

Increased Efficiency: Without tools, running a business can take a lot of time. More repetitive tasks can be handled by AI, liberating workers to concentrate on more important work.

Enhanced Communication with Customers: Today's clients expect the appropriate offers at the right time, which can be challenging for organizations that must do their own in-house data analysis. AI automation has the capacity to process vast volumes of client data, enabling the creation of tailored interactions that enhance customer experience.

Cost Savings: By removing the need for human labor in routine and repetitive operations, automated AI systems can save operating costs for companies and organizations.

Error Reduction: AI automation reduces the possibility of human oversight in quality control, data entry, and analysis processes, producing outputs that are more accurate.

Enhanced Decision-making: Automation powered by AI can process commercial and industry data far more quickly than humans. Businesses can gain assistance with forecasting, future product trends, and other industry insights by feeding AI with data. Their decision-making can then be informed by this data.

Applications in Technology:

In the context of AI, automation is the application of AI methods and technology to carry out operations and procedures without the need for direct human involvement. The following are some crucial facets of AI automation:

- RPA
- Autonomous vehicles
- Smart home automation
- Cybersecurity
- Agricultural automation

1.5.1.8   AI in Healthcare

AI in healthcare involves the application of ML algorithms to analyze, interpret, and understand complex medical data. AI aims to augment human capabilities by offering innovative approaches to disease diagnosis, treatment, and prevention. A primary goal of AI in healthcare is to identify the relationship between clinical data and patient outcomes. AI is being employed in various areas, including drug discovery, personalized medicine, treatment protocol development, diagnostics, and patient monitoring. As the use of AI in healthcare is relatively recent, research into its applications across different industries and medical fields is ongoing.

Significance:

Faster Detection and Disease Detection: AI is able to accurately and efficiently evaluate patient data and medical imaging, which helps with the early and accurate detection of a number of diseases, such as neurological disorders, cancer, and cardiac issues.

Improved Treatment Planning: AI helps medical professionals create more individualized and efficient treatment plans by considering each patient's particular genetic composition and past medical records.

Medication Management: AI improves medication safety and patient outcomes by helping patients manage their medications by discovering drug interactions, sending reminders, and keeping track of adherence.

Drug Development and Discovery: AI speeds up the process of finding new drugs, which could cut down on the time and expense it takes to introduce them to the market.

Saves Workers' Time: By automating repetitive procedures, AI allows users to concentrate on more intricate and patient-centered responsibilities. The administrative demand on healthcare staff can be decreased by using AI to automate administrative processes like insurance processing, billing, and appointment scheduling.

Applications of AI in Healthcare:

AI is being used more and more in the healthcare industry to enhance patient outcomes, expedite processes, and promote medical research. Here are a few well-known uses of AI in healthcare:

- Medical imaging analysis
- Electronic health records (EHR) management
- Robot-assisted surgery
- Radiology and pathology
- Genomic data analysis
- Telemedicine and remote monitoring

1.5.2 AI APPLICATION AREAS

AI is increasingly indispensable in modern society. It offers efficient solutions to complex problems across various industries, including entertainment, finance, healthcare, and education. AI has penetrated numerous markets, with applications in the following sectors:

AI in Astronomy: AI can be helpful for understanding and solving complex universe problems such as how it works and the origin. AI is used in autonomous spacecraft, rovers for navigation, and data analysis on other planets.

- AI in Healthcare: In recent years, AI has become increasingly beneficial to the healthcare industry. AI tools assist doctors in diagnoses and can alert them to deteriorating patient conditions, enabling timely medical intervention.
- AI in Education: AI can streamline the grading and assessment process, allowing teachers to focus on instructions. In the future, AI-powered virtual tutors could provide personalized support to students at any time and place.
- AI in Social Media: AI excels at organizing and managing large datasets. Social media platforms like Instagram, Snapchat, and LinkedIn generate billions of data points that require efficient storage and management. AI analyzes this data to identify emerging trends, popular hashtags, and user preferences.
- AI in Finance: AI-powered algorithms are used for high-frequency trading and investment decision-making. AI models are used to help in assessing credit risks and detecting fraudulent transaction.
- AI in Data Security: Given the rapid increase in cyberattacks, data security is paramount for businesses. AI can enhance data security by identifying and mitigating threats. AI-powered tools like AEG bot and AI2 platforms can effectively detect software vulnerabilities and cyberattacks.
- AI in Robotics: AI-powered robots are prevalent in numerous industries, including manufacturing, healthcare, and logistics.
- AI in Travel: The travel industry is leveraging AI-powered chatbots to provide human-like customer service, enhancing response times and offering services like booking travel arrangements, and suggesting hotels, flights, and optimal routes.

These are just few examples of AI applications across various domains. The field continues to expand into new areas, creating innovative solutions across multiple industries.

1.6 FUTURE SCOPE OF AI

The scope of AI is expected to influence our daily life, and it is estimated that it will help the economy by about $15.7 trillion globally. The following are the trends estimated to be achieved by AI in the near future.

1. **Self-driving vehicles will be able to drive better than humans:** Due to the emerging progress in the transportation industry, Tesla and its release of Dojo, a supercomputer, will surely become operational within the next decade. It is also expected that by 2025 8 million driverless and self-automated cars will be on the roadway, creating $800 billion jobs in the automobile industry.
2. **AI will work as a human:** Fields such as NLP and sentiment analysis are at its peak because generative AI is capable of creating a human-like input with the vast amount of data fed into the system. All these facts ensure that in the near future, AI will be able to work with human intelligence.

3. **AI will potentially make the health sector better:** According to the US healthcare industry, 23% think that the advancements in AI with the ML model will help achieve better and faster outcomes. With large data sets, its predictive analysis will benefit patients and doctors in getting the insights.
4. **Deepfakes may become a problem in society:** Fake videot and audio samples might be distributed rapidly because of people's prejudices, anxieties, and reservations.
5. **AI might affect in massive job losses:** Udacity CEO Gabe Dalporto has predicted that more than 1 billion people will lose their jobs due to AI by 2030. Job functions like as driving an auto or truck, operating heavy machineries, and rehearsing law will become increasingly automated. As a result, many of these positions will become obsolete.
6. **The metaverse:** The metaverse is about simulation. Incorporations can act, within tightly defined parameters, as our agents and our companions, and some may indeed be considered as coworkers. By 2050, we will be unfit to tell the difference between a real person and an AI-generated one.

2 Problem-Solving Methods and Search Strategies

2.1 INTRODUCTION

Artificial intelligence (AI) utilizes search algorithms as a fundamental approach to problem-solving, wherein these algorithms systematically navigate through potential solutions in order to identify an optimal one. These algorithms find extensive application across a wide spectrum of AI domains, such as path finding, game playing, planning, search space analysis, and optimization. Whether it's determining the shortest route between two points, strategizing in complex games, charting out future actions, or comprehending the structure of search spaces, search algorithms play a pivotal role in these AI tasks by enabling efficient exploration and decision-making. Here are some of the most well-known problem-solving techniques in AI:

1. **Uniformed/Blind Search**
   a. Breadth-first search (BFS)
   b. Depth-first search (DFS)
   c. Uniform cost search (UCS)
   d. Iterative deepening depth-first search
   e. Bidirectional search
2. **Informed Search**
   a. Best-first search
   b. A* search

2.1.1 UNIFORMED/BLIND SEARCH

Uniformed/blind search refers to a category of search algorithms that do not have prior knowledge about the structure of the search space or the location of the goal state. This algorithm works on the information available during the search process.

Examples of uniformed or blind search algorithms include BFS, DFS, UCS, iterative deepening DFS, and bidirectional search. These algorithms are also called as "blind search" because they make decisions about which node to explore next, ignoring additional information like heuristics or cost estimates.

DOI: 10.1201/9781003532170-2

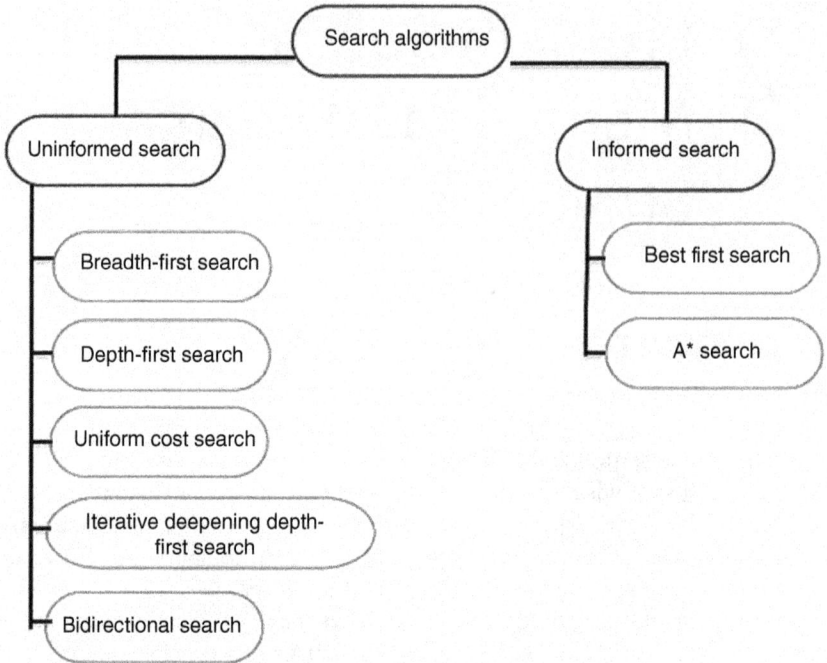

FIGURE 2.1   Categorization of Search Algorithms.

a. **Breadth-First Search:** BFS is used for finding the shortest path by exploring all nodes at a given level before moving to the next level, considering all possible paths with a uniform cost. BFS uses queue data structure to keep track of the node to be explored. The BFS will visit the node and mark it as visited and places it into the queue. Then the BFS will visit the nearest and unvisited nodes and mark them. The remaining nearest and unvisited nodes on the graph will be analyzed marked and added to the queue. These items will be deleted from the queue as they are received and printed as the result.

Its implementation in Python is given below. Data structures are used in queue and store unvisited nodes.

INPUT:

```
# Import the deque class from the collections module
# deque is used for efficient queue operations
from collections import deque
def bfs(graph, start):
```

```python
    # Initialize a set to keep track of visited vertices
    visited = set()

    # Create a queue and add the starting vertex
    queue = deque([start])

    # Mark the starting vertex as visited
    visited.add(start)

    # Continue until the queue is empty
    while queue:
        # Remove and return the leftmost vertex from the
queue
        vertex = queue.popleft()

        # Print the current vertex (part of BFS traversal)
        print(vertex, end=' ')

        # Explore all neighbors of the current vertex
        for neighbor in graph[vertex]:
            # If the neighbor hasn't been visited yet
            if neighbor not in visited:
                # Mark it as visited
                visited.add(neighbor)
                # Add it to the queue for future
exploration
                queue.append(neighbor)

# Define the graph as an adjacency list
graph = {
    'A' : ['B', 'C'],
    'B' : ['A', 'D', 'E'],
    'C' : ['A', 'F'],
    'D' : ['B'],
    'E' : ['B', 'F'],
    'F' : ['C', 'E']
}

# Print a message indicating the start of BFS
print("Breadth-First Search starting from vertex 'A':")

# Call the BFS function with the graph and starting ver-
tex 'A'
bfs(graph, 'A')
```

OUTPUT:

Output   Clear

Breadth-First Search starting from vertex 'A':
A B C D E F
=== Code Execution Successful ===

b. Depth-First Search: DFS is used for finding the shortest path by exploring as deeply as possible along one branch of the search tree before backtracking. It can be carried out by using stack data structure.

For example, we connected components 1 -> 2 -> 3.
    Then we connected component 4 -> 5.
    The final connected component is vertex 6.
    Graph G is disconnected here and has the components given below.
    Its implementation in Python is given below.

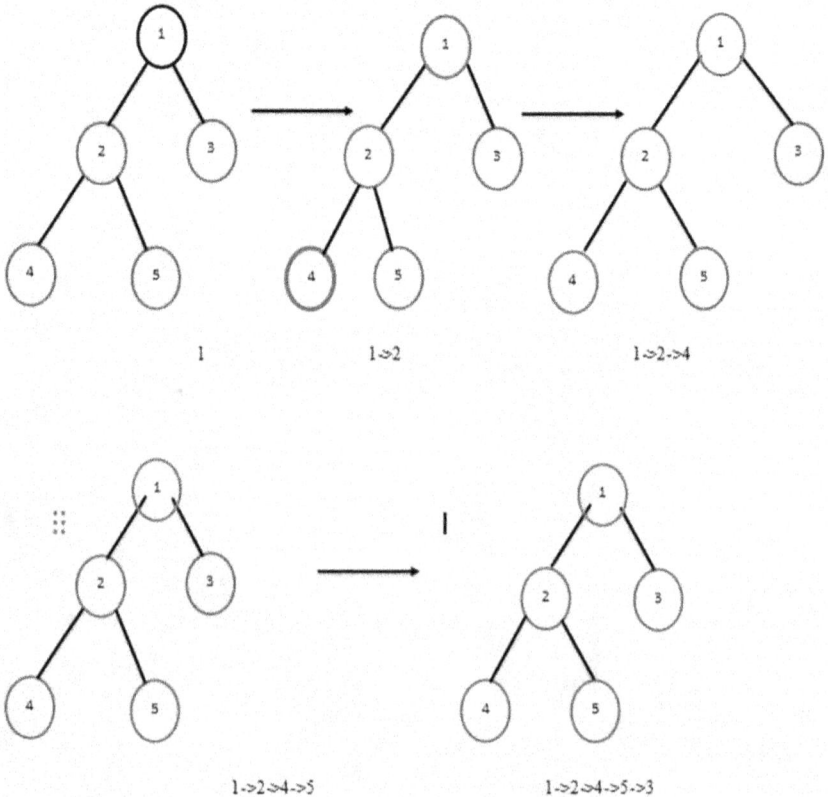

FIGURE 2.2   DFS Traversal.

INPUT:

```python
def dfs(graph, start, visited=None):
    # If this is the first call, initialize the visited
set
    if visited is None:
        visited = set()

    # Mark the current vertex as visited
    visited.add(start)

    # Print the current vertex (part of DFS traversal)
    print(start, end=' ')

    # Explore all neighbors of the current vertex
    for neighbor in graph[start]:
        # If the neighbor hasn't been visited yet
        if neighbor not in visited:
            # Recursively call DFS on the neighbor
            dfs(graph, neighbor, visited)

# Define the graph as an adjacency list
graph = {
    'A' : ['B', 'C'],
    'B' : ['A', 'D', 'E'],
    'C' : ['A', 'F'],
    'D' : ['B'],
    'E' : ['B', 'F'],
    'F' : ['C', 'E']
}

# Print a message indicating the start of DFS
print("Depth-First Search starting from vertex 'A':")

# Call the DFS function with the graph and starting ver-
tex 'A'
dfs(graph, 'A')
```

OUTPUT:

Output   Clear

```
Depth-First Search starting from vertex 'A':
A B D E F C
=== Code Execution Successful ===
```

c. **Uniform Cost Search:** UCS is primarily used for finding the shortest path in a weighted graph. UCS is effective in cases when different costs are available for each edge. A UCS is implemented by using priority queue. It selects the child node with the lowest total cost and adds it to the priority queue. If a lower cost path to an already visited node is discovered, the cost of that node is updated in the priority queue.

d. **Iterative Deepening DFS:** Iterative deepening DFS is a combination of BFS and DFS. It performs a series of DFS iterations, each with an increasing depth limit. In the first iteration, the depth limit is 0, which means it explores nodes only at the initial state. If the goal state is not found at this depth, the search proceeds to the next iteration with a depth limit of 1, then 2, and so on. It explores as far as possible along a single branch, and if the depth limit is reached, it backtracks to the previous level to explore other branches.

e. **Bidirectional Search:** Bidirectional search algorithm runs two searches simultaneously. One for the forward search (from the start state) and one for the backward node (from the goal state). The goal is to meet in the middle and find a common state that connects the two searches.

2.1.2 INFORMED SEARCH

Informed search is also known as heuristic search because it uses a heuristic function to guide the search process. Here, heuristic function is the cost of moving from a starting state to a goal state. It is represented by h(n).

2.1.2.1 Heuristic Functions

A heuristic function is like a tour guide that helps in an efficient search process. Common heuristic functions include the following:

Manhattan Distance: Useful for grid-based environments.
Euclidean Distance: Suitable for continuous space problems.
Diagonal Distance: A compromise between Manhattan and Euclidean distances.
Custom Heuristics: Tailor-made heuristics for specific problem domains.

These algorithms are designed to make more informed decisions about which paths to explore within a search space.

Search algorithms represent a foundational and indispensable component of AI, serving as a methodical problem-solving approach. Whether tasked with identifying the shortest distance between two points, formulating intricate game strategies, devising prospective action plans, or comprehending the intricate structures within search spaces, these algorithms assume a central role in facilitating the efficient exploration of possibilities and informed decision-making.

2.2 STATE SPACE REPRESENTATION

1. **Definition of State Space:** State space encompasses all possible configurations of a relevant object or system.

2. **Initial States:** In state space representation, one or more initial states are specified as the starting point for a problem-solving process.
3. **Goal States:** Goal states represent the expected solutions to the problem. These are the desired outcomes.
4. **Action Rules:** A set of rules is defined to describe the available actions or operators in the problem space.
5. **Key Considerations:** During the process of defining a state space search, several considerations come into play:
   - Determining the generality of the rules and the effort required to solve the problem.
   - Deciding whether to pre-compute certain aspects or represent them in rule sets.
   - Employing appropriate control strategies to navigate the problem space from initial states to goal states.
   - Identifying any assumptions that may not be explicitly stated in the problem description.

Problem Solution

State space representation defines a problem as a set of states, with the solution being a path from the initial state to a goal state. In some cases, simply reaching the goal state is sufficient. A cost function assigns a numerical value to each path, reflecting the cost of applying operators to transition between states. The quality of a solution is determined by the cost function, with an optimal solution having the lowest cost among all possible solutions. Depending on the problem and its requirements, the goal might be to find any solution, the optimal solution (lowest cost), or all possible solutions. The significance of cost depends on the specific problem context and the nature of the desired solution.

Problem Description

- A problem description comprises the following elements:
- The current state of the world or system.
- The actions or movements that can transition one state into another.
- The desired goal state of the world.

2.2.1 STATE SPACE

The state space is explicitly or implicitly defined and should include all necessary information for problem-solving while excluding unnecessary details.

Initial State: The initial state is the starting point for the problem-solving process.

Goal State: The goal state defines the desired conditions that need to be fulfilled. It represents a complete or partial description of the desired state of the world.

Operators: Operators are actions that transition a state to another. They have two components: preconditions and effects. Preconditions define the necessary conditions for an operator to be applicable, while effects describe the resulting state after the operator is executed.

Elements of the Domain: Elements of the domain are the components or entities relevant to the problem. Knowledge of the starting point is essential for understanding the problem.

Problem-Solving: Problem-solving entails identifying a series of actions that can transform the current state into a desired goal state.

Restrictions: Restrictions are related to the quality of the solution, which can be any, optimal, or all based on the problem requirements. Quality restrictions may involve finding the shortest or least expensive sequence, or simply identifying any valid sequence as quickly as possible.

Few case studies of state space representation are as follows:

- Traveling Salesman Problem

The traveling salesman problem (TSP) is a classic computational problem where a salesman must visit each city in a given list exactly once, minimizing the total travel distance. The problem is represented as a graph, with cities as nodes and distances between cities as edges. The goal is to find the shortest possible route that visits all cities and returns to the starting point. A state in this problem is represented as a pair of cities and the distance between them.

Initial State (S_0):

At the beginning of the journey, the salesman starts at a specific city—let's say City 1. None of the cities other than City 1 is visited yet.

State Space (S):

The state space encompasses all possible combinations of cities visited by the salesman, starting from the initial city. These states can be understood as different permutations of cities, excluding the starting city. These permutations indicate the order in which the cities are visited.

Operators (Actions):

In the context of the TSP, operators symbolize the choices the salesman makes to transition between states. The primary operator involves selecting the next city to visit from the pool of unvisited cities. This choice modifies the sequence in which cities are visited.

Transition Model:

The transition model defines how the salesman's state changes when an operator is applied. For instance, when the salesman picks the next city to visit, the state updates to reflect the new order in which cities have been visited.

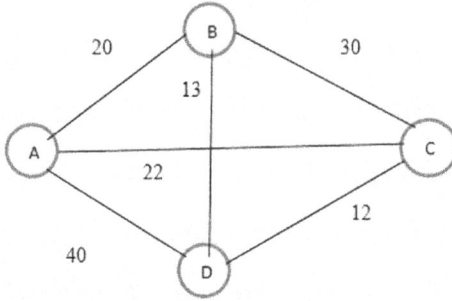

FIGURE 2.3 Connected Cities and Distances.

Goal State (S$_i$):

Goal state signifies the completion of the tour, where every city has been visited once, and the salesman returns to the starting city. This final state is
characterized by a permutation of all cities, with the starting city appearing
as both the first and the last city in the sequence.

Let us now understand with an example.
The nodes represent cities, and the edges represent the distance between them.

Starting point: A

To find: The shortest possible route starting from A, covering all the nodes and
returning back to A (origin).

STATE SPACE

Initial state (State A): {A--B, A--C, A--D}

Possible routes

1. A→B→D→C→A
2. A→B→C→D→A
3. A→C→B→D→A
4. A→C→D→B→A
5. A→D→C→B→A
6. A→D→B→C→A

The best routes in this case are route 1 and route 4. Let's go step by step starting with
node A.

Step 1: We select the starting node, that is, A.

A

Step 2:

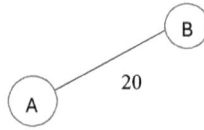

Step 3:

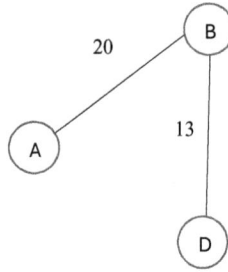

Step 4:

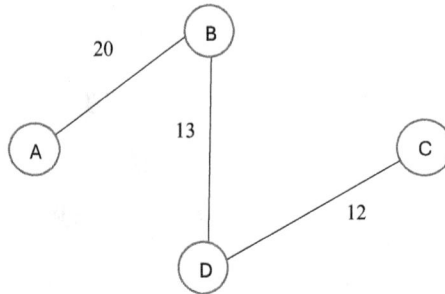

Step 5:

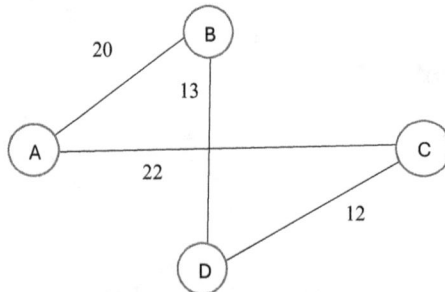

This is the final route, which costs 20 + 13 + 12 + 22 = 67.

- EIGHT-PUZZLE PROBLEM

Eight-puzzle problem is one of the classic problems solved by AI. In the below context, we are going to see how this problem is represented by AI with the help of a concept, i.e., "state space representation."

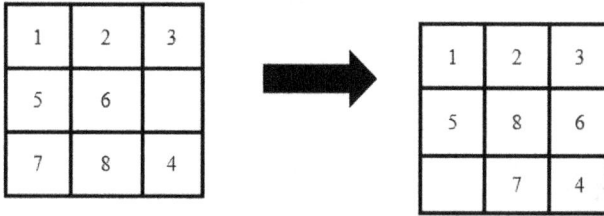

FIGURE 2.4 Eight-Puzzle Problem.

Let us understand what an eight-puzzle game is.

Eight puzzle is a 3 x 3 grid game with eight numbered tiles and one blank space. The problem is to rearrange the tiles in the initial state so that we can reach the goal state. Steps involve sliding the tiles on the adjacent blank space. The solution to this problem is found by finding the minimum number of sequential moves required to reach the goal state from the actual initial state.

Example:

State Space: Eight-Puzzle Problem

The state space of an eight-puzzle problem is somewhat large but finite. It performs 9! permutations, which is approximately 362,880 different states. The state space representation of an eight-puzzle problem includes the following points:

1. **State**

    The states in an eight-puzzle problem can be initial state and goal state, where every new state is generated on each possible move of the tile. Here the states represented in the figure are our states.

2. **Space**

    All the possible states generated by sliding the tile.

3. **Search**

    Search for the successive state in an eight-puzzle problem can be performed with the help of various search algorithms such as BFS, DFS, and various heuristic search techniques. Heuristic search provides faster solutions than uninformed searches.

4. **Operators**

    Operators in eight-puzzle problems are used to slide the tile on the black space, which are
    * Moveup
    * Movedown
    * Moveleft
    * Moveright

5. **Search Tree**

Various possible states of eight-puzzle problems are represented in the form of a search tree. In the search tree, each root node represents the initial state, and each node in the search tree represents all possible states of the puzzle.

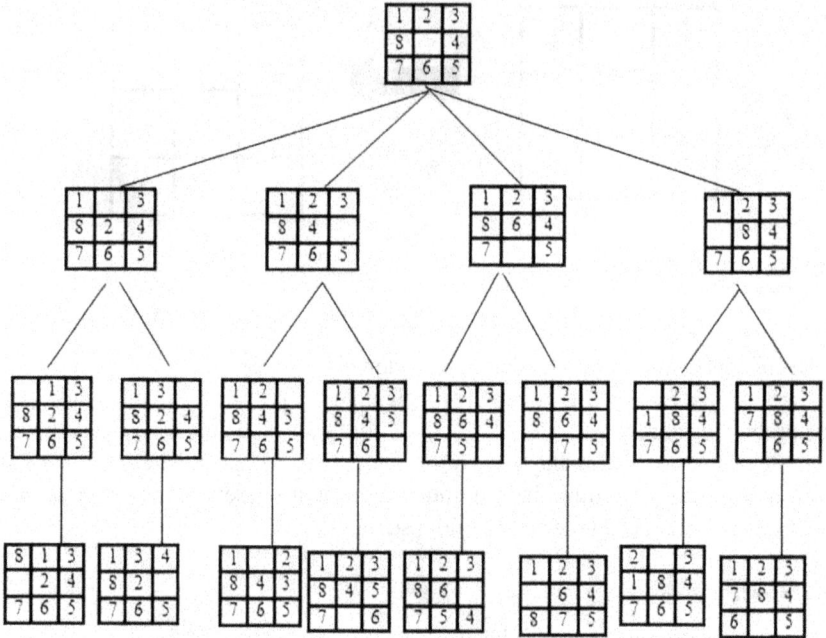

FIGURE 2.5   Space State Search Tree of an Eight-Puzzle Problem.

The search tree for an eight-puzzle problem is given below.
Implementation of an eight-puzzle problem in Python is given below.

```
# FOR PRIORITY QUEUE OPERATIONS
import heapq
class PuzzleState:
    def __init__(self, board, parent=None):
        self.board = board
        self.parent = parent
        self.cost = 0 if parent is None else parent.cost
+ 1
        self.lower_bound = self.calculate_misplaced_tiles()

    # LOWER BOUND CALCULATION (HEURISTIC)
    def calculate_misplaced_tiles(self):
        goal = [1, 2, 3, 4, 5, 6, 7, 8, 0]
        return sum(1 for i in range(9) if self.board[i]
!= goal[i] and self.board[i] != 0)

    # COMPARISON FOR PRIORITY QUEUE (BRANCH AND BOUND
PRIORITIZATION)
```

```
    def __lt__(self, other):
        return (self.cost + self.lower_bound) < (other.
cost + other.lower_bound)

    def __eq__(self, other):
        return self.board == other.board

    # GENERATE BRANCHES (POSSIBLE MOVES)
    def get_neighbors(self):
        moves = [('LEFT', -1), ('RIGHT', 1), ('UP', -3),
('DOWN', 3)]
        empty_index = self.board.index(0)
        for move, offset in moves:
            new_position = empty_index + offset
            if 0 <= new_position < 9 and abs(empty_index
% 3 - new_position % 3) <= 1:
                new_board = self.board[:]
                new_board[empty_index], new_board[new_posi-
tion] = new_board[new_position], new_board[empty_index]
                yield PuzzleState(new_board, self)

# BRANCH AND BOUND ALGORITHM
def solve_puzzle(initial_state):
    open_set = []
    closed_set = set()
    heapq.heappush(open_set, initial_state)
    while open_set:
        # SELECT NODE WITH LOWEST BOUND
        current = heapq.heappop(open_set)

        # CHECK FOR GOAL STATE
        if current.board == [1, 2, 3, 4, 5, 6, 7, 8, 0]:
            solution_path = []
            while current.parent:
                solution_path.append((None, current.
board))
                current = current.parent
            return solution_path[::-1]

        closed_set.add(tuple(current.board))

        # BRANCH: EXPLORE NEIGHBORS
        for neighbor in current.get_neighbors():
            if tuple(neighbor.board) not in closed_set:
```

```
                        # BOUND: PRUNE OR EXPLORE BASED ON LOWER
BOUND
                    if neighbor not in open_set or neighbor.
cost + neighbor.lower_bound < open_set[open_set.index-
(neighbor)].cost + open_set[open_set.index(neighbor)].
lower_bound:
                        heapq.heappush(open_set, neighbor)

    return None


# USAGE AND SOLUTION DISPLAY
initial_board = [1, 2, 3, 4, 0, 5, 7, 8, 6]
initial_puzzle_state = PuzzleState(initial_board)
solution = solve_puzzle(initial_puzzle_state)

# Print initial state and solution
print("Initial State:")
for i in range(0, 9, 3):
    print("+---+---+---+")
    print(f"| {initial_board[i] if initial_board[i] != 0
else ' '} | {initial_board[i+1] if initial_board[i+1]
!= 0 else ' '} | {initial_board[i+2] if initial_
board[i+2] != 0 else ' '} |")
print("+---+---+---+")

if solution:
    print("\nSolution:")
    for step, (move, board) in enumerate(solution, 1):
        print(f"Step {step}: {move if move else ''}")
        for i in range(0, 9, 3):
            print("+---+---+---+")
            print(f"| {board[i] if board[i] != 0 else
' '} | {board[i+1] if board[i+1] != 0 else ' '} |
{board[i+2] if board[i+2] != 0 else ' '} |")
        print("+---+---+---+")
    print(f"Solution found in {len(solution)} moves.")
else:
    print("\nNo solution found.")
```

```
    Output                                          Clear

    Initial State:
    +---+---+---+
    | 1 | 2 | 3 |
    +---+---+---+
    | 4 |   | 5 |
    +---+---+---+
    | 7 | 8 | 6 |
    +---+---+---+

    Solution:

    Step 1: RIGHT
    +---+---+---+
    | 1 | 2 | 3 |
    +---+---+---+
    | 4 | 5 |   |
    +---+---+---+
    | 7 | 8 | 6 |
    +---+---+---+

    Step 2: DOWN
    +---+---+---+
    | 1 | 2 | 3 |
    +---+---+---+
    | 4 | 5 | 6 |
    +---+---+---+
    | 7 | 8 |   |
    +---+---+---+

    Solution found in 2 moves.

    === Code Execution Successful ===
```

2.3   PROBLEM CHARACTERISTICS

AI aims to create intelligent machines capable of mimicking human cognitive functions like natural language processing, problem-solving, and decision-making. When selecting an AI approach for a specific problem, the problem has to categorized into one of given below characteristics.

Can the problem be decomposed into smaller subproblems?
Are the solution steps reversible or irrelevant?
Is the problem's environment predictable?
Is the optimal solution absolute or relative?
Is the solution a final state or a path?
What is the significance of knowledge in solving the problem?
Does the task require human input?

1. Can the problem be decomposed into smaller subproblems?

Yes, many of the complex problems can be divided into smaller, more manageable sub-problems. This approach is widely used in problem-solving, which is known as decomposition. Decomposable problems can be solved by tackling each subproblem individually and making it easier to find a solution using the divide and conquer approach.

Example: Symbolic integration.

$$\int(x^2+4x+\sin^2x.\cos^2x)dx$$

$$\int x^2dx \qquad \int 4xdx \qquad \int\sin^2x.\cos^2xdx$$

$$\int(1-\cos^2x)\cos^2xdx$$

$$\int\cos^2xdx \qquad -\int\cos^{4x}dx$$

2. Are the solution steps reversible or irrelevant?

The reversibility of the solution steps varies between problems. In some cases, steps can be undone or ignored if they prove to be incorrect or lead to dead ends. However, in other problems, this may result in a different or incomplete solution.

Example: a) Eight-puzzle problem

The eight-puzzle allows for reversible moves, enabling the exploration of different tile arrangements. In contrast, some problems, like chess, have irreversible moves where actions cannot be undone once performed.

1	2	3
8		4
7	6	5

Initial state: goal state:

1	2	6
3		7
8	4	5

b) In water jug problems, moves can be undone.

3. Is the problem's environment predictable?

The predictability of a problem's environment depends on its nature. Some problems have deterministic outcomes, meaning the result can be predicted with certainty based on given rules and conditions. For example, the water jug problem is deterministic, involving only one person and predictable outcomes.

4. Is the optimal solution absolute or relative?

The quality of a good solution can be absolute or relative. Solutions can vary depending on the problem and individual perspectives. An absolute solution is considered sufficient once found, while a relative solution requires comparison with other possibilities to determine the best option, often based on cost.

Example: Traveling salesman problem: This problem seeks the shortest route among all problem routes, making it a relative.

In the water jug problem, we need not bother about other solutions once the solution is found. Hence it is absolute.

5. Is the solution a final state or a path?

The solution of a particular problem can either be a specific state or a path, depending on the nature of the problem. In some problems, appropriate outcome is a specific state or a configuration that fulfils the problem requirement. The nature of a problem often determines whether the solution is more about achieving a specific state or following a particular path.

Example: In a maze-solving problem, the outcome is the path from the starting point to the ending point.

6. What is the significance of knowledge in solving a problem?

Knowledge plays a critical role in guiding a problem-solving process. The knowledge in problem-solving varies based on the complexity and nature of the problem. In many problems, extensive domain-specific knowledge is required to recognize the pattern, constraints, and possible solutions.

Example: Chess requires deep knowledge of the game rules and strategic principles to make informed moves.

7. **Does the task require human input?**

Many problems require human interaction depending on the nature of the problem and the system tools used to address it. some problems can be solved entirely by automated systems, while others may benefit from human guidance, creativity, and expertise. Human interaction is often necessary in a complex or subjective problem domain where the system may try to replicate human judgment and understanding.

Example: Chess is a conversational problem, involving back-and-forth communication between the computer and the user to provide information or assistance. Unlike other problem types, chess does not require additional human intervention.

2.4 PRODUCTION SYSTEM AND CONTROL STRATEGIES

2.4.1 PRODUCTION SYSTEM

Production systems are the rules of the form C→A, where the left-hand side is the condition and right-hand side is the action. C→A implies the condition for which action is needed to be performed.

If one adopts a system with a production rule and rule interpreter, then that system is known as a production system. It helps in structuring the program in a way that facilitates describing and performing the search process.

Production system is a model of computation that provides pattern-directed search control using a set of production rules, working memory, and recognize–act cycle.

It has four parameters:

- Set of Rules: It consists of the if-then conditions that tell us what action should be performed when such conditions occur.
- Knowledge Base: Stores the value according to the specific tasks; that is, it stores the information related to the condition.
- Control Strategy: It specifies the order in which the rules are to be compared to the databases so that the conflict can be resolved in the minimum requirement/time.
- Rule Applier: It applies the rules on the basis of the control strategy.

Steps to Resolve a Problem:

1. Reduce the problem in the form of a precise statement. It should clearly show its states and goals.
2. A problem can be solved by searching a path through space so that we can reach the goal state from the start state.
3. The process of solving a problem can be modeled through a production system.

Advantages of a Production System:

- It is an amazing tool for structuring AI problems.
- It is highly modular; that is, it gives the flexibility to change, delete, or remove the rules.
- The production rules are expressed in the natural form, which makes the rules easy to understand.

Characteristics of a Production System:

1. Monotonic Production System: The application of one rule never prevents the later application of another rule; that is, rules are independent of each other.
2. Non-Monotonic Production System: It is not applicable for a production system.
3. Partially Commutative Production System: If the application of a particular set of rules transforms from state X to state Y, then allowable permutation of those rules also transforms from state X to state Y.
   Example: X→Y, then their permutations, e.g., (r1, r2), will also transform from X→Y.
4. Commutative Production System: It is both monotonic and partially commutative.

	Monotonic	**Non-monotonic**
Partially commutative	Theory pruning (solving ignorable problems)	Robot navigation (changes occur but can be reversed)
Non-partially commutative (if changes occur, then they are irreversible)	Chemical synthesis	Bridge

2.4.2 CONTROL SYSTEM

Control strategies refer to the methods and techniques used to manage, regulate, and ensure the desired behavior, performance, and safety of AI systems. These strategies are important for controlling AI systems, especially when AI systems have the ability to adapt, learn, or make autonomous decisions. It tells us about which rule has to be applied next while searching for a solution for a problem within a problem space.

Here are some common control strategies in AI:

1. **Feedback Control:**
   It is a fundamental strategy that involves continuous monitoring of the performance of an AI and making adjustments to keep it on track with the desired objectives.
2. **Reinforcement Learning:**
   It is a type of control strategy where AI agents learn behavior through interactions with their environment. They receive rewards or punishments based on their actions, which guide their learning process.
3. **Proactive Control:**
   It involves predicting potential issues and taking action to prevent them before they occur. It aims to anticipate problems and maintain system performance.
4. **Rule-Based Control:**
   It employs predefined rules or policies to enforce specific behaviors or constraints on AI systems. It's often used to ensure ethical behavior, compliance with regulations, or predefined standards.

5. **Model Predictive Control (MPC):**
   It is a control strategy that uses predictive models to optimize system performance while adhering to constraints. It repeatedly solves optimization problems to determine the best control actions.
6. **Explainable AI (XAI):**
   It is a control strategy that focuses on making AI systems transparent and interpretable. It aims to provide users with insight into how AI decisions are made, making it easier to trust and control the system.
7. **Adaptive Control:**
   It allows AI systems to adjust their behavior or parameters based on changing conditions or environments. It's often used in systems that need to operate in dynamic and uncertain settings.

Implementing control strategies in AI involves the following:

1. Objective Definition: Clearly define goals and constraints.
2. Strategy Selection: Choose a suitable control strategy.
3. Data Collection: Set up sensors and data sources.
4. Policy/Rules Development: Create control policies or algorithms.
5. Monitoring and Feedback: Continuously assess AI behavior.
6. Control Algorithm Design: Generate corrective actions.
7. Reference Values: Set desired states and error thresholds.
8. Adaptation: Implement mechanisms for dynamic adjustments.
9. Safety and Ethics: Incorporate constraints for responsible behavior.
10. Testing and Optimization: Validate and fine-tune control strategies.
11. User Interface: Develop tools for monitoring and intervention.
12. Training and Documentation: Train personnel and document procedures.
13. Deployment: Integrate control strategies into AI systems.
14. Continuous Monitoring: Regularly review and adapt strategies.
15. Contingency Planning: Prepare for unexpected situations.

2.5   INFORMED AND UNINFORMED SEARCH

Uninformed and informed search are two primary approaches to problem-solving in AI. Uninformed search algorithms explore the search space systematically without prior knowledge of the goal, treating all paths equally. Examples include BFS and DFS. These algorithms are simple but can be inefficient in large spaces. Informed search algorithms leverage heuristic functions, which estimate the distance to the goal, to guide the search toward promising paths. A* is a well-known informed search algorithm that uses a combination of the actual cost and estimated cost to prioritize states. While informed search is generally more efficient, the quality of the heuristic function significantly impacts its performance.

2.5.1   GENERATE AND TEST METHOD

Generate and test is a heuristic search process based on DFS with backtracking, which guarantees finding a solution if it is successful and a solution is found. In this

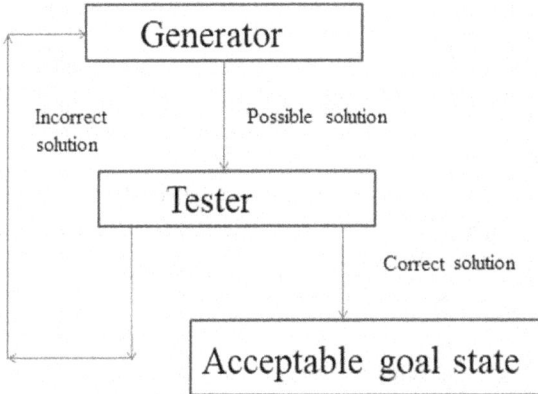

FIGURE 2.6   Generate and Test Method.

process, all solutions are generated and the best ones are tested. It ensures that the best solution is checked for all possible solutions.

It is also called the British Museum Search Algorithm because it seems to randomly search or walk through the exhibits in the British Museum. It is done with a heuristic function because all solutions are systematically generated in the algorithm of generating and testing, but if there is at least one way that will lead us to the result, it is not considered correct. Heuristics does this by ranking each option and often does it well. Developing methods and experiments is useless when solving complex problems. However, one method that can be improved in difficult cases is to reduce the search space by combining the construction and testing of the search with other strategies.

Algorithm

Identify a potential solution. This could involve selecting a specific point within the problem area or devising a route starting from an initial state.

Next, verify if this candidate solution is valid by checking the selected point or the endpoint of the created path against the defined acceptable goal states.

If a valid solution is identified, stop the process. If not, return to the first step.

Scenario: Imagine you're a chef looking to create a new dessert with three unique ingredients you can choose from a basket of five fruits (apple, banana, orange, mango, and kiwi). You want to find a combination that tastes delicious.

Generate:

1. **State Representation:** A state here represents a single dessert consisting of three chosen fruits. We can represent it as a list of three fruits (e.g., [apple, banana, mango]).
2. **Solution Generation:** Here's the generate part. You can simply pick three fruits at random from the basket (five fruits) to create a possible dessert (state). This random selection can be repeated to generate multiple dessert options (states).

Test:

1. **Evaluation Function:** This is where you define what makes a dessert delicious. It can be subjective (your taste preference) or objective (nutritional balance). Let's say you simply want a variety of flavors (not three of the same fruit).
2. **Testing the Generated State:** You would then evaluate each generated dessert (state) against your criteria. If a dessert has three different fruits, it's a valid solution (delicious dessert).

Process:

1. You keep generating random dessert options (states) until you find one that meets your criteria (a solution with three different fruit).
2. If after a set amount of tries you haven't found a solution, you might need to adjust your criteria or try to generate more options.

Limitations:

- This is a basic generate-and-test approach. With a larger basket of fruit, randomly generating three unique fruit can become inefficient (especially if there are many repeated picks).
- The efficiency depends on the size of the search space (possible combinations) and how easy it is to evaluate solutions.

This method is simple to implement but can be slow for large search spaces. It's a good choice for problems where there's no clear path to a solution and random exploration might be helpful.

2.5.2   Hill Climbing Method

It is one of the local search algorithms that move in the direction of increasing value to find the best and optimal solution for the problem. It is terminated when it reaches a peak value where no neighbor has a higher value. It mainly used to optimize the problem. Traveling salesman is one of the popular examples of the hill climbing method in AI. In this problem, the salesman always tries to find the minimum cost root to reach the destination, and this method helps him find the optimal path. Since it is always possible to find a better next state than the previous one, it is considered a greedy algorithm as well. If good heuristics is available, then this search is used. It is an efficient algorithm because we don't have to maintain any type of graph and search trees as it operate on a single state.

Current State: The state at which the agent is currently available.
Local Maxima: The state that is better than the previous one.
Global Maxima: The state that is always best; that is, no state is better than this.
End: No further move occurs.

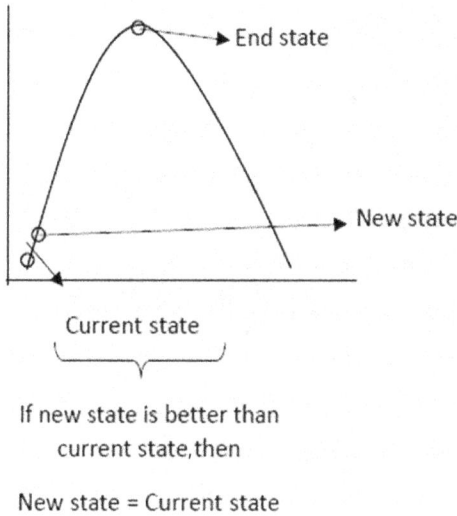

FIGURE 2.7 Hill Climbing Method.

Types as given below:

Simple Hill Climbing: It is one of the simplest ways to implement hill climbing. This algorithm compares the current state with the next state. If the next state is better than the current state, it updates the current state with the next state. If the next state is not optimal than the current, then the current state remains as it is. It always tries to find a better state than the previous one. It is less time-consuming, but the solution is not always guaranteed.

Steepest-Ascent Hill Climbing: In this method, the algorithm first examines all the neighboring nodes of the current state and selects the node that is close to the goal state. This algorithm takes more time than others due to its search for all neighbors.

Stochastic Hill Climbing:

This algorithm does not examine all its neighbors before starting to move. This algorithm chooses any random node and decides whether to choose the current state or not. If it does not start, it examines other states.

Special Features of Hill Climbing:

- It does not backtrack the search space, and it does not remember the previous state.
- It is a greedy algorithm.
- It is a variant of the generate and test method.

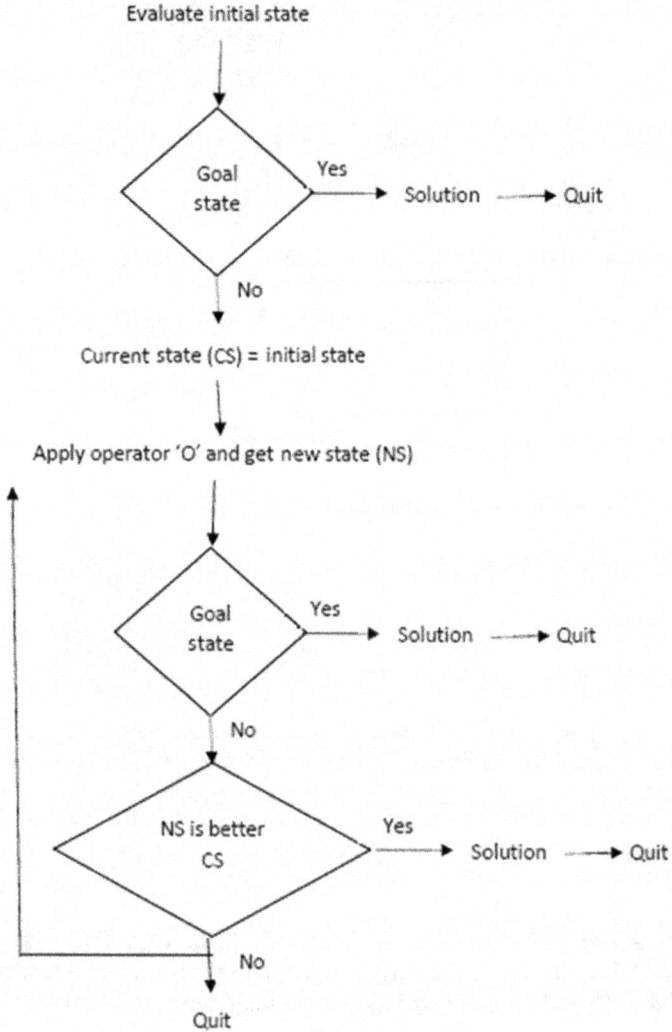

FIGURE 2.8 Flowchart of Simple Hill Climbing.

Problems in Hill Climbing:

- Local maxima:
  a. Local maxima is a peak state in landscape that is better than it previous state, but another state that is better than local maxima is also present.
  b. Backtracking method is the solution of local maxima as the backtracking algorithm can backtrack and search paths.
- Plateau: It is a flat area of search space in which all neighbor states of the current state contain the same value. Due to the same set of value, it is impossible to find the best way. The solution for plateau is to take big steps

or very little steps while searching to solve the problem. Select the step that is far away from the current state.

• Ridges: A ridge is special form of local maxima. It has an area that is higher than its surrounding area, but it has a scope and cannot be reached in a single move. Bidirectional search is used to find a solution move in different directions.

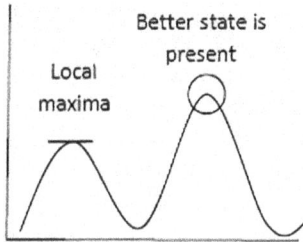

FIGURE 2.9   Trap of System in Local Maxima.

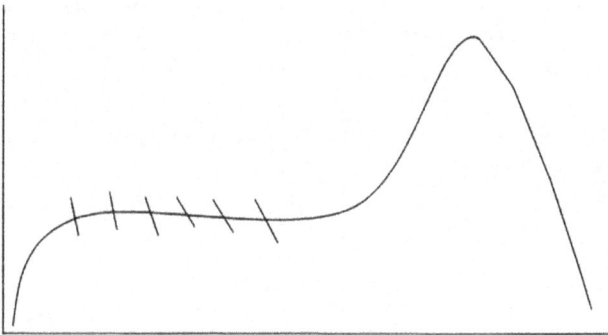

FIGURE 2.10   After Plateau Solution.

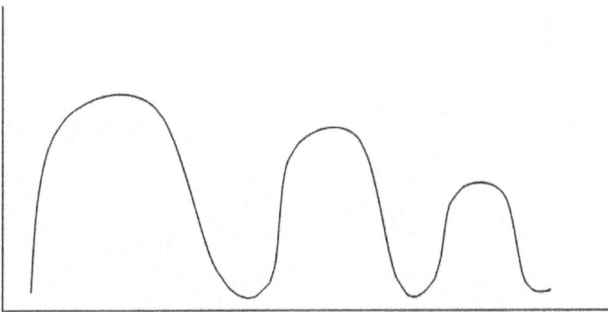

FIGURE 2.11   Ridges.

2.5.3 Best-First Search and A* Search

Best-first search is a widely used algorithm in computer science and AI. It is primarily employed in various applications, such as path finding, puzzle solving, and decision-making. Best-first search is characterized by its ability to efficiently navigate through a search space by selecting the most promising nodes to explore first.

2.5.3.1 Understanding Best-First Search

Best-first search is a graph search algorithm that works by exploring the most promising nodes first. Unlike some other search algorithms, best-first search does not necessarily follow a rigid order, like DFS or breadth-first search. Instead, it evaluates nodes based on a heuristic function, which estimates the desirability of each node.

The algorithm maintains an open list of nodes, which initially contains the start node. It then iteratively selects the most promising node from the open list based on the heuristic value and expands it. The expansion involves generating all possible successor nodes and evaluating them with the heuristic function. The best successor is then added to the open list, and the process continues until the goal node is reached or the open list becomes empty.

a. **Best-First Search:** Best-first search finds solutions based on a specific evaluation function or heuristic function h(n). It consistently chooses the most favorable path available at the current moment. Here f(n) = h(n), where h(n) = estimated cost from node n to the goal node.

We start from source "S" and search for goal "I" using the best-first search. We use the given costs for the same.

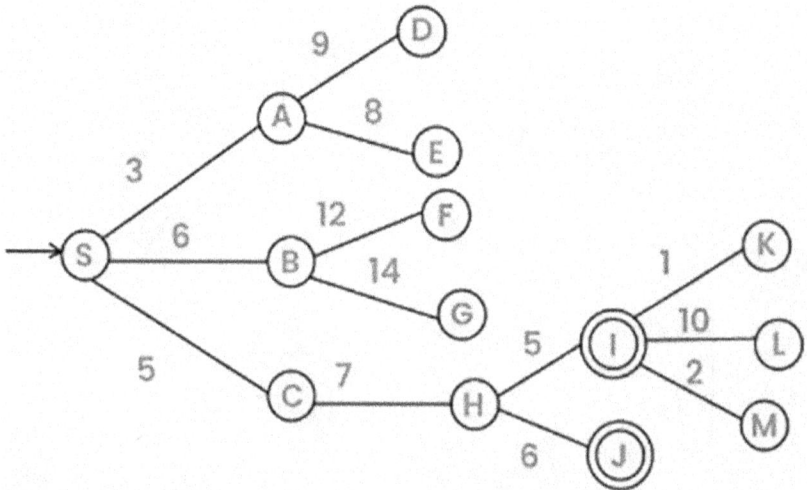

FIGURE 2.12   Graph.

The priority queue initially contains S.

Remove S from the priority queue and process unvisited neighbors of S to the priority queue. The priority queue has {A, C, B}.

Remove A from the priority queue and process unvisited neighbors of A to the priority queue.

The priority queue has {C, B, E, D}.

Remove C from the priority queue and process unvisited neighbors of C to the priority queue.

The priority queue now has {B, H, E, D}.

Remove B from the priority queue and process unvisited neighbors of B to the priority queue.

The priority queue now has {H, E, D, F, G}.

Remove H from the priority queue.

Since our goal "I" is a neighbor of H, we return.

Key Characteristics of Best-First Search

1. **Heuristic Function:** The effectiveness of best-first search relies on the accuracy of the heuristic function. A good heuristic provides an informed estimate of the cost or distance from a node to the goal. In many cases, best-first search uses admissible heuristics, which never overestimate the true cost, to guarantee optimality.

2. **Open List:** Best-first search maintains an open list, which is a priority queue that stores the nodes to be explored. The priority of each node is determined by the heuristic value: the lower the value, the higher the priority.

3. **Completeness:** Best-first search is a complete algorithm, meaning it will always find a solution if one exists. However, it may not be efficient in terms of time and space in some cases.

4. **Optimality:** If best-first search uses an admissible heuristic, it is guaranteed to find an optimal solution, i.e., the shortest path or the best solution according to the given heuristic.

Best-first search is a versatile and effective algorithm with a wide range of applications in computer science and AI. Its ability to efficiently explore search spaces by selecting the most promising nodes first, based on a heuristic function, makes it a valuable tool for solving complex problems. When combined with admissible heuristics, best-first search guarantees optimality, making it a crucial component in many real-world systems.

2.5.4 A* SEARCH ALGORITHM

The A* search algorithm is a widely used and highly efficient path-finding algorithm in computer science and AI. It is essential for solving problems like route planning, maze solving, and even game AI development. In this comprehensive guide, we will delve into the A* search algorithm, its principles, and how to implement it effectively.

Understanding the Basics of A* Search:

A* (pronounced as "A star") is a combination of two essential components:

1. **G-Cost (g(n)):** The cost of reaching a particular node from the start node. It is the total cost incurred from the start node to the current node.
2. **H-Cost (h(n)):** The estimated cost from the current node to the goal node. It is an educated guess of how far the current node is from the goal.

The A* algorithm balances these two factors by selecting the nodes with the lowest total cost, which is defined as the sum of the G-Cost and H-Cost. The algorithm is guided by the principle that it should explore nodes with lower total costs first, making it both efficient and optimal.

A* Algorithm Workflow

1. **Initialize Open and Closed Lists:** Formulate two lists: the open list and the closed list. The open list includes nodes that are pending evaluation, while the closed list consists of nodes that have already been assessed.
2. **Add the Start Node to the Open List:** Start the search by adding the starting node to the open list. Set its G-Cost to zero.
3. **While the Open List Is Not Empty:**
   a. Identify the Node with the Lowest F-Cost: Find the node in the open list that has the lowest total cost (F-Cost).
   b. Transfer the Selected Node to the Closed List: Take the node out of the open list and add it to the closed list.
   c. Check if the Selected Node Is the Goal Node: If it is, the path has been located. Backtrack from the goal node to trace the optimal path.
   d. Generate Successor Nodes: Expand the selected node by generating its neighboring nodes.
   e. For Each Neighbor:
      i. Calculate the G-Cost: Calculate the G-Cost for the neighbor node.
      ii. If the neighbor is in the closed list and the new G-Cost is lower, update it: If the neighbor is already in the closed list but can be reached with a lower G-Cost, update its values.
      iii. If the neighbor is not in the open list, add it: If the neighbor is not in the open list, calculate its F-Cost, add it to the open list, and set the current node as its parent.
      iv. Continue to the next neighbor.
4. **Path Not Found:** If the open list has become empty and the goal node has not been reached, that means there is no path from the start to the goal node. **A* Search:** A* search is widely used to find the optimal path from a starting state to a goal state in a search space, taking into account both the cost to reach a node from the initial state (g) and an estimate of the cost from that node to the goal state (h). It is given by

$$f(n) = g(n) + h(n)$$

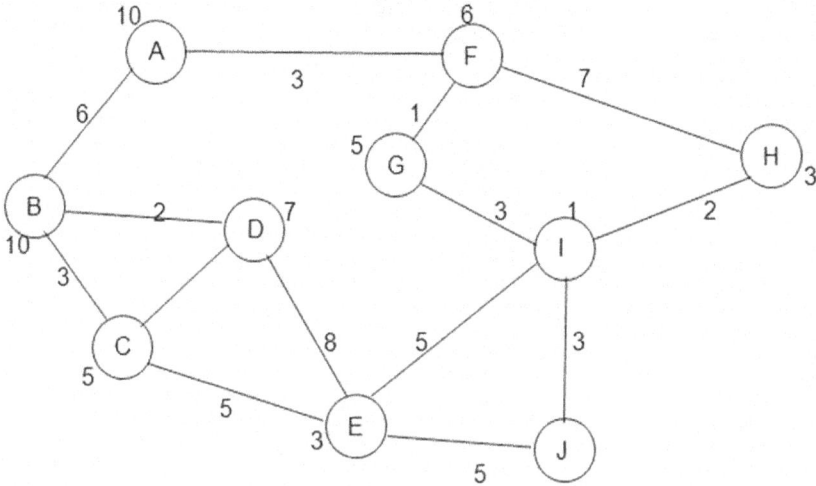

FIGURE 2.13 Graph.

Consider the following graph.

Step 01: We begin with node A. Nodes B and F are accessible from node A. The A* algorithm calculates f(B) and f(F). f(B) equals 6 plus 8, resulting in 14. f(F) equals 3 plus 6, resulting in 9. Because f(F) is less than f(B), we proceed to node F. The path is A to F.

Step 02: Nodes G and H can be reached from node F.
A* algorithm calculates f(G) and f(H).

$$F(G) = (3 + 1) + 5 = 9$$
$$F(H) = (3 + 7) + 3 = 13$$

Since f(G) < f(H), it now moves to node G.
Step 03: Node I can be reached from nodes G and H.
A* algorithm calculates f(I).
From node G,

$$f(I) = (3 + 1 + 3) + 1 = 8$$

From node H,

$$f(I) = (3 + 7 + 2) + 1 = 13$$

Since f(I) from node G < f(I) from node H, we move to node I from node G.
Therefore, Path A → F → G → I.
This is the required shortest path from node A to node I.
The A* search algorithm is a versatile and efficient approach to path-finding problems. By understanding its underlying principles and following the workflow, you

can apply A* to a wide range of applications, from games to logistics and robotics, to find the shortest and most optimal paths.

The implementation of A* in Python is given below:

```python
import heapq

class Node:
    def __init__(self, name):
        self.name = name
        self.edges = {}
        self.g = float('inf') # cost from start node to
current node
        self.h = 0 # heuristic cost from current node to
goal node
        self.f = float('inf') # total cost (g + h)
        self.parent = None

    # COMPARISON METHOD FOR PRIORITY QUEUE
    def __lt__(self, other):
        return self.f < other.f

class Edge:
    def __init__(self, node, cost):
        self.node = node
        self.cost = cost

class AStar:
    def __init__(self, start_node, goal_node):
        self.start_node = start_node
        self.goal_node = goal_node
        self.open_list = []
        self.closed_list = set()

    # HEURISTIC FUNCTION
    def calculate_heuristic(self, node):
        return abs(ord(node.name) - ord(self.goal_node.
name))

    def run(self):
        # INITIALIZE START NODE
        self.start_node.g = 0
        self.start_node.h = self.calculate_heuristic(-
self.start_node)
        self.start_node.f = self.start_node.g + self.
start_node.h
        heapq.heappush(self.open_list, self.start_node)
```

```
        while self.open_list:
            # SELECT NODE WITH LOWEST F-SCORE
            current_node = heapq.heappop(self.open_list)
            self.closed_list.add(current_node)

            # CHECK FOR GOAL
            if current_node == self.goal_node:
                path = []
                while current_node:
                    path.append(current_node.name)
                    current_node = current_node.parent
                return path[::-1]

            # EXPLORE NEIGHBORS
            for edge in current_node.edges.values():
                neighbor = edge.node
                tentative_g = current_node.g + edge.
cost
                if neighbor not in self.closed_list or
tentative_g < neighbor.g:
                        neighbor.parent = current_node
                        neighbor.g = tentative_g
                        neighbor.h = self.calculate_
heuristic(neighbor)
                        neighbor.f = neighbor.g + neighbor.h
                        heapq.heappush(self.open_list, neighbor)
        return None

# Usage
if __name__ == "__main__":
    # Create nodes
    node_a = Node("A")
    node_b = Node("B")
    node_c = Node("C")
    node_d = Node("D")
    node_e = Node("E")

    # Create edges
    node_a.edges = {"B": Edge(node_b, 2), "C": Edge(node_c,
3)}
    node_b.edges = {"D": Edge(node_d, 2), "E": Edge
(node_e, 4)}
    node_c.edges = {"D": Edge(node_d, 1)}
    node_d.edges = {"E": Edge(node_e, 1)}
```

```
# RUN A* ALGORITHM
astar = AStar(node_a, node_e)
path = astar.run()
print("Shortest path:", path)
```

Output   Clear

Shortest path: ['A', 'C', 'D', 'E']

=== Code Execution Successful ===|

3.5.4 Means–Ends Analysis: Means–ends analysis is a problem-solving technique commonly used in AI to narrow down the search space in AI applications. This method employs strategies that can reason both forward and backward, making it suitable for addressing large, complex problems. It functions by breaking down larger problems into smaller, more manageable subproblems and then solving these smaller parts sequentially.

Central to this technique is the evaluation of differences between the current state and the desired goal, with the aim of reducing these disparities. An essential aspect of intelligence is the ability to identify a series of actions that lead to a desired outcome. A problem-solving system should be connected to its environment through input (afferent) sensors and output (efferent) actions. A means-ends analysis system also incorporates memory to store information about the environment's state, sensors, and actions.

Case: Goal Stack Planning

Goal stack planning involves organizing goals and subgoals in a hierarchical manner. We start at the goal state and try fulfilling the preconditions required to be satisfied first. We iterate over the goals and subgoals until we reach the initial state. A stack is used to hold these goals and the actions that we need to perform.

Algorithm

1. Push the original goal on stack.
2. Repeat following until the stack is empty.
   a. If stack-top is a compound goal, push its subgoals.
   b. If stack-top is a single unsatisfied goal, replace it with action and its preconditions.
   c. If stack-top is action, pop and extend the knowledge base with action effects.
   d. If stack-top is a satisfying goal, pop it from the stack.

Heuristic Guidance

Heuristics in MEA serve as problem-solving strategies that guide the selection and application of means to achieve goals. Heuristics are the rules of thumb or guiding principles that expedite the decision-making process, helping navigate through the solution space more efficiently.

   a. **Subgoal Ordering**

      Subgoal ordering involves prioritizing or ordering the resolution of sub-goals based on certain criteria. This can include factors such as dependencies between subgoals, the ease of resolution, or the significance of a subgoal in achieving the overall objective.

   b. **Difference Reduction**

      Difference reduction focuses on identifying the differences between the current state and the desired goal state. The heuristic strategy involves selecting the means that reduce these differences incrementally, guiding the system toward the goal.

   c. **Means Refinement**

      Means refinement involves continuously improving and optimizing the selected means during the problem-solving process. This heuristic ensures that the chosen means are not only effective in achieving the subgoals but also are refined iteratively to enhance efficiency.

Algorithmic Implementation

Initialization

The algorithm begins with the input of the problem description, including the initial state and the desired goal state.

   i. Create an empty goal stack to present the hierarchy of goals and subgoals.
   ii. Push the top-level goal into the goal stack.
   iii. Initialize the current state to the initial state of the problem.

Means Identification

At each iteration, pop the top goal from the goal stack.

   i. Identify potential means (actions or subgoals) that can be applied to achieve the current goal.
   ii. Apply heuristics to guide the selection of most suitable means.
   iii. Evaluate the effectiveness of each potential means based on the heuristics. If means refinement is part of the strategy, adjust the chosen means to optimize the solution path.

Iteration

   a. Check if the current state satisfies the goal at the top of the stack. If yes, mark the goal as achieved and proceed to the next iteration.

b. If the goal is not achieved, apply the selected means to transition the system to a new state. Update the current state based on the side effects of the chosen means.

c. If subgoals are generated in the process, push them onto the goal stack, maintaining the hierarchical structure.

d. Repeat the process from b. until the top level goal is marked as achieved.

The algorithm terminates once the top level goal is achieved. The sequence of means and subgoals that lead from the initial state to the goal state represents the solution path.

Extensions and Enhancements to MEA

Backward Chaining

Backward chaining is an extension of MEA that reverses the problem-solving direction. Instead of starting with the initial state and progressing toward the goal, backward chaining starts with the goal and works backward to identify the means necessary to achieve it.

Backward chaining is particularly useful in scenarios where the final goal is known, and the challenge lies in determining the prerequisite conditions or subgoals to reach that goal.

Forward Chaining

In contrast to backward chaining, forward chaining starts with the initial state and progresses toward the goal. It iteratively applies means to achieve subgoals, gradually building toward the top-level goal.

Forward chaining is effective when the initial state is known, and the challenge is to determine the sequence of actions or subgoals that lead to the desired outcome.

Domain Knowledge

The basic MEA algorithm can be enhanced by incorporating domain-specific knowledge. This involves leveraging information about the problem domain to guide the selection of means and improve the efficiency of problem-solving.

Incorporating domain-specific knowledge enhances the adaptability of MEA by tailoring the problem-solving approach to the intricacies of a particular domain. This is especially valuable when dealing with complex and specialized problem spaces.

2.5.5   PROBLEM REDUCTION AND AO* ALGORITHM

AI has redefined problem-solving strategies, offering innovative techniques such as problem reduction and the AO* algorithm. Problem reduction, a key AI approach, involves simplifying intricate problems by dividing them into manageable subproblems, streamlining the overall solution process. The AO* algorithm, a pivotal search algorithm in AI, extends the capabilities of the renowned A* algorithm, enhancing search efficiency and solution optimization. By integrating these techniques, AI systems can effectively address complex tasks, contributing significantly to the development of intelligent problem-solving methodologies.

Problem Reduction:

Problem reduction is a critical technique in the field of AI that serves to simplify complex problems by decomposing them into smaller, more manageable subproblems. This method is crucial in AI because it allows for the effective resolution of intricate tasks that may otherwise be too challenging or time-consuming to solve directly.

The significance of problem reduction in AI lies in its ability to streamline the problem-solving process. By breaking down complex problems into simpler components, AI systems can address each subproblem independently, making the overall task more feasible and comprehensible. This approach not only reduces the computational burden but also enables the application of specific algorithms or techniques tailored to each subproblem. As a result, AI systems can efficiently navigate and resolve complex real-world issues, ranging from automated planning and reasoning to natural language processing and computer vision. Overall, problem reduction plays a crucial role in enhancing the efficiency and effectiveness of AI systems, making it an indispensable strategy in the realm of AI.

Why Problem Reduction Is Needed?

Problem reduction optimizes the allocation of computational resources, ensuring that the AI system operates effectively within resource constraints. By facilitating a systematic and targeted approach to addressing multifaceted real-world issues, problem reduction significantly contributes to the overall effectiveness of AI applications.

How Problem Reduction Is Performed in AI?

Problem reduction is typically performed through a systematic approach that involves several key techniques:

- **Decomposition:** Breaking down complex problems into simpler subproblems that are more manageable and easier to solve.
- **Abstraction:** Focusing on the essential aspects of the problem while ignoring unnecessary details, allowing for a more streamlined analysis.
- **Dependency Analysis:** Identifying and understanding the relationships and dependencies among different components of the problem to determine their interconnections and dependencies.
- **Heuristic Evaluation:** Employing heuristic techniques to guide the problem-solving process and prioritize subproblems based on their estimated potential for solution optimality.
- **Constraint Satisfaction:** Ensuring that the solutions generated for each subproblem adhere to a set of predefined constraints or conditions, thus maintaining the integrity of the overall problem-solving process.

AO* Algorithm:

The AO* (A-star-Optimal) algorithm is an extension of the A* algorithm, commonly used in AI for path finding and graph traversal. It aims to improve the efficiency and optimality of the search process. AO* achieves this by integrating problem reduction heuristics and additional techniques to guide the search more effectively toward the optimal solution. The algorithm incorporates a heuristic function to estimate the cost of reaching the goal from a particular node, thus guiding the search toward the most promising paths. It also prioritizes node expansion based on the cost incurred so far and the estimated cost to reach the goal, ensuring an optimal solution. The use of problem reduction heuristics allows AO* to streamline the search process, making it a powerful tool for solving complex optimization and path-finding problems in various AI applications.

The AO* algorithm is a type of best-first search used for finding optimal solutions in AND–OR graphs. Unlike A*, it works on graphs with alternative paths (OR) and mandatory subgoals (AND).

AND–OR Graph: A graph with two types of nodes:
   o   **AND Node:** Requires all its child nodes to be reached to achieve the goal.
   o   **OR Node:** Only one child node needs to be reached to achieve the goal.
f(n): Evaluation function, sum of actual cost (g(n)) from the start to the current node and the estimated cost (h(n)) from the current node to the goal.
Open List: Stores nodes to be explored, ordered by f(n).
Closed List: Stores explored nodes.

Steps in Algorithm:

Steps:

1. **Initialize:** Put the starting node in the open list with f(n) based on the heuristic.
2. **Loop:**
   o   Select the node with the lowest f(n) from the open list.
   o   If it's a goal node, you have the optimal solution. Stop.
   o   If it's an OR node, expand it by adding all its children to the open list with f(n) calculated.
   o   If it's an AND node:
      –   Expand all its children.
      –   For each child, check if it's already in the closed list with a lower f(n).
      –   If yes, skip it (better path found previously).
      –   If no, add it to the open list with f(n) calculated.
   o   Update f(n) of the parent node based on the best child's f(n) (propagation). This ensures the most promising path is explored first.
   o   Move the selected node to the closed list.

Imagine you need to travel from City A to City G. You can either drive (D) or take a train (T). Driving allows a detour to City E (optional, OR node). A train goes directly to City G or City F (alternative, OR node). We have estimated travel times (heuristics) between cities.

Graph:

```
A
/\
D T
/\/\
B E F G
```

Travel Times:

- A-B: 1
- A-D: 2
- B-E: 3
- D-E: 1
- T-F: 4
- T-G: 5
- E-G: 2
- F-G: 1

Solution:

1. Start with A, f(A) = 0 + estimated travel time to G (let's say 7) = 7.
2. Explore A's children (D and T).
   o D: f(D) = 2 + estimated travel time to G (let's say 5) = 7.
   o T: f(T) = 0 + 5 = 5 (lower than D, becomes priority).
3. Explore T's children (F and G).
   o G is the goal, so stop! The optimal path is A -> T -> G with total cost 5.

We started with the most promising option (train) based on the heuristic. Since T led directly to the goal, we didn't need to explore the detour via driving (D). The algorithm also ensured the best path within the train option (T -> G) by updating the parent node's (T) f(n) based on the child's (G) actual cost.

This is a simplified example. In real-world scenarios, the heuristics might not be perfect, and the algorithm might explore some unnecessary paths before finding the optimal solution. However, AO* guarantees an optimal solution eventually and is efficient for problems with alternative paths and mandatory subgoals.

- **Optimal Path Selection:** After reaching the goal node, trace back the path from the goal node to the start node using the recorded parent nodes, thus determining the optimal path.

Connection between AO* and Problem Reduction:

The AO* algorithm is closely connected to problem reduction in AI as it integrates problem reduction heuristics to enhance search efficiency. By breaking down complex problems into manageable subproblems, AO* prioritizes relevant nodes, thus guiding the search toward the most promising solutions. Its heuristic evaluation and optimal path selection rely on problem decomposition, ensuring an effective and targeted approach to complex problem-solving. This integration allows AO* to streamline the search process, leading to the efficient resolution of intricate tasks within AI applications.

Problem reduction is indispensable for managing complex tasks, optimizing resource allocation, and applying specialized techniques, enabling AI systems to navigate intricate real-world challenges effectively. Meanwhile, the AO* algorithm's integration of problem reduction heuristics enhances search efficiency, prioritizing relevant nodes and guiding the search toward optimal solutions. Its practical applications in robotics, logistics, and gaming underscore its significance in enabling efficient pathfinding solutions and advancing intelligent systems. Together, these methodologies drive the development of sophisticated AI systems.

2.5.6 CONSTRAINT SATISFACTION

Constraint satisfaction is the process of finding a solution through a set of constraints that impose conditions that the variable must satisfy. Depending on the type of constraints under consideration, several strategies are employed in constraint satisfaction. Constraints on a finite domains are widely employed, to the extent that issues based on constraints on a finite domain are usually identified with constraint satisfaction problems (CSPs). Typically, searches are used to tackle these kinds of issues; specifically, local or backtracking searches are used. Another family of approaches employed in similar situations is constraint propagation; generally speaking, most of them are incomplete, meaning they may show the problem as unsatisfactory or solve it, but not always. In addition, constraint propagation techniques are applied in conjunction with search to reduce the complexity of a particular issue. Real or rational numbers are other types of restrictions that are taken into consideration; issues involving these constraints are solved.

Constraint encapsulation into programming languages was developed in the 1980s and 1990s. Prolog was the first language designed specifically to facilitate constraint programming. Since then, constraint-programming libraries—like Choco for Java—have been made accessible in languages other than C++ or Java.

In the 1970s, the science of AI introduced constraint satisfaction as a generic issue. The field dates back to Joseph Fourier in the 19th century, however, when the constraints were expressed as multidimensional linear equations defining (in)equalities. George Dantzig's 1946 invention of the simplex algorithm for linear programming, a special case of mathematical optimization, made it possible to determine workable solutions to problems with hundreds of variables.

The key components of constraint satisfaction include the following:

1. **Variables:** These are the things or entities to which values must be allocated in order to meet the restrictions. Generally, there is a range of values that can be assigned to each variable.
2. **Domains:** The collection of all potential values that a variable can have is known as its domain. In a Sudoku problem, for instance, every cell represents a variable with a range of integers from 1 to 9.

Constraints: Relationships or requirements that must be met between the variables are known as constraints. These limitations can be stated as equations, logical statements, or any other kind of relation. The combinations of variable assignments that are allowed and not allowed are specified by constraints.

1. **Constraint Satisfaction Problem:**

A group of objects whose state must meet several restrictions or limits is referred to as a CSP in mathematics. Constraint satisfaction techniques address the homogeneous collection of finite constraints over variables that CSPs describe as entities in a problem.

Formal Definition of CSP:

Formally, a CSP is defined as a triple, where

- $X = \{X1, \ldots, Xn\}$ is a set of variables;
- $X = \{V1, \ldots, Vn\}$ is a set of their respective domains of values; and
- $X = \{C1, \ldots, Cn\}$ is a set of constraints.

CSP Algorithm:

The backtracking algorithm is a DFS technique that gradually explores the search space of potential solutions until a solution that fulfills all the requirements is found. Before continuously attempting to assign values to the other variables, the technique first selects one variable and assigns a value to it. If at any moment a variable cannot be provided a value that satisfies the requirements, the procedure goes back to the previous variable and attempts a different value. The algorithm is complete after every assignment has been tried or a solution that fulfills every requirement has been found.

A modified version of the backtracking method that uses some form of local consistency to reduce the search space is the forward-checking algorithm. The method maintains a list of the remaining values for each unassigned variable and applies local constraints to remove conflicting values from these sets. After a variable is given a value, the algorithm looks at its neighbor to determine if any of the remaining values becomes inconsistent. If they do, the program eliminates those neighbors from the sets. If a variable has no more values after a forward check, the algorithm reverses the direction.

- Local consistency and inference are two techniques used by algorithms for propagating constraints to reduce the size of the search space. These algorithms work by propagating limitations across variables and using the gathered data to remove inconsistent values from the variable domains.

Algorithm Steps
- Choose an unassigned variable.
- Assign a value from its domain.

- Check if the assignment violates any constraints with already assigned variables.
  - If yes, backtrack: Undo the assignment and try a different value for the same variable.
  - If no, proceed to the next unassigned variable.
- Repeat steps 2–4 until all variables are assigned or a dead end is reached (no valid value for the current variable).

2. **Constraint Propagation:**

Constraint propagation techniques improve backtracking by reducing the search space. The idea is to remove inconsistent values from variable domains before assigning them. This avoids exploring paths that will ultimately lead to failure. Here are some common constraint propagation techniques:

- **Arc Consistency (AC-3):** This algorithm ensures that for any two variables connected by a constraint, no value in one variable's domain leads to a violation when paired with any value in the other variable's domain.

Constraint propagation can significantly reduce the search space for backtracking, making it more efficient for complex problems.

Here's an example of a CSP:

Problem: Assigning colors (red, green, and blue) to three houses such that no two neighboring houses have the same color.
Variables: House 1, House 2, House 3.
Domains: {Red, Green, Blue} for each house.
Constraints: House 1–House 2 (colors must be different), House 2–House 3 (colors must be different).

This problem can be solved using backtracking with constraint propagation (AC-3) for efficiency.

These are just two basic algorithms for solving CSPs. There are many variations and more advanced techniques depending on the specific problem characteristics.

Constraint Graph:

A constraint graph is a graphical representation of a CSP. A constraint graph has the following elements:

1. **Nodes:** Each node in the graph represents a variable in the CSP.
2. **Edges:** An edge between two nodes represents a constraint between the corresponding variables. If variables X and Y have a constraint, there is an edge between the nodes representing X and Y in the graph.

In constraint satisfaction research in AI and operation research, constraint graphs and hypergraphs are used to represent the relationship among constraints in a CSP.

A constraint graph is a special case of a factor graph that allows for the existence of free variables.

Constraint Hypergraph:

A constraint fulfillment problem's constraint hypergraph is a hypergraph in which variables are represented by the vertices and constraints are represented by the hyperedges. If the matching variables are those found in a constraint, then a group of vertices forms a hyperedge.

1. Primal Constraint Graph:

The graph where each node represents a variable of the issue and an edge connects two nodes if the corresponding variables appear together in a constraint is known as the primal constraint graph, also known as the primal graph or the Gaifman graph, of a constraint fulfillment problem.

In the real world, the constraint hypergraph's primary graph is the primal constraint graph.

Advantages of CSPs:

1. Problem Modeling:
   Adaptability:
   CSPs are capable of modeling a variety of real-world issues, such as puzzles, scheduling, resource allocation, and configuration. They can be used in a variety of fields because of their adaptability.
   Natural Representation:
   A large number of issues across various fields can be naturally represented as CSPs, which facilitate comprehension and problem-solving for problem-solvers.
2. Effective Problem-Solving:
   Optimization:
   By establishing objective functions and incorporating them into the constraints, CSPs can be applied to optimization problems. This makes it possible to identify solutions that meet particular requirements or those that are ideal.
   Heuristics:
   A number of algorithms and heuristics have been devised to solve CSPs effectively, which makes them useful in cases of huge and difficult problems.
   Incremental Problem-Solving (CSP): In dynamic situations, partial solutions can be developed and refined over time, thanks to CSP solutions' ability to be built incrementally.
3. Real-World Applications:
   Scheduling:
   To maximize resource usage and reduce conflicts, CSPs are utilized in timetabling, personnel scheduling, project management, and other scheduling issues.

Configuration: CSPs are used in product configuration, which includes adjusting hardware, software, or services to meet the needs of the client.

Circuit Design:

By guaranteeing that components adhere to particular specifications and limitations, CSPs support the design of electronic circuits.

In robotics, CSPs are useful for motion planning, which is the process of guiding a robot through a given area while avoiding obstacles and adhering to mobility restrictions.

Natural Language Processing:

CSPs are utilized for tasks such as word sense clarification and grammar correction.

4. Decision Support:

Diagnosis and Troubleshooting:

By modeling the relationships between symptoms and likely causes such as constraints, CSPs can be utilized to diagnose system flaws.

Resource Allocation:

CSPs help in efficiently allocating resources like labor, equipment, and funds to ensure maximum utilization.

5. Collaborative Problem-Solving in Multi-Agent Systems:

In multi-agent systems, CSPs are used to simulate agent interactions and promote cooperation and bargaining.

Building Consensus:

CSPs can assist parties in coming to an agreement by identifying solutions that meet the needs and preferences of all parties.

6. Educational Objectives:

Teaching Tool:

CSPs are used in AI and computer science courses to teach problem-solving strategies, algorithms, and heuristics.

7. Development and Research:

Algorithm Development:

In the fields of AI and optimization, researchers use CSPs as a framework to create and test novel algorithms and methods.

CSPs are useful for prototyping and testing novel approaches to problem-solving before implementing them in more complicated systems.

Problems in CSPs:

Combinatorial Explosion in CSPs:

There can be a huge number of alternative assignment combinations, creating a large search space. Pruning strategies and clever heuristics are essential for controlling this explosion.

Local Minimum:

Occasionally, a CSP algorithm may become trapped in a situation where a solution is actually there but unable to be found. Methods such as reverse engineering and intelligent variable and value selection assist in reducing this issue.

2.5.7 CASE STUDIES ON PRODUCTION SYSTEM

Example 1: Let's construct a basic production system to categorize geometric shapes based on their properties:

Knowledge Base Rules:

Rule 1: If a shape has three sides and three angles, then it is a triangle.
Rule 2: If a shape has four equal sides and four right angles, then it is a square.
Rule 3: If a shape has four sides and opposite sides are parallel, then it is a parallelogram.

Working Memory (Initial Facts):

The shape has three sides.
The shape has three angles.

Inference Engine:

The inference engine would match the first rule (Rule 1) based on the given facts, place it on the agenda, and fire it. This would update the working memory with the new fact: "The shape is a triangle."

Expert Systems: Classic production systems in AI often incorporate expert systems. These systems emulate the problem-solving capabilities of human experts within specific fields. They employ a rule-based approach, where an inference engine processes a knowledge base of rules to draw conclusions and offer expert advice. Examples of expert systems include medical diagnosis systems and financial advisory systems.

Manufacturing Control Systems:

In manufacturing, AI-powered production systems are utilized to supervise and optimize process performance. Rules guide machine adjustments, inventory management, and quality control parameters. These systems enhance efficiency and responsiveness in dynamic manufacturing environments.

Customer Support Chatbots:

Customer support chatbots leverage production rules to interact with users based on predetermined criteria. The chatbot's responses to user inquiries are governed by rules that dictate its actions, such as providing information or escalating the issue to a human supervisor. These systems improve customer satisfaction and streamline support operations.

3 Knowledge Representation

Knowledge representation is a fundamental aspect of artificial intelligence (AI) that deals with the organization and structuring of information to facilitate machine understanding and reasoning. In this chapter, we focus on the key subtopics of knowledge representation: ontologies, objects, and events.

There are many subtopics in the field of knowledge representation:

1. Ontologies:

Ontologies are a crucial component of knowledge representation in AI. They provide a structured way to define and represent concepts, entities, and their interrelationships within a specific domain. An ontology comprises a controlled vocabulary of terms and a formal description of how these terms relate to one another. Ontologies serve as a shared understanding of a domain, enabling machines to reason and make inferences based on this structured knowledge.

2. Objects:

Objects represent entities or things in the world that AI systems need to understand and manipulate. Objects in knowledge representation are characterized by their properties, attributes, and relationships with other objects. They serve as a foundation for representing real-world entities in a structured manner, allowing AI systems to reason about and interact with them. In AI, object-oriented knowledge representation is used in applications such as robotics, computer vision, and expert systems.

Objects play a crucial role in AI knowledge representation, providing a structured way to model and represent entities, concepts, and their attributes within a given domain. They are fundamental in organizing information and facilitating reasoning in various AI applications. Here are some key uses of objects in AI knowledge representation:

a. **Entity Modeling:** Objects represent entities or things in the world. In AI systems, these entities can range from physical objects like cars or animals to abstract concepts like ideas or events. Objects allow AI systems to work with these entities in a structured manner.

b. **Attribute Representation:** Each object can have attributes that describe its characteristics or properties. For example, a "car" object may have attributes like "color," "model," and "year." This attribute–value representation is vital for capturing essential information about objects.

DOI: 10.1201/9781003532170-3

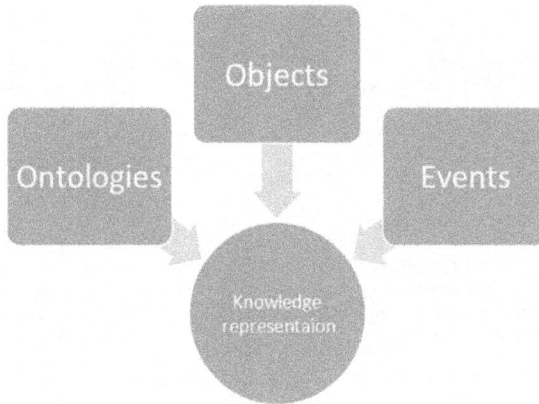

FIGURE 3.1 Knowledge Representation.

c. **Relationship Modeling:** Objects can be related to one another through relationships. These relationships describe how objects interact or are connected. For instance, a "person" object can have a "works for" relationship with a "company" object, indicating employment.
d. **Hierarchical Organization:** Objects can be organized hierarchically, creating a structured taxonomy. This hierarchy helps in classifying and categorizing objects based on their similarities and differences. For example, a taxonomy of animals might include objects like "mammals," "birds," and "reptiles."
e. **Ontology Development:** In building ontologies, which are formal representations of knowledge in a specific domain, objects play a central role. They define the classes or concepts in the ontology and their associated properties and relationships.
f. **Reasoning and Decision Support:** Objects, their attributes, and relationships enable AI systems to perform reasoning and decision-making. For instance, a diagnostic system might use objects representing symptoms, diseases, and patient information to make medical diagnoses.

In summary, objects are a foundational element of AI knowledge representation, serving as a structured way to model and work with entities, concepts, and their attributes and relationships in a domain. They are integral to various AI applications, enabling systems to organize, reason about, and interact with the world in a more intelligent and context-aware manner.

III) Events:

Events in knowledge representation refer to occurrences or happenings that can be observed and described. Events are essential for capturing the dynamic aspects of the world, such as processes, actions, and changes. Representing events involves specifying

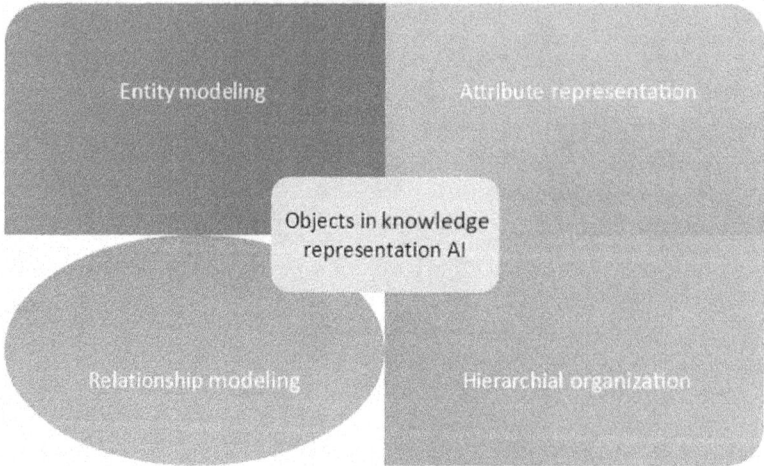

FIGURE 3.2   Applications of Objects in AI.

their participants, time, and the conditions under which they occur. Understanding events is crucial for AI systems that need to model and reason about dynamic scenarios, such as natural language understanding, process automation, and monitoring systems.

Events are essential elements in AI knowledge representation, particularly when dealing with dynamic and temporal aspects of a domain. They allow AI systems to capture, model, and reason about processes, changes, and occurrences. Here are some key uses of events in the knowledge representation of AI:

1. **Process Modeling:** Events are used to model and represent processes and workflows. This is crucial in areas like business process management and industrial automation.
2. **Temporal Reasoning:** Events help AI systems reason about the sequence of events over time. Temporal reasoning is essential in scheduling, planning, and tracking changes in dynamic environments.
3. **Change Detection:** Events enable the detection and monitoring of changes in a system. For example, they are used in intrusion detection systems to identify suspicious events in network traffic.
4. **Causal Inference:** Events can be used to establish causal relationships between different occurrences, helping AI systems understand why certain events happen as a result of others.
5. **Event Detection in Text:** In natural language processing (NLP), events are used to extract and understand actions, occurrences, and developments in text, facilitating tasks like information extraction and event summarization.
6. **Event-Based Reasoning:** AI systems can use events to reason about actions and their consequences. This is valuable in automated planning and decision support.

Some of the uses of events in AI:

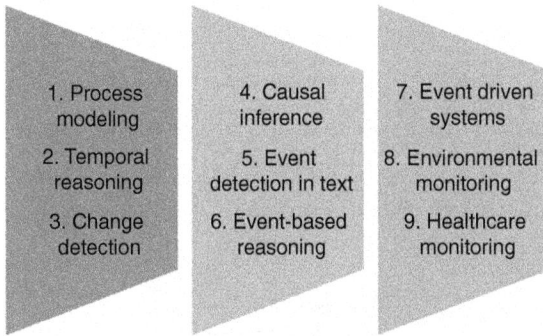

FIGURE 3.3 Events in AI.

In AI, the use of events is paramount for understanding and modeling processes, changes, and temporal dynamics in various domains. They enable AI systems to make sense of and respond to the evolving and dynamic nature of the world.

Knowledge Representation and Mapping:

- Knowledge and Representation:
  - o Knowledge is the important element, or we can say it is the information that current computer AI uses so that from the given knowledge that AI may infer some useful statistical data for any organization or its use.
  - o Knowledge is information that prevails in the world. Representation is the way knowledge is represented in different formats, e.g., encoding. It defines a system's performance in any computational tasks.
- Types of Knowledge:

The diagram illustrates the steps AI takes to achieve its objectives. It begins with the perception component, which collects information from various sources such as audio, video, text from platforms like Instagram, and social media.

Subsequently, the learning component plays a crucial role in acquiring knowledge from the data gathered by perception. This process enables the AI system to adapt and improve its performance.

However, the core of AI lies in the knowledge representation and reasoning components. These two aspects are pivotal in enabling the machine to mimic human-like activities. While they operate independently, they are also integrated to enhance the AI's capabilities.

Finally, the planning and execution phases rely heavily on the analysis of the knowledge represented and reasoned upon. These stages are where AI translates its acquired intelligence into practical actions to achieve its intended goals.

❖

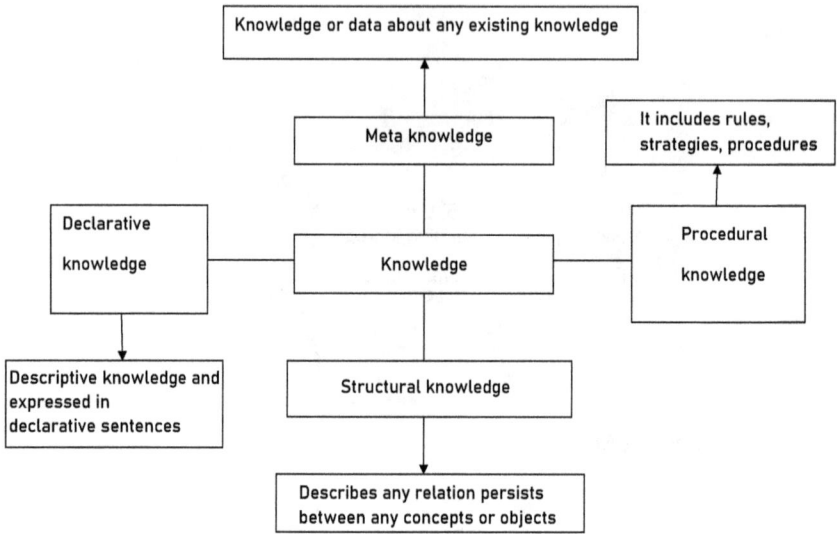

FIGURE 3.4   AI Knowledge Cycle.

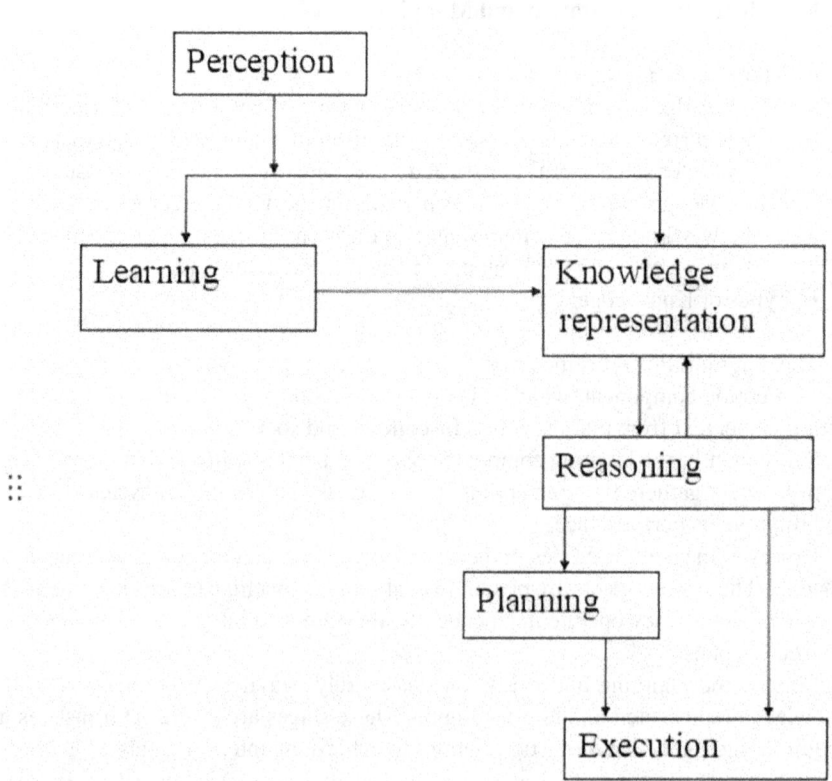

FIGURE 3.5   AI Components.

3.1 KNOWLEDGE REPRESENTATION USING PREDICATE LOGIC

3.1.1 KNOWLEDGE

Knowledge is any information or data that is well-organized and well-structured and can be processed in such a way that it is efficient for an intelligent system to understand, process, and infer results from. It also enables the system to act upon the data and make necessary judgments or decisions.

Knowledge includes facts, concepts, rules, relationships, and all inferred or derived results about a particular domain or problem. With this knowledge, an AI system can solve problems, make informed decisions, and perform necessary tasks and jobs.

There are two main types of knowledge in AI:

Declarative Knowledge: This represents facts and information about a particular domain or a problem. It includes statements about objects, their properties, and the relationships between them.

It answers questions like, "What is?"

Procedural Knowledge: This focuses on how to perform tasks and actions. It also includes rules, procedures, algorithms, and strategies for solving problems or for achieving goals.

It answers questions like, "How can I?"

3.1.2 KNOWLEDGE REPRESENTATION

In AI, knowledge representation is the process of encoding, structuring, and organizing knowledge in such a format that can be easily used by an AI system to make calculated decisions and reasoning. Knowledge representation allows machines to store, manipulate, and access information relevant to a particular task or domain, and due to this reason, knowledge representation is a fundamental component of AI systems.

3.1.3 PREDICATE LOGIC

Predicate logic is a mathematical model used in AI for reasoning with predicates. We use predicates to model facts and use them to reason facts and derive results from the facts or take informed decisions.

Some key components of predicate logic are as follows.

Predicates: Predicates are statements or properties that can be true or false depending on the values of their arguments. In predicate logic, predicates are represented by symbols or letters, often followed by variables. For example,

P(x) might represent the predicate "x is a prime number."

Variables: Variables are placeholders that can take on various values. In predicate logic, variables are often denoted using letters, such as x, y, or z. They are used to represent objects or elements in the domain of discourse.

Quantifiers: We use two quantifiers in predicate logic: the universal quantifier ($\forall$) and the existential quantifier ($\exists$). These quantifiers allow us to make statements about all or some elements in a domain.

Universal quantifier ($\forall$) is used to express that a statement is true for all elements in the domain. For example, $\forall x\ P(x)$ might mean "For all values of x, P(x) is true."

Existential quantifier ($\exists$) is used to express that a statement is true for at least one element in the domain. For example, $\exists x\ P(x)$ might mean "There exists at least one value of x for which P(x) is true."

3.1.4 Knowledge Representation Using Predicate Logic

We can represent knowledge in predicate logic using the aforementioned components. For example,

Rajesh is a soldier.
Suresh is a doctor.

The above facts or statements can be represented as

Rajesh is a solider.
Soldier(Rajesh)
Suresh is a doctor.
Doctor(Suresh)
We now use quantifiers to represent more complex facts.

Universal Quantifier ($\forall$):

$\forall x$: means "For all x."
This means that something is true for all possible values of a variable: in this case x.

For example:

Ketan knows everyone.
$\forall x$: knows (Ketan,x)
Existential Quantifier ($\exists$):
$\exists x$: means there exists some.
This means that there is some possible value of x for which this is true.

For example:

Somebody knows Ketan.
$\exists x$: knows(x, Ketan)

We can also use both quantifiers separately:

For example:

Everybody loves somebody.
$\forall x: \exists y: loves(x, y)$

3.1.5 REPRESENTING FACTS IN LOGIC

Logic provides a precise language for expressing facts and knowledge. It eliminates vagueness, which ensures that statements are clear and well-defined. Logic allows for the formalization of facts and relationships, making it possible to represent knowledge systematically. Logical representation enables automated inference and reasoning. Logic allows us to check for inconsistencies in a set of facts. Logic is used to represent problems, constraints, and goals. To represent facts in logic, we use a structured approach that involves the following components.

Statements and Predicates:

Facts are expressed as statements. Predicates, typically written as "P(x)," convey properties or relationships.

Constants and Variables:

Constants denote specific objects or elements within the domain, such as "John" or "Alice." Variables, like "x," are used to represent general elements and can stand for any specific object.

Quantifiers:

We use quantifiers, like $\forall$ (for all) and $\exists$ (there exists), to specify the extent of a statement's validity.

Logical Connectives:

Logical connectives, including $\land$ (AND), $\lor$ (OR), (NOT), $\rightarrow$ (IMPLIES), and $\leftrightarrow$ (IF AND ONLY IF), are employed to combine and manipulate facts. These connectives enable the formation of more intricate statements.

Functions:

Functions can represent relationships involving mappings between objects or entities. For example, the function "Age(x)" might denote the age of an individual, allowing for the representation of various attributes or characteristics.

Rules and Constraints:

Beyond simple facts, logic can be used to express rules, constraints, and dependencies among facts. These rules define how facts interrelate and can be employed for logical reasoning.

3.2   USING PREDICATE LOGIC RESOLUTION ALGORITHM AND DEDUCTION

Predicate Logic Resolution Algorithm: The key concept of predicate logic inference is the resolution algorithm. It is employed to reconcile discrepancies, establish the veracity of an argument, and extract new information from previously acquired knowledge. There are two main steps in the algorithm:

Conversion to Clausal Form: Prior to applying resolution, we change the predicate logic statements into clausal form. Through the reduction of complex assertions into a series of clauses (disjunctions of literals), the representation is made simpler.

For instance:

$\forall x(P(x) \lor Q(x)) \land P(a)$ is the original predicate logic statement.

Form of Clause: $\{P(x) \land Q(x), P(a)\}$

a. **Resolution Rule:** Utilizing complimentary literals (a literal and its negation) in various clauses, the resolution rule enables the deduction of a new clause. The procedure is followed until a resolution is no longer achievable after this new clause is introduced to the group of clauses.

For instance:

Clauses given: $\{P(x) \lor Q(x), P(a)\}$
Step of Resolution: $\{Q(a)\}$

The Deduction Process:

The process of drawing conclusions from premises through the application of logical rules and inference mechanisms is known as deduction, and it is a fundamental idea in both AI and logic. Deduction in predicate logic is the process of making inferences about the world and drawing new conclusions from known facts.

Modus Ponens: A straightforward method of inference that allows us to conclude that B is true if we have premises in the form of "If A then B."

$(A \Rightarrow B)$ and A is true.

For instance:

Concepts: $A \Rightarrow B$, A

Conclusion: B

b. **Resolution:** As was previously mentioned, the resolution algorithm is an effective technique for predicate logic deduction. It lets us resolve complementary literals to get new clauses.

For instance:

$$\{P(x) \lor Q(x), P(a)\} \text{ are the clauses.}$$

Inference: $\{Q(a)\}$

c. **Universal and Existential Quantifiers:** Using quantifiers to make deductions requires thinking through the range of variables. While existential quantification ($\exists$) requires the introduction of new variables to satisfy the statement, universal quantification ($\forall$) allows us to instantiate variables to specific values.

For instance:

The hypothesis is: $\forall x \ \text{Human}(x) \Rightarrow \text{Mortal}(x)$.
Conclusion: Socrates, a human, $\rightarrow$ Socrates, a mortal

Resolution Algorithm

Before learning resolution theorem, every fact in predicate needs to be converted in clause form.

Conversion to Clause Form

1. To eliminate $\rightarrow$ from fact.
   $X \rightarrow Y \equiv \neg X \lor Y$
2. Reduce the scope of each (negation) to a single term.
   $\neg(X \lor Y) \equiv \neg X \land \neg Y$
   $\neg(X \land Y) \equiv \neg X \lor \neg Y$
   $\neg \forall p: X \equiv \exists p: \neg X$
   $\neg \exists p: X \equiv \forall p: \neg X$
   $\neg \neg X \equiv X$
3. Now variables should to be standardized and each quantifier should bind with a unique variable.
   $(\forall p: X(p)) \lor (\exists p: Y(p)) \equiv (\forall p: X(p)) \lor (\exists q: Y(q))$
4. All quantifiers should be moved to the left without changing their relative order.
   $(\forall p: X(p)) \lor (\exists q: Y(q)) \equiv \forall p: \exists q: (X(p) \lor (Y(q))$
5. To remove $\exists$, Skolem constant or functions must be introduced. Depending on information, $\exists$ can be either replaced by constant or parameterized function.

∃p: X(p) ≡ X(c) Skolem constant

∀p: ∃q X(p, q) ≡ ∀p: X(p, f(p)) Skolem function

6. Drop quantifier ∀

∀p: X(p) ≡ X(p)

7. Now convert the formula into a conjunction of disjuncts (CNF). It will allow the separation of the clause corresponding to each conjunct.

(X ∧ Y) ∨ Z ≡ (X ∨ Y) ∧ (Y ∨ Z)

Example of Conversion:

∀x: [Rom (x) → (**Pomp(x)** ∧ **dislike (x, Caes))**]

Step 1: In the above expression, eliminate → and ⇔. It will become

∀x: [Rom (x) ∨ (Pomp(x) ∧ dislike (x, Caes))]

Step 2: Move to each term in braces and reduce the scope.

∀x: [**Rom (x)** ∧ (**Pomp(x)** ∧ **dislike (x, Caes))**]

∀x: [**Rom (x)** ∧ (**Pomp(x)** ∨ **dislike (x, Caes))**]

- Demonstration of Step 3 for standardization to bind unique quantifiers with variables.

∀x: [[∀y: **animal_all (y)** → **cares(x, y)**] → [∃y: **cares(y, x)**]]

After this step, a new variable z is introduced with ∃ as y was bonded with both quantifiers.

∀x: [[∀y: **animal_all (y)** → **cares(x, y)**] → [∃z: **cares(z, x)**]]

Demonstration of Step 4: Move all quantifiers to the left without changing their relative order.

∀x: [[∀y: **animal_all (y)** ∧ **cares(x, y)**] ∨ [∃z: **cares(z, x)**]]

After applying Step 4, the above statement becomes

∀x: ∀y: ∃z: [**animal_all (y)** ∧ **cares(x, y)** ∨ **cares(z, x)**]

This statement is said to be in PNF (prenex normal form).

Demonstration of Step 5: Skolemization to remove ∃ quantifier.

∃y: **king (y) transformed into King (S1)**

There exist a value y that satisfies king, so Skolem constant S1 is introduced.

Example of Skolem function

∃y: ∀x: better (**y, x**)

The value of y that satisfies "better" depends on the particular value of x, so parameterized function has to be introduced.

∀x: better (**f(x)**, x)

Demonstration Step 6: Dropping of prefix ∀.

∀x: ∀y: ∀z: [Rom (x) ∨ know (x, y) ∨ dislike(y, z)]

After the prefix is dropped,

[Rom (x) ∨ know (x, y) ∨ dislike(y, z)]

Example to demonstrate Step 7: Convert the formula into a CNF.

Rom (x) ∨ ((dislike (x, caes) ∧ loyalto (x, caes))

P ∨ (Q ∧ R) ≡ (P ∨ Q) ∧ (P ∨ R)

CLAUSE 1 (Rom (x) ∨ (dislike (x, caes)) ∧

CLAUSE 2 (Rom (x) ∨ loyalto (x, caes))

Unification: It is the process of matching two literals and finding whether they both can become identical with some substitution.

- Example 1:

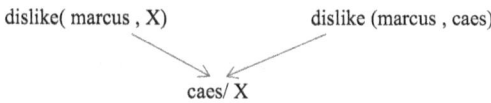

- Example 2:

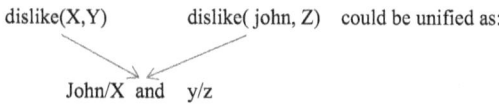

Unification

$$\text{UNIFY}(p, q) = \text{unifier } \theta \text{ where SUBST}(\theta, p) = \text{SUBST}(\theta, q)$$

$$\forall x: \text{knows}(John, x) \rightarrow \text{hates}(John, x) \text{ knows}(John, Jane)$$

$$\forall y: \text{knows}(y, Leonid)$$

$$\forall y: \text{knows}(y, \text{mother}(y))$$

$$\forall x: \text{knows}(x, Elizabeth)$$

UNIFY(knows(John,x), knows(John, Jane)) = {Jane/x} UNIFY(knows(John, x), knows(y, Leonid)) = {Leonid/x, John/y}
UNIFY(knows(John, x), knows(y, **mother(y)**)) = {John/y, **mother(John)**/x}
UNIFY(knows(John, x), knows(**x**, Elizabeth)) = **FAIL**
Resolution Algorithm: When multiple related facts are present, they can be used for inference mechanism. To apply resolution algorithm, prepossessing steps discussed above must be applied to convert into CNF. If any sentence is not in the clausal form, then convert it into the clausal form.

Resolution Algorithm Steps:

1. Start with negation of the proposition that is to be proved.
2. Combine the related facts and apply unification if needed.
3. Repeat until contradiction is found or no progress can be made:
e.g.,

$$X(\mathbf{p}) \lor Y(p) \qquad\qquad Z(r) \lor \neg\, X(\mathbf{P})$$

$$Y(p) \lor Z(p)$$

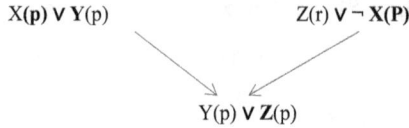

If the result is empty clause (E), then the contradiction has been found and the fact is true.

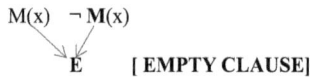

$$M(x) \quad \neg\, M(x)$$

$$E \qquad [\text{ EMPTY CLAUSE}]$$

Example

1. Marcus was a man.
2. Marcus was a Pomp.
3. All Pomp were Rom.
4. Caes was a king.
5. All Pomp were either loyal to Caes or disliked him.
6. Everyone is loyal to someone.
7. People only try to assassinate the king they are not loyal to.
8. Marcus tried to assassinate Caes.

1. "Marcus was a man"
   man(marcus)------------- 1
2. "Marcus was a Pomp"
   pomp (marcus)------------- 2
3. "All Pomp's were Rom"
   => $\forall x1: pomp(x1) \rightarrow rom(x1)$.
   => $\forall x1:$ **pomp(x1)** $\lor$ **rom(x1)**
   pomp (x1) $\lor$ **rom(x1)**---------------- 3
4. "Caes was a king"
   king (caes)----------------   4
5. "all Rom's were either loyal to caes or disliked him"
   => $\forall x2: rom(x2) \rightarrow [loyal\_to(x2, caes) \lor dislike(x2, caes)]$
   => $\forall x2: rom(x2) \lor loyal\_to(x2, caes) \lor dislike(x2, caes)$
   => $rom(x2) \lor loyal\_to(x2, caes) \lor dislike(x2, caes)$
   rom (x2) $\lor$ loyal_to **(x2, caes)** $\lor$ **dislike (x2, caes)**------ 5
6. "Everyone is loyal to someone"
   => $\forall\, x3: \exists\, y1: loyal\_to\, (x3, y1)$.
   Let f(x3) be a Skolem function, then
   => $\forall x3: loyal\_to(x3, f(x3))$.
   => $loyal\_to(x3, f(x3))$
   loyal_to $(x3, f(x3))$---------------- 6
7. "People only try to assassinate king they are not loyal to."
   => $\forall x4: \forall y2: [man(x4) \land king(y2) \land try\_assassinate(x4, y2)] \rightarrow loyal\_to(x4, y2)$
   => $\forall x4: \forall y2: [man(x4) \land king\, (y2) \land try\_assassinate(x4, y2)] \lor loyal\_to(x4, y2)$
   $\Rightarrow \forall x4: \forall y2: man(x4) \lor king(y2) \lor try\_assassinate(x4, y2) \lor loyal\_to(x4, y2)$

Let f(x4) be Skolem function, then

$\Rightarrow$ => $\forall$x4: man(x4) $\lor$ ruler(f(x4)) $\lor$ try_assassinate(x4, f(x4)) $\lor$ loyal_to(x4, f(x4))

$\Rightarrow$ man(x4) $\lor$ ruler(f(x4)) $\lor$ try_assassinate(x4, f(x4)) $\lor$loyal_to(x4, f(x4))

man(x4) $\lor$ ruler(f(x4)) $\lor$ try_assassinate(x4, f(x4)) $\lor$loyal_to**(x4, f(x4))**------- 7

8. "Marcus tried to assassinate Caesar"

try_assassinate(marcus, caes)

try_assassinate(marcus, caes)------------ 8

To prove: marcus dislike caes

That is

dislike(marcus, caes)

•   Assume

$\neg$ dislike(marcus, caes) $\neg$ **roman (x2) $\lor$ loyal_to (x2 , caes) $\lor$ dislike (x2 , caes)**

x2 / marcus

⫬ **dislike (marcus , caes)**

$\neg$ **rom (marcus) $\lor$ loyal_to (marcus, caes)** $\neg$ pompeian (x1) $\lor$ **rom(x1)**

x1 / marcus

pomp (Marcus) $\neg$ **pomp (marcus) $\lor$ loyal_to (marcus, ceas)**

loyal_to **(marcus, caes)**

$\neg$ **man(x4) $\lor$ $\neg$ king(f(x4)) $\lor$$\neg$ try_assassinate(x4 , f(x4))**

x4/ marcus f(x4)/ caes

$\neg$ **man(marcus) $\lor$ $\neg$ ruler(caes) $\lor$$\neg$ try_assassinate(marcus , caes)**

try_assassinate(marcus ,   caesar)

$\neg$ **man(marcus) $\lor$ $\neg$ ruler(caes)**

man(marcus)

$\neg$ **ruler(caes)**   **ruler(caes)**

E

Since we get an empty clause, i.e., contradiction, our assumption is that **dislike**(marcus, caes) is false; hence, dislike(marcus, caes) must be true.

3.3 FORWARD VERSUS BACKWARD CHAINING IN AI

AI encompasses a diverse array of problem-solving techniques, among which forward and backward chaining are prominent inference methods. These techniques play a crucial role in knowledge representation and reasoning systems. This section will delve into the concepts of forward and backward chaining, highlighting their key characteristics and applications, while emphasizing the importance of originality and integrity in academic and professional pursuits.

Forward Chaining:

Forward chaining, often referred to as data-driven reasoning, is an inference method that starts with the available data and iteratively applies rules and facts to derive conclusions. In this approach, the system uses the existing information to make deductions, gradually building toward a final goal or conclusion. Forward chaining is particularly useful in scenarios where there is an abundance of data and a need to explore multiple potential outcomes. In a forward chaining system, the process commences with the known facts or data. These initial facts are then matched against a set of rules to draw preliminary conclusions. If the derived conclusions lead to further inferences, the process continues iteratively until no more conclusions can be drawn. This method is akin to a domino effect, where one piece of information triggers the next logical step. It is particularly advantageous in scenarios where there is a wealth of data available, allowing the system to explore numerous potential outcomes and possibilities.

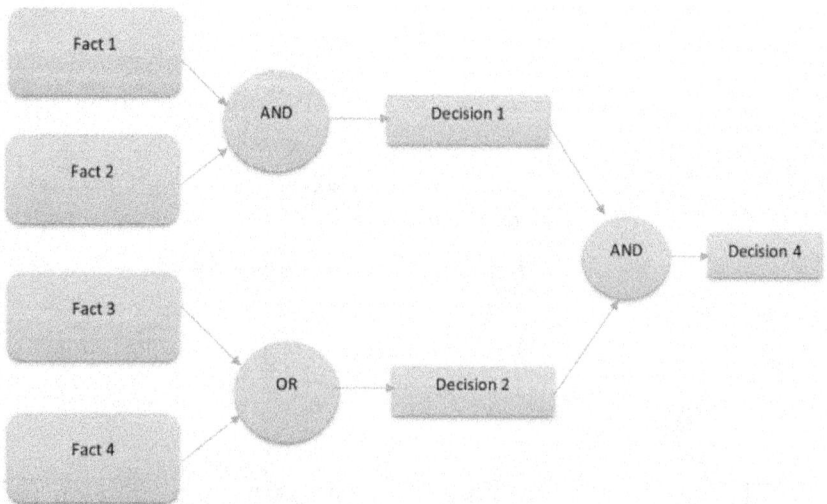

FIGURE 3.6 Forward Chaining.

Applications of Forward Chaining:

- Diagnostic Systems: Forward chaining is extensively employed in medical diagnosis systems, where symptoms and test results are used to determine potential ailments.
- Production Systems: It finds application in rule-based production systems, such as expert systems, where a set of rules guides decision-making.

Backward Chaining:

Conversely, backward chaining, also known as goal-driven reasoning, starts with a goal or a desired outcome and works backward through a series of rules to find the necessary conditions or facts that lead to that goal. This approach is especially effective when there is a predefined objective and the system must identify the supporting evidence or conditions. In contrast, backward chaining starts with a specific goal or desired outcome in mind. The system then works in reverse, seeking the conditions or facts necessary to achieve that goal. By recursively applying rules in the reverse order, the system traces back through the chain of reasoning until it identifies the initial conditions required to satisfy the goal. This approach is highly effective in situations where a clear objective is defined, and the focus is on discerning the underlying causes or prerequisites.

Applications of Backward Chaining:

- Expert Systems: Backward chaining is employed in expert systems for troubleshooting, helping identify the root cause of a problem by tracing back from the observed symptoms.
- Planning and Robotics: In AI planning and robotics, backward chaining is utilized to establish a sequence of actions that leads to a specific goal.

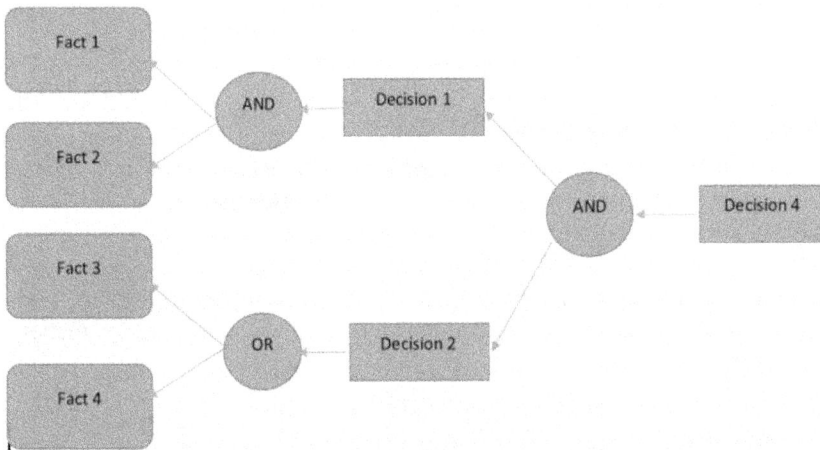

FIGURE 3.7 Backward Chaining.

Originality and Integrity in Academic Pursuits:

When discussing forward and backward chaining in AI, it is imperative to underscore the significance of originality and integrity in academic and professional endeavors. Plagiarism, the act of presenting someone else's work or ideas as one's own, is a breach of ethical standards and hinders the progress of knowledge. Therefore, it is essential to ensure that all written and verbal expressions are appropriately cited, giving due credit to the original authors and sources.

Benefits and Trade-offs:

Both forward and backward chaining possess distinct advantages and are suitable for different problem-solving scenarios. Forward chaining excels in situations where there is an abundance of data, allowing for a comprehensive exploration of potential solutions. Conversely, backward chaining is highly efficient when the objective is clearly defined, as it concentrates efforts on identifying the critical conditions for goal attainment. The choice between these methods depends on the specific nature of the problem and the available data.

Forward and backward chaining are fundamental techniques in AI, each offering unique approaches to reasoning and problem-solving. While forward chaining starts with available data and iteratively applies rules, backward chaining begins with a goal and works backward to establish the required conditions. Understanding the distinctions between these methods is crucial for effectively applying them in various AI applications. Furthermore, upholding originality and integrity is paramount in academic and professional pursuits, promoting a culture of ethical and innovative research. In summary, forward and backward chaining are pivotal reasoning methods in the realm of AI. Understanding their principles and applications empowers AI practitioners to employ the most suitable approach for a given task. It is imperative to uphold academic and professional integrity by avoiding plagiarism and ensuring that all sources are appropriately cited. This fosters a culture of originality and ethical research, ultimately driving the progress and innovation of AI technologies.

3.4   SLOT AND FILLER STRUCTURE

The terms "slot" and "filler" are often used for information extraction and knowledge representation in the context of AI and NLP. They describe how information is structured and how it is extracted from text or data.

a. **Slot:** A slot can be described as a predefined category or attribute that serves to represent a specific type of information, with the aim of extraction or comprehension by an AI system. Slots are like placeholders used to store a specific piece of information. For example, in a restaurant management context, some slots can be "Date," "Time", "Location," and "Party size."

b. **Filler:** The filler, which is also called a value or an argument, is the particular piece of information that gets stored in a "slot." It can be called as the actual data or content associated with a specific slot. Again, taking the example of restaurant reservation, if slot is "Date," then its filler could be "Saturday, October 22th."

In practical terms, slot–filler pairs are used to extract structured information from unstructured text or speech. This information extraction process is a fundamental part of various NLP tasks, such as chatbots, virtual assistants, and information retrieval systems.

For example, consider the following sentence: "I would like to book a table for two at an Italian restaurant on Saturday at 7 PM." In this sentence, the slots and fillers can be identified as follows:

- Slot: "party size" - Filler: "five"
- Slot: "restaurant type" - Filler: "South Indian"
- Slot: "date" - Filler: "Saturday"
- Slot: "time" - Filler: "7 PM"

By extracting slots and their corresponding fillers from the input text, the AI system can understand and act upon the user's request effectively, such as making a restaurant reservation. Structured information representation enables the AI system to enhance the accuracy of processing user queries and providing responses.

Hierarchy:

1. Weak Slot and Filler Structure:

The knowledge in slot and filler systems comprises sets of entities and their attributes, forming a structure known as a weak slot and filler structure. Typically, this refers to a pattern where a slot represents a category or attribute, and its relationship with its corresponding filler is often loosely defined or lacks specificity. They are "Knowledge-poor" as the structure contains knowledge that is not specific.

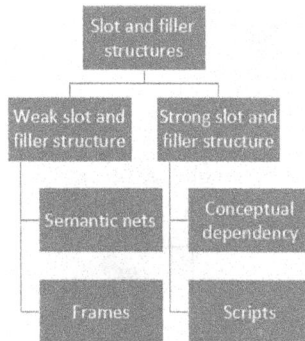

FIGURE 3.8 Slot and Filler Structures.

There are two types of weak slot and filler structure:

a. **Semantic Nets**: In the semantic net, a set of nodes are connected to each other by a set of labeled arcs to represent the information. These act as an alternative for predicate knowledge in knowledge representation. A semantic net consists of nodes, links, and link label.
   - Nodes represent various values of the attributes of the object.
   - Arcs represent relations among nodes.

Inheritance association (is a relation) can be described using a semantic network. Semantic networks provide direct indexing for objects, categories, and the link between them.

Intersection Search: By spreading activation from two nodes and observing where the activation intersects, we can seek relationships among objects. Due to these various connections, the connection between blue color and India can be found.

Partitioned sematic nets are used to represent quantified expressions.

Simple binary predicates, such as "isa (Person, Mammal)" can be easily expressed in semantic nets. For more intricate nonbinary predicates, one can make use of versatile predicates like "isa" and "instance."

To convert predicates with three or more places into a binary form, a new object can be created that represents the entire predicate statement. Then, binary predicates can be introduced to depict relationships with this newly created object.

- Example score (England, India, 300–350)

b. **Frames:** A frame consists of attributes, which are called slots, along with their associated values used to describe an entity in the world. Natural language understanding requires inference, i.e., assumptions about what is typically true of the objects or situations under consideration. Such information is coded into structures known as frames.

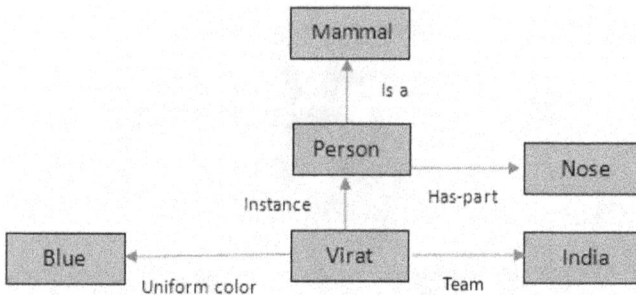

FIGURE 3.9   Example of Semantic Net.

FIGURE 3.10 Example of Semantic Net.

- A frame is similar to a record structure, and corresponding to the fields and values are slots and slot fillers. Here procedures are attached to slots, which are called "procedural attachments." They are mainly of three types: 1) if needed, 2) defaults, and 3) if added.
- One frame by itself isn't very helpful. To make them more useful, we connect several frames together in a frame system. We do this because sometimes the value of one detail in one frame talks about or points to another frame.
- The types of frames are 1) procedural frames and 2) declarative frames.
- Frame system can be understood easily with the help of set theory. Frame can be represented as a class or an instance. Considering an example of cricket—batsman, bowler, and team can be considered as classes, and Virat and India can be instances(entities).

Example: Frame for Book

Slot	Filler
Publisher	Pearson
Title	AI-A modern approach
Author	Stuart Russel

2. **Strong Slot and Filler Structure:**

A strong slot and filler structure involves precise and well-defined relationships between slots (categories or attributes) and their corresponding fillers (specific data values). This structure is often used in cases where the data must adhere to clear patterns and constraints for effective information extraction and processing.

a. **Conceptual Dependency (CD):** It is a structured frame (strong slots and fillers) used for the representation of complex and high-level knowledge for solving complex problems.

- It has a collection of symbols that contain knowledge and information.
- It acts as a theoretical model representing information types about events found in NLP.
- Various primitives used in CD are
    1) ATRANS
    2) PTRANS
    3) PROPEL
    4) MOVE
    5) GRASP
    6) XPEL
    7) MTRAN
    8) MBUILD
    9) ATTEND
    10) INGEST

The symbols in CD have specific meanings:

- Arrows show the direction of dependency.
- Double arrows denote a two-way link between an actor and an action.
- p signifies past tense.
- ATRANS represents one of the basic acts within the theory, indicating the transfer of possession.
- O signifies the object case relation.
- R represents the recipient case relation.

b. **Scripts:** It describes a sequence of events in particular consents.

Scripts are frames like structures used to represent commonly occurring events such as going to a movie.

- o   t contains a set of slots and information.
- o   If particular scripts are known to be appropriate in a given situation, then it is very useful for determining whether the event has occurred or not.
- o   Script indicates how events are mentioned or related to each other.
- o   The key components of a script include the following:

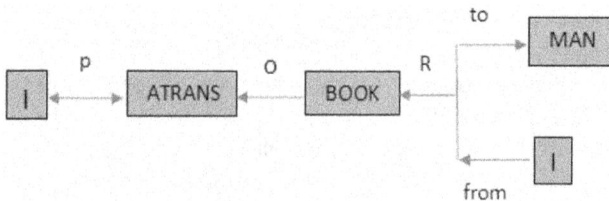

FIGURE 3.11   Simple Conceptual Dependency Representation.

- Script Name: This serves as the title.
- Track: It represents special situations or specific variations.
- Roles: These are the people or participants involved in the events described in the script.
- Entry Condition: It specifies the prerequisites needed for executing the script.
- Props: These are nonliving objects used in the script.
- Scenes: These are the actual sequences of events.
- Result: It defines the conditions that will be true after the events described in the script have occurred.

3. **Advantages (Slot and Filler Structure):**
   a. The efficiency of monotonic inheritance is notably enhanced through these structures compared to pure logic, and they also readily accommodate non-monotonic inheritance.
   b. The reason for this ease is rooted in the structured format of knowledge within slot and filler systems, which organize information as entities and their attributes.
   c. This structured approach facilitates the swift retrieval of attribute values since assertions are indexed by the entities they represent.
   d. Structured Knowledge: Slot and filler structures organize information in a structured manner, making it easier for AI systems to comprehend and manipulate data.
   e. Efficient Retrieval: Information retrieval is efficient as the value for a specific attribute is quickly obtained, thanks to the indexed nature of assertions.

4. **Disadvantages (Slot and Filler Structure):**
   a. Lack of Formal Semantics: Slot and filler structures may not have well-defined formal semantics, so it becomes difficult to perform complex mathematical reasoning unlike predicate and propositional logic.
   b. Scalability Issues: While they are more scalable than predicate logic, slot and filler systems can still face scalability challenges when dealing with very large or complex knowledge bases.

5. **Applications:**
   o Some common applications of slot and filler structures include the following:
   - NLP
   - Creating knowledge bases
   - Question-answering systems
   - Expert systems

3.5 ISSUES IN KNOWLEDGE REPRESENTATION

Issues in knowledge representation include difficulties in handling incomplete or ambiguous information, ensuring representation consistency and accuracy, managing the scalability of knowledge basis, addressing contextual awareness and situational adaptability, and mitigating potential biases or ethical concerns within the represented knowledge, all of which can impact the effectiveness and reliability of AI systems.

1. Important Attributes:

There are two attributes, **"instance"** and **"isa"**, that are of general importance. These attributes are important because they support property inheritance and organizing information in a structured manner.

- **Instance Attribute:**
  The "instance" attribute is used to define the relationships between specific objects and the more general categories to which they belong. It allows to specify that a particular object is an instance of a broader category.
  Example: "Harry Potter and the Philosopher's Stone" **instance** "Book." This states that this specific book is an instance of the class "Book."
- **Isa Attribute:**
  The "isa" attribute is used to express class–subclass relationships or inheritance. It defines that one class is a subclass of another, indicating a hierarchical relationship.
  Example: Dog **isa** Mammal. This states that the class "Dog" is a subclass of the more general class "Mammal."

These attributes simplify knowledge representation and reasoning in AI systems by allowing for the efficient propagation of attributes, which is essential for tasks like classification, reasoning, and problem-solving.

2. Relationships among Attributes:

The relationship between the attributes of an object, independent of the specific knowledge it encodes, may hold properties like inverses, existence in an Isa hierarchy, single-valued attributes, and techniques for reasoning about values.

- **Inverses:**
  Inverse attributes define a reciprocal relationship between objects. This allows for a bidirectional understanding of relationships, where knowing one attribute implies knowledge about its inverse.
  Example: The inverse of the attribute "hasFather" might be "isChildOf."
- **Existence in an Isa Hierarchy:**
  In this hierarchy, attributes defined for a superclass are inherited by its subclasses.
  Example: If superclass "Animal" has an attribute "hasLegs," all subclasses like "Cat" and "Dog" inherit this attribute.

- **Single-Valued Attributes:**
  Attributes can be single-valued, meaning they associate one value with an object.
  Example: An attribute "Age" associated with an object "Person" might have a single value such as "30."
- **Techniques for Reasoning about Values:**
  To support reasoning, various techniques are employed, including deductive reasoning, rule-based inference, and probabilistic reasoning.
  Example: Age of person cannot be greater than the age of their parents.

The combination of these properties ensures that knowledge representation systems are capable of efficiently capturing and processing information about objects and their attributes.

3. Choosing the Granularity:

High-level facts may not be adequate for inference, while low-level primitives may require a lot of storage.
Choosing the granularity of knowledge representation refers to determining the level of detail or abstraction at which information is encoded. The granularity can significantly impact how effectively an AI system operates.
In practice, a hybrid approach may be adopted, where fine-grained data is used for real-time monitoring and immediate intervention, while coarse-grained data is used for broader traffic management strategies and long-term planning.
Example: Online Product Catalog:

- Fine-Grained Granularity: Each product is represented with detailed attributes such as the product's name, brand, model, price, weight, color, dimensions, materials used, and customer reviews.
- Coarse-Grained Granularity: Each product is represented more succinctly. For instance, each product listing includes only the product's name, a brief description, and the price.

4. Representing Set of Objects:

Representing a set of objects in knowledge representation involves defining a collection of objects that share a common characteristic or relationship.
There are several methods for representing sets of objects, including list or array, logical predicate, graphs or networks, and data structures.
The choice of representation methods depends on the specific requirements of the application and the level of complexity needed to describe the set and its relationships.
Example: Set of cities with population greater than 1 million.

- List or Array: ["Mumbai," "Delhi," "Kolkata," "Bangalore," . . .]
- Logical Predicate: $\{x \mid x \text{ is a city and population}(x) > 10000000\}$

5. Finding the Right Structure as Needed:

Finding the right structure in knowledge representation involves selecting an appropriate representation format or schema to best match the requirements of a given application or problem domain.

It is a balance between the specific requirements of your application and the available tools and methods for representation. It often involves a combination of domain knowledge, experimentation, and adaptation based on the evolving needs of the system or application.

Example: Creating a customer relationship management (CRM) system involves structuring customer data as profiles with attributes like contact information, purchase history, and interactions, facilitating personalized communication and state strategies.

4 Data and Preprocessing
The Heart of Machine Learning

4.1 INTRODUCTION TO MACHINE LEARNING

A significant area of artificial intelligence (AI) is machine learning (ML). One of the pioneers of AI, Arthur Samuel is often cited for his explanation of ML. According to him, "the field of study that gives the computer the ability to learn without being explicitly programmed" is ML.

The main principle of this definition is that the system should be able to learn on its own without the need for explicit programming. How is that even possible? It is well known that creating programs that teach computers how to perform computations is necessary for them to be completed.

In traditional programming, a thorough program design, such as an algorithm or flowchart, is made after the problem is understood, and then the programs are generated using an appropriate programming language. This method might be challenging to use for a variety of real-world issues, including complex image recognition applications, games, and riddles.

AI made an effort to comprehend these issues and manually create general-purpose rules. To build intelligent systems, these rules were put into a software and made logical. An expert system is a concept for creating intelligent systems via the application of logic and reasoning, transforming the knowledge of an expert into a collection of guidelines and instructions. The expertise of numerous doctors was turned into a system and used to create an expert system for medical diagnosis, similar to MYCIN. This strategy did not, however, yield much progress because the systems lacked true intelligence. The majority of antibiotics have names that finish in "mycin," which is where the word "mycin" originated.

Because the aforementioned method still relied on human knowledge and did not actually demonstrate intelligence, it was impractical in many fields. After then, the focus switched to data-driven systems and ML. The primary objective of AI is to construct intelligent systems using a data-driven technique, where data is used as input to create intelligent models. These models can be used to predict output for new input data. In order to accurately anticipate the unknown data, ML aims to automatically learn a model [1] or a set of rules from the provided dataset. Like people making decisions based on experience, computers build models based on patterns they see in the input data. These data-filled models are then used by computers to make predictions and make decisions. The learned model is the computer equivalent of human experience.

DOI: 10.1201/9781003532170-4

A model is a clear explanation of the patterns found in data, such as the following [2]:

- Mathematical equations
- Relational diagrams like trees/graphs
- Logical if/else rules
- Groupings called clusters

In conclusion, a formula, process, or representation that may provide data judgments can be called a model. Patterns and models differ in that the former are local and only apply to specific attributes, while the latter are global and fit the whole set of data. A model can be useful, for instance, in determining whether or not a certain email is spam. The key element is that the provided data is automatically used to construct the model.

Tom Mitchell is another AI pioneer. His definition of ML states, "A computer program is said to learn from experience E, with respect to task T and some performance measure P, if its performance on T measured by P improves with experience E." The three key elements of this definition are task T, performance measure P, and experience E.

For instance, task T can involve identifying an object in a picture. With a training dataset of thousands of photos, the machine can learn about objects. We refer to this as experience E. Therefore, the goal is to apply experience E to the object detection task T. Precision and recall are two performance metrics that indicate how well the system can identify an object. To enhance the system's performance, a course correction can be implemented based on the performance metrics.

Computer system models are analogous to human experience. Experience is based on data. People acquire experience in different ways. They acquire knowledge by memorization. They study others and try to emulate them. Books and teachers are two great sources of knowledge for humans. They also pick up a lot of knowledge by trial and error. When faced with a new issue after gaining knowledge, people look for previous circumstances, create heuristics, and apply those to make predictions. But in systems, experience is acquired by the following procedures:

1. Collection of data
2. After information is acquired, abstract notions are created using that information. Concept generation is done through abstraction. This is comparable to how people conceptualize objects; for instance, they can describe the appearance of an elephant.
3. The abstraction is transformed into a useful kind of intelligence by generalization. You may think of it as an ordering of all possible concepts. Thus, classification of concepts, drawing conclusions from them, and developing heuristics are all part of generalization, which is a useful component of intelligence. Heuristics are well-informed approximations for each task. For instance, one's formation of heuristics or human experience is the reason behind running into or encountering danger. It happens in the same way in machines. Although they often work, heuristics can also be ineffective.

Since it is only a "rule of thumb," heuristics are not to blame. The process of making a course correction involves taking assessment measurements. Evaluation verifies that the models are comprehensive and makes any necessary course corrections to provide superior formulations.

4.2 NEED FOR ML

ML is an emerging and rapidly advancing field. It enables top management to derive insights from both structured and unstructured data stored across various organizational archives, aiding in decision-making processes.

In the past, the full potential of this data was not leveraged. This was partly due to data being dispersed across different archival systems, making integration challenging for organizations. Additionally, there were limited software tools available to extract valuable information from the data.

Business organizations are now adopting the latest technology, ML, to address these issues. The rise of ML can be attributed to three main factors:

High volume of data: Companies like Facebook (now Meta), Twitter, and YouTube generate massive amounts of data each year, with the data volume expected to double annually.

Decreased storage costs: The cost of hardware has significantly dropped, facilitating the capture, processing, storage, distribution, and transmission of digital information.

Advanced algorithms: The development of deep learning has introduced many sophisticated algorithms for ML.

As ML gains popularity and is readily adopted by businesses, it has become a leading technology trend.

4.3 TYPES OF ML

Based on Figure 4.1, there are four categories of ML.

Understanding data is crucial before exploring the many forms of ML. Two categories of data exist: labeled and unlabeled. Although it can also be shown as a data point, data is usually displayed in a tabular format. Each row in a table is a data point, while the columns stand for characteristics/attribute/feature or traits. The trait we are trying to predict among these attributes is the label. To demonstrate labeled data, consider the Iris flower dataset, also known as Fisher's Iris dataset. This dataset contains 50 samples of Iris flowers [3], with four attributes: sepal length, sepal width, petal length, and petal width. The target variable is called class, with three possible classes: *Iris sentosa*, *Iris virginica*, and *Iris versicolor*. Thus, the data in Table 4.1 is labeled data, where each row has an assigned value for the target variable.

Data may be in the form of images also. Various deep learning models can be used for this data.

Unlabeled data comes without a label. Figure 4.2 shows labeled and unlabeled image data.

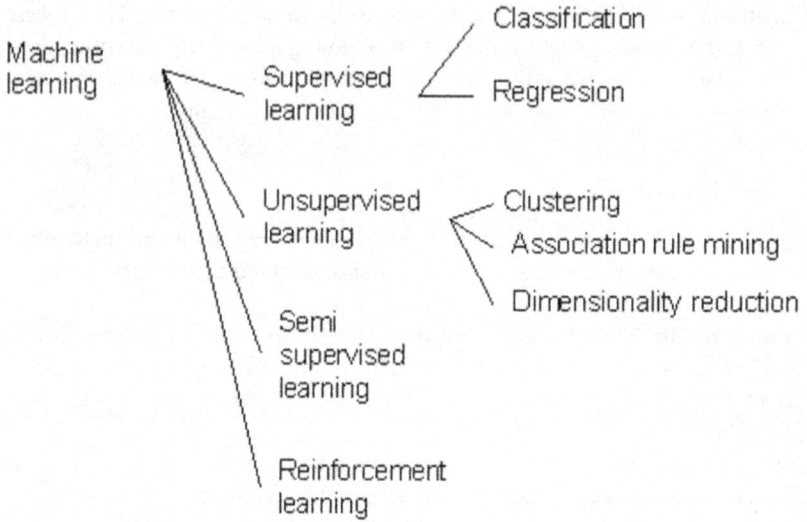

FIGURE 4.1 Types of ML.

TABLE 4.1
Iris Dataset Example

Petal Length	Petal Width	Sepal Length	Sepal Width	Class
5.5	4.2	1.4	0.2	Sentosa
7	5.2	1.7	1.4	Versicolor
7.3	4	1.8	1.8	Virginica

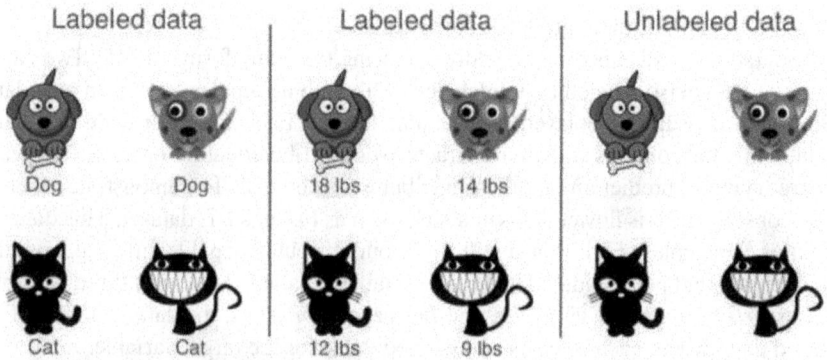

FIGURE 4.2 Example of Labeled and Unlabeled Data.

4.3.1 SUPERVISED LEARNING

Supervised algorithms utilize labeled datasets. As implied by the name, supervised learning involves a supervisory or instructional component. This supervisor supplies labeled data, enabling the model to be built and generate test data.

In supervised learning algorithms, the supervisor communicates the information that the learner is supposed to know. The learner understands the received information without the supervisor knowing whether the information has been grasped by the learner or not. The supervisor tests the learner by asking a set of questions. Typically, supervised learning employs two techniques:

- Classification: Predicting the "label" or "class" of discrete data is the goal of classification, a supervised learning technique, for instance, identifying an image as a dog or a cat. A classification algorithm uses a set of labeled images (e.g., cats and dogs) to build a model that can classify unseen new images.

Two stages of classification are involved. The learning algorithm uses a labeled dataset in the first step, referred to as the training stage, to identify patterns and create a model. The second step involves testing the built model with fresh or unidentified samples and labeling them. This process defines classification.

For instance, using the Iris dataset, if a test sample is given as (6.3, 2.9, 5.6, 1.8,?), the classification model will predict a label for it. Other examples of classification include image recognition, disease diagnosis such as cancer classification, plant classification, email spam detection, and sentiment analysis.

Key classification algorithms include the following:

- Decision trees
- Random forests
- Support vector machines
- Naive Bayes
- Artificial neural networks and deep learning models like convolutional neural networks (CNNs)
- **Regression:** Regression models forecast continuous variables like prices, in contrast to categorization techniques. Stated differently, they forecast actual values. Regression models use an input of x and produce a model as a fitted line, denoted by $y = f(x)$. In this case, y is the dependent variable and x is the independent variable, which may have one or more qualities. Sales of a product, e.g., may vary depending on the sale week. Using the training data, linear regression fits a line, as in product sales = 0.66 × Week + 0.54.

The regression coefficients in this equation, which were obtained from the data, are 0.66 and 0.54. This model has the advantage of predicting product sales (y) for weeks that are not known (y). To forecast revenues for the eighth week, for instance, you would enter 8 in place of x.

Models for classification and regression are both classified as supervised algorithms. They employ the principles of testing and training and include a supervisory component. Regression models predict continuous variables, like product pricing, while classification models concentrate on giving discrete labels, like classes or categories. This is the main distinction between the two types of models.

4.3.2   Unsupervised Learning

This kind of learning entails self-training. As the name suggests, neither teachers nor supervisors are involved. Without a guide, learning occurs mostly through self-instruction using a trial-and-error methodology. With unlabeled data, self-learning takes place when the algorithm looks at samples and data and recognizes patterns based on grouping principles. This grouping ensures that similar objects are clustered together. Examples of unsupervised learning algorithms include cluster analysis, association rule mining, and dimensionality reduction.

- **Cluster analysis** aims to group objects into distinct clusters based on their attributes. Objects within the same cluster share similarities, while they significantly differ from objects in other clusters. Key clustering algorithms include the following:
  - ➢ k-means
  - ➢ Hierarchical clustering
  - ➢ DBSCAN
- **Dimensionality reduction** involves taking high-dimensional data and transforming it into a lower-dimensional form by exploiting data variance. This process reduces the dataset to fewer features without losing its generality. Principal component analysis (PCA) is a frequently employed method for dimensionality reduction.
- **Association rule mining** discovers interesting associations and relationships among large datasets. These rules indicate how frequently an itemset appears in a transaction, such as in market basket analysis. These insights help retailers identify items that are often purchased together. A priori algorithm is commonly used to find association rules.

4.3.3   Semi-Supervised Learning

A dataset may occasionally have a significant portion of unlabeled data mixed together with a lesser quantity of labeled data. Because data labeling is an expensive and difficult operation for humans, semi-supervised algorithms can be used. These techniques provide pseudo-labels to the unlabeled data, enabling the training of models using a combination of labeled and pseudo-labeled data.

4.3.4   Reinforcement Learning

Reinforcement learning emulates human behavior by providing an environment for an agent to interact with and learn from. Instead of relying on data, the agent navigates the environment to acquire knowledge. Similar to how humans use their senses to perceive the world and take actions, reinforcement learning enables the agent, which could be a human, animal, robot, or software program, to interact with the environment to receive rewards. These rewards allow the agent to accumulate experience, with the goal of maximizing the reward, which can be either positive or negative (in the form of punishment). When rewards are higher, behaviors are reinforced, facilitating learning. Reinforcement learning finds applications in various domains, including gaming, robotics, and autonomous vehicles.

4.4   UNDERSTANDING DATA

All facts are data. In computer systems, bits encode facts present in numbers, text, images, audio, and video. Data can be directly human-interpretable, such as numbers or text, or be diffused, such as images or videos that can be interpreted only by a computer.

Data by itself is meaningless. It needs to be processed to generate any information. A string of bytes is meaningless. Only when a label is attached, such as the height of a person, does the data become meaningful. Information is defined as processed data that has been given patterns, associations, and relationships. One way to extract information from sales data analysis is to identify the product that sold in larger amounts during the last quarter of the year.

4.4.1   BIG DATA

Data whose volume is less and can be stored and processed by a small computer is called small data. Big data, on the other hand, is data whose volume is much larger. It must satisfy the 6Vs: volume, velocity, variety, veracity, validity and value. Big data is measured in terms of petabytes (PB) and exabytes (EB). One exabyte is 1 million terabytes. The high arrival speed of data and its increase in volume are noted as velocity of data. Data comes in different forms ranging from text, graphs, audio, video, and maps to composite data. Data also comes from various resources such as human conversation, transaction records, and old archive data. Data sources can be open/public, social media, and multimodal. The veracity of data deals with aspects such as conformity to facts, truthfulness, believability, and confidence in data. Veracity of data is one of the important aspects of data as there may be many sources of error such as technical, typographical, and human. Validity is the accuracy of data for taking decisions. Value is the characteristic of big data that indicates the quality of the information that is extracted from the data; it influences the decisions that are taken based on it.

In big data, there are three kinds of data:

- **Structured data:** Here, data is stored in an organized manner such as a database, where it is available in the form of a table, and can be retrieved in an organized manner using tools like SQL.
- **Unstructured data:** This includes video, image, and audio. It also includes textual documents, programs, and blog data. Nowadays, 80% of data is unstructured data.
- **Semi-structured data**: This type of data is partially structured and partially unstructured. Examples are XML/JSON data, RSS feeds, and hierarchical data.

Once a dataset is assembled, it must be stored in a structure that is suitable for analysis. Data can be stored in flat files in plain ASCII or EBCDIC format. Comma-separated values (CSV) and tab-separated values (TSV) are popular spreadsheet formats for storing data.

Data can be stored in database files, which consist of original data and metadata. Each set of tables in a relational database has rows and columns. With the use of several tools like database administrator, query processing, and transaction manager, a database management system seeks to manage data and enhance operator performance. Transactional, time-series, and spatial are a few types of databases where different types of data are stored.

The World Wide Web (WWW) provides diverse, worldwide online information. Algorithms can be used to mine interesting patterns of information in WWW. eXtensible Markup Language (XML) is a machine-interpretable data format that can be used to present data that needs to be shared across platforms. Dynamic data enters and exits the observing environment as a data stream. Massive amounts of data, a dynamic nature, fixed order movement, and real-time constraints are typical traits of a data stream. Really Simple Syndication (RSS) is a format for sharing instant feeds across services. JavaScript Object Notation (JSON) is another useful data interchange format that is often used for many ML algorithms.

4.5   DATASET AND DATA TYPES

One way to think about a dataset is as a compilation of data entities. These entities could be records, documents, samples, observations, cases, points, vectors, patterns, or events. Each record encompasses multiple attributes, which can be described as the defining characteristics or properties of an entity. Let's contemplate the dataset showcased in the example in Table 4.2.

There should be a value assigned to each attribute. We refer to this as measurement. The type of attribute determines the data types, often referred to as measurement scale types. The data types are shown in Figure 4.3.

Data can be broadly divided into two categories:

- **Categorical or qualitative data** can be nominal or ordinal. In Table 4.2, student ID is nominal data. Because they are symbols, nominal data cannot be handled like numerical data. The average student ID, for instance, defies

---

TABLE 4.2
Student Placement Dataset

Student ID	CGPA	Interactiveness	Practical Knowledge	Communication Skills	Job Offer
1	>9	Yes	Very good	Good	Yes
2	>8	No	Average	Moderate	No
3	<8	No	Good	Poor	No

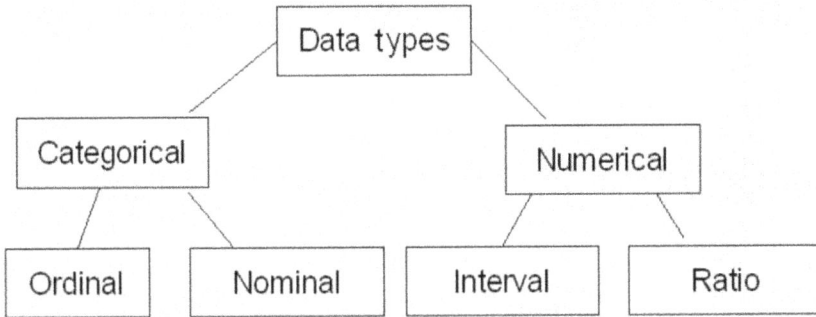

FIGURE 4.3 Types of Data.

statistical interpretation. Likewise, job offer (Yes, No) and interactiveness (Yes, No) are also nominal data. Nominal data types provide only information but have no order. Only operators like (=, ≠) are meaningful for this data.

Ordinal data provides information and has a natural order. For example, communication skill (good, average, and poor) is ordinal data. Regardless of value, poor is certainly less than average, and average is less than good. This data can be transformed in any way to produce a different value.

- **Numerical or quantitative data** can be classified as discrete or continuous. Another classification is interval and ratio. Discrete data is recorded as integers. Employee identification number such as 10011 is discrete data. Continuous data can be fitted into a range and includes decimal points, for example, height. Age is a continuous data as height, age can be 120.3 cm, 12.5 years, respectively. Interval data consists of numerical values where the distinctions between values hold significance. For instance, the disparity between 30 and 40 degrees is meaningful. Permissible operations solely include addition and subtraction. Conversely, ratio data encompasses meaningful differences and ratios. The key disparity between ratio and interval data lies in the position of zero on the scale. For instance, consider the conversion between centigrade and Fahrenheit scales. The zero points on both scales do not align, distinguishing this as interval data.

4.6 DATA PREPROCESSING

In the real world, the available data is "dirty." By this, we mean

- Incomplete data
- Outlier data
- Data with inconsistent value
- Inaccurate data
- Data with missing values
- Duplicate data

This "dirtiness" of data can be caused by

- Equipment malfunction
- Inconsistency with other recorded data, thus leading to deletion
- Data not entered due to misunderstanding
- Certain data may not be considered important at the time of entry
- Not registering history or changes in the data

As data preprocessing enhances the quality [4] of the data, it also enhances the quality of data mining techniques. This means improving accuracy, completeness, consistency, timeliness, believability, and interpretability of data. The raw data must be preprocessed to give accurate results. The process of detection and removal of errors in data is called data cleaning. Some of the data errors include human errors such as typographical errors or incorrect measurement and structural errors like improper data formats. Additional causes of data errors include attribute duplication and omission. A random component that causes a value to be distorted or an incorrect object to be introduced is referred to as noise. Typically, noise is present in data that involves spatial or temporal components. Deterministic distortions, appearing as streaks, are recognized as artifacts.

Consider Table 4.3. "Bad" or "dirty" data can be observed in this table.

It can be observed that data such as salary "" is incomplete. Date of birth for Shreya, Tanu, and Pragnay is missing. Rishika's age is recorded as 8, but her date of birth is stated as 10/10/2006. This is called inconsistent data. Shreya's salary is −1500. It cannot be less than 0. It is an instance of noisy data.

Inconsistent data occurs due to problems in conversion, inconsistent formats, and differences in units. Outliers are data points that display distinct characteristics and possess unusual values compared to the rest of the dataset. For instance, Shreya's age recorded as 136 could potentially be a typographical error. It's essential to differentiate between noise and outlier values. Outliers may indeed represent legitimate data and can even be of interest to ML algorithms. These errors often occur in the data collection stage. They must be removed so that ML algorithms yield better results as the quality of results is determined by the quality of input data. This removal process is called data cleaning.

TABLE 4.3
"Dirty" Data Example

Student ID	Name	Age	Date of Birth	Fever	Salary
1	Shreya	136		Low	−1500
2	Tanu	18		High	Yes
3	Rishika	8	10/10/2006	Yes	""
4	Pragnay	17		High	Yes

4.6.1 MISSING DATA ANALYSIS

The primary data cleaning process is missing data analysis [5]. Data cleaning procedures aim to rectify data inconsistency, smooth out noise while detecting outliers, and fill in missing data values. This enables ML to avoid overfitting of models. Following are a few techniques to solve the problem of missing data:

- Tuples lacking information—particularly the class label—are ignored. A rise in the percentage of missing values renders this strategy ineffective.
- The data tables can be examined by the domain expert, who can also perform analysis and manually enter the numbers. This takes time, though, and it might not be possible for big data sets.
- The properties that are lacking can be filled up with a global constant. The missing value could be "infinity" or "unknown." However, certain ML algorithms may use these labels to produce false positives.
- For every sample in the same class, use the attribute mean. In this case, the missing values for each tuple in this group are replaced by the average value.
- To fill in the missing value, use the value that is most likely to occur. Other techniques, such as decision tree prediction and classification, can yield the most likely value.

4.6.2 REMOVAL OF NOISE

A random error or fluctuation in a measured value is called noise [6]. It can be removed using binning. Binning is a technique that sorts and distributes the given data values into equal frequency bins in order to eliminate it. Buckets are another name for the bins. The neighbor values are used by the binning procedure to smooth the noisy data.

Several often employed strategies include "smoothing by mean," in which the bin mean eliminates the bin values; "smoothing by bin median," in which the bin median substitutes the bin values; and "smoothing by bin boundary," in which the closest bin boundary substitutes the bin value. Bin boundaries are the highest and lowest values.

Binning methods may be used as a discretization technique. For example, applying binning technique using bins of size 3 on data {12,14,19,22,24,26,28,31,34}:

Smooth by equal frequency bin method:

Bin1: 12,14,19
Bin2: 22,24,26
Bin3: 28,31,32

Smooth by mean method:

Bin1: 15,15,15
Bin2: 24,24,24
Bin3: 30.3,30.3,30.3

Smooth by bin boundary method:

Bin1: 12,12,19
Bin2: 22,22,26
Bin3: 28,32,32

4.6.3 DATA INTEGRATION AND DATA TRANSFORMATION

The process of combining data from several sources into one data source is known as data integration. Finding and eliminating redundancies that result from data integration is the primary objective of data integration. To enhance the efficiency of ML algorithms, data transformation procedures carry out tasks such as normalization or standardization. Data must be transformed in order for it to be processed. In normalization, the performance of ML algorithms is enhanced by scaling attribute values to fit within a range (e.g., 0–1). Some of the normalization techniques used are as follows:

- **Min–Max Procedure (MinMax Scaler):** Using this normalization technique, each variable V is normalized to a new range, say 0–1, by dividing its difference with the minimum value within the range. Often, neural networks require this kind of normalization.

$$V' = \frac{V - min_A}{max_A - min_A}(new\_max_A - new\_min_A) + new\_min_A \qquad (1)$$

Consider the marks {88,90,92,94}. To convert these marks to the 0–1 range, normalization can be applied as
For mark 88:

$$v' = \frac{(88-88)}{(94-88)} * (1-0) + 0 = 0$$

For mark 90:

$$v' = \frac{(90-88)}{(94-88)} * (1-0) + 0 = 0.33$$

For mark 92:

$$v' = \frac{(92-88)}{(94-88)} * (1-0) + 0 = 066$$

For mark 94:

$$v' = \frac{(94-88)}{(94-88)} * (1-0) + 0 = 1$$

So the marks {88,90,92,94} are mapped to a new range {0,.33,.66,1}.

Z-Score Normalization (Standard Scaler): This procedure scales the difference between the field value and mean value by the standard deviation of the attribute.

$$v' = \frac{v - \mu_A}{\sigma_A} \tag{2}$$

For example, applying z-score normalization in {10,20,30}, mean and standard deviation of this data are required. The mean of 10,20,30 is 20, and the standard deviation is 10.

$$\text{Z-score of } 10 = \frac{(10 - 20)}{(10)} = -1$$

$$\text{Z-score of } 20 = \frac{(20 - 20)}{(10)} = 0$$

$$\text{Z-score of } 30 = \frac{(30 - 20)}{(10)} = 1$$

Z-scores are used to detect outliers. Z-score function is extremely sensitive to outliers as it is dependent on the mean.

4.6.4 DATA REDUCTION

While reducing the quantity of the data, data reduction yields identical outcomes. Data reduction can be done in a variety of methods, including dimensionality reduction, feature selection, wavelet transform, and sampling.

- **Discrete wavelet transform (DWT)** transforms the given data vector to a numerically different data vector. The transformed vector is of the same size as the original, but the wavelet transformed vector can be truncated. The strongest wavelet coefficients, i.e., wavelet coefficients larger than some specified threshold, can be retained and the rest can be set to 0. This helps in data compression. As many data values become 0 after applying this transform, data becomes sparse and computation becomes very fast in wavelet space. Inverse DWT can be applied on a given set of wavelet coefficients, which gives an approximation of the original data.
- **PCA** creates an alternative reduced set of variables from the original data, resulting in dimensionality reduction of data. Original data is projected into smaller spaces, and the projection that captures the largest amount of variation in data is found. It works only on numeric data. Data is first normalized to make it more consistent and to make all attributes or variables in the same range. Eigenvectors [7] of the covariance matrix are found. These

eigenvectors define the new space, i.e., k orthogonal vectors, which are k principal components of data, where $k \leq n$. These principal components are considered in decreasing order of "significance" or strength. Weak components are those with low variance, and strong components have high variance. Therefore, strong components give more information to ML models. Since only strong components are stored, the size of data is reduced.

- **Feature subset selection** helps in feature reduction as attributes are redundant and sometimes irrelevant. There are heuristic methods for feature selection:
  - **Step-wise forward selection [5]:** Since the reduced set begins with an empty set of features, it operates in a forward manner. The feature that performs best in the original version is chosen and added to the smaller set. Iteratively, the set gains the best of the remaining original features.

Initial attribute set = {A1, A2, A3, A4, A5, A6}
  Initial reduced set: {}

— {A1}
—-{A1,A4}
—-Reduced attribute set {A1,A4, A6}
- **Step-Wise Backward Elimination:** It works in the backward direction as it starts with a full set of features as the reduced set. The worst of the remaining original features are removed at each step iteratively.
Initial attribute set = {A1, A2, A3, A4, A5, A6}
Initial reduced set: {A1, A2, A3, A4, A5, A6}
— {A1, A4, A5, A6}
—-Reduced attribute set {A1, A4, A6}
- **Combination of Forward Selection and Backward Elimination:** It combines both techniques discussed above. Here, the best features are added and the worst features are removed from the remaining data.
- In sampling [6], a representative subset of data is selected, which helps reduce data. Taking out samples randomly can result in poor performance as data may be skewed. So adaptive sampling methods must be used for better performance. Some sampling techniques are as follows:
  - **Simple random sampling:** Here you choose any item with equal probability.
  - **Sampling without replacement:** Here, an item is removed from a population after selection.
  - **Sampling with replacement:** Here, an item is not removed from the population after selecting it. It means that the same sample can appear again.
  - **Cluster sampling:** Data is clustered, and a cluster is randomly selected from the population.
  - **Stratified sampling:** This works well for skewed data. Here, the dataset is partitioned and samples are drawn from each partition (proportionally or in approximately the same percentage of the data).

4.6.5 DIMENSIONALITY REDUCTION USING PYTHON

For each data sample that chooses a set of primary features, the number of feature variables is reduced using the unsupervised ML technique known as dimensionality reduction. One of the popular dimensionality reduction methods offered in Sklearn is PCA.

By examining the features of the original dataset, PCA [8, 9] is a statistical technique that linearly projects the data into a new feature space. Picking out the "principal" qualities of the data and creating features based on them is the primary idea. It will provide us with a new dataset that is small in size but which has all of the same information as the original dataset. Computations become fast with a reduced dataset.

Here, we use the Iris dataset for explanation. It has one target variable, flower category, and four independent variables: sepal length, sepal width, petal length, and petal width. We reduce the feature space from four independent variables to two, using PCA. So these two PCA components will have all the information contained by the four independent variables.

First, import the libraries and load the Iris dataset. Then, separate the x and y variables; x contains sepal length, sepal width, petal length, and petal width, and y contains species. The pca() method and fit_transform() are used on x data. Features are scaled using StandardScalar().

```
from sklearn.preprocessing import StandardScaler
import matplotlib.pyplot as plt
import seaborn as sns
import pandas as pd
df = sns.load_dataset('iris')
x = df.drop('species', axis =1)
y = df['species']

x = StandardScaler().fit_transform(x)
x = pd.DataFrame(x)
from sklearn.decomposition import PCA
pcatwofeatures = PCA()
x_pca = pcatwofeatures.fit_transform(x)
x_pca = pd.DataFrame(x_pca, columns=['PCA1','PCA2','PCA3
','PCA4'])
print(x_pca.head())
explained_variance = pca.explained_variance_ratio_
print(explained_variance)

plt.figure(figsize=(10, 10))
sns.scatterplot(x_pca['PCA1'], [0] * len(x_pca), hue=y,
s=50)

plt.figure(figsize=(10, 10))
sns.scatterplot(x_pca['PCA2'], [0] * len(x_pca), hue=y,
s=50)
```

```
plt.figure(figsize=(10, 10))
sns.scatterplot(x_pca['PCA3'], [0] * len(x_pca), hue=y,
s=50)
plt.figure(figsize=(10, 10))
sns.scatterplot(x_pca['PCA4'], [0] * len(x_pca), hue=y,
s=50)
```

Output:

```
PCA1 PCA2 PCA3 PCA4
0 -2.264703 0.480027 -0.127706 -0.024168
1 -2.080961 -0.674134 -0.234609 -0.103007
2 -2.364229 -0.341908 0.044201 -0.028377
3 -2.299384 -0.597395 0.091290 0.065956
4 -2.389842 0.646835 0.015738 0.035923

[0.72962445 0.22850762 0.03668922 0.00517871]
```

PCA1 gives very accurate information, PCA2 gives less information compared to PCA1, and PCA3 gives less information compared to PCA2 as shown in the below figures.

Here, we can see that of the four features, the first two principal components explain 96% of the variance of data, which is visible in Figures 4.4 and 4.5. We can see that PCA1 separates the Sentosa class clearly from Virginica and Versicolor and others. Virginica and Versicolor are tougher to classify, but we should still get most

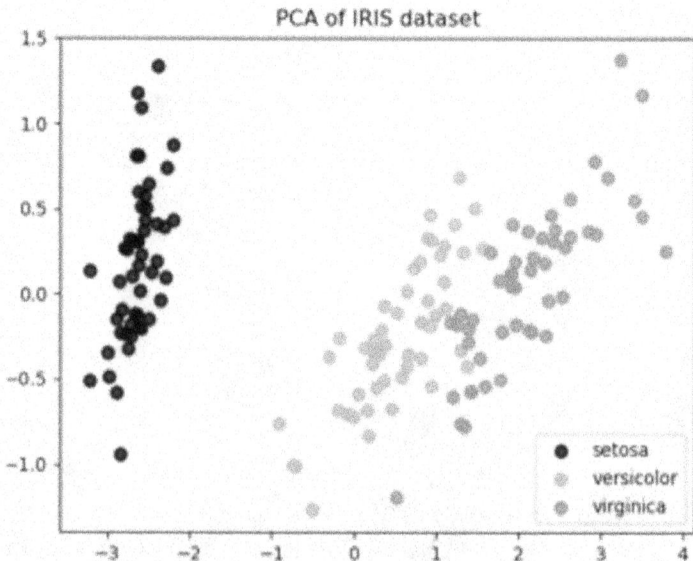

FIGURE 4.4   Iris Flower Categorization Using PCA1.

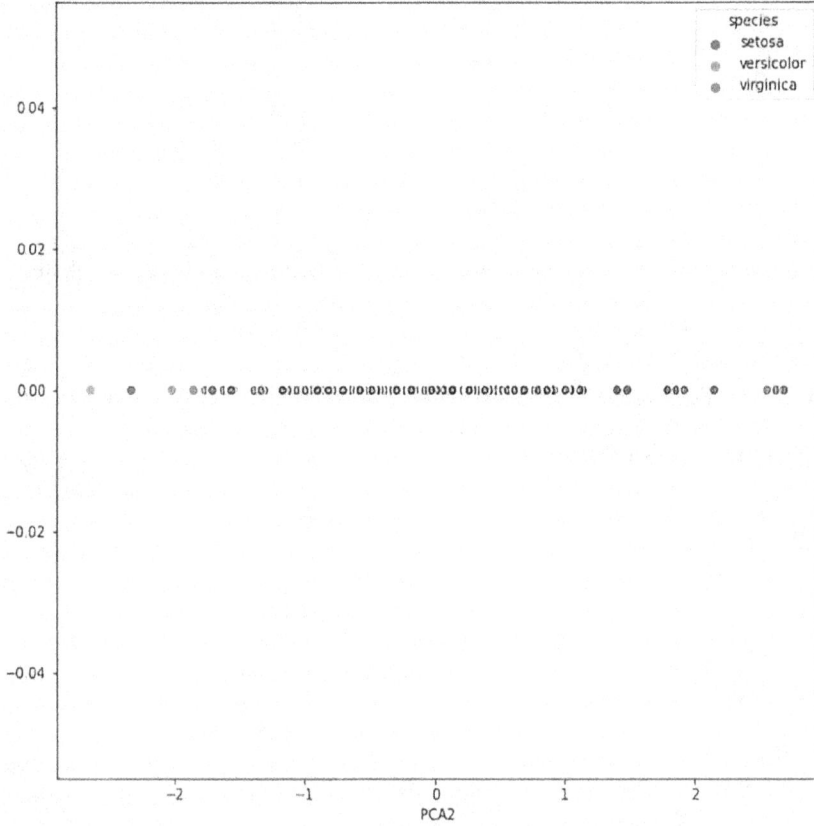

FIGURE 4.5   Iris Flower Categorization Using PCA2.

of the classifications correct only with a single principal component. Other principal components PCA2, PCA3, and PCA4 do not help much to classify the data clearly.

4.6.6   DATA PREPROCESSING IN PYTHON

Here, a few data preprocessing operations are performed in Python on the Fitness - Fitness.csv dataset. Missing values in the dataset are checked first. They can be replaced using the different strategies discussed above. Here, missing values are present in the AGE feature, which is replaced with the mean of the same feature. The dataset is uploaded to Google Colaboratory and then preprocessing [10] is performed.

4.6.6.1   Handling Missing Data Values

First, upload the .csv file to Google Colaboratory.

```
import io
from google.colab import files
```

```
import pandas as pd
import numpy as np
uploaded= files.upload()
datadf=pd.read_csv(io.BytesIO(uploaded['Fitness - Fit-
ness.csv']))
print("ORIGINAL DATA")
print(datadf.isnull().sum())
print(datadf)
```

This will print data attributes with the count of null values for each attribute.

Output:

Fitness - Fitness.csv (text/csv) - 390 bytes, last modified: n/a - 100% done
Saving Fitness - Fitness.csv to Fitness - Fitness (3).csv
ORIGINAL DATA
ID 0
Age 0
Gender 0
MaritalStatus 0
Fitness 0
Income 0
MilesRun 0
Fit 0
dtype: int64
ID Age Gender MaritalStatus Fitness Income MilesRun Fit
0 ST19 32 Female Single 4 34562 114 yes
1 ST19 33 Male Single 3 29342 75 no
2 ST19 21 Female Partnered 3 43214 65 yes
3 ST19 19 Male Single 3 30987 84 yes
4 ST19 22 Male Partnered 2 53234 46 yes
5 ST19 22 Female Partnered 3 28345 64 no
6 ST19 24 Male Partnered 3 36432 74 no
7 ST19 25 Female Single 3 30987 86 yes
8 ST19 24 Male Single 4 31234 142 yes

The .csv file has some missing values in the AGE attribute.

```
# The data file with missing values
uploaded= files.upload()
df1=pd.read_csv(io.BytesIO(uploaded['Fitness - Fitness1.
csv']))
print("DATA WITH MISSING VALUES IN AGE FEATURE")
print(df1.isnull().sum())
x = df1.iloc[:, :-1].values
print(x)
```

Output:

Fitness - Fitness1.csv(text/csv) - 388 bytes, last modified: n/a - 100% done
Saving Fitness - Fitness1.csv to Fitness - Fitness1 (3).csv
DATA WITH MISSING VALUES IN AGE FEATURE
ID 0
Age 2
Gender 0
MaritalStatus 0
Fitness 0
Income 0
MilesRun 0
Fit 0
dtype: int64
[['ST19' 32 'Female' 'Single' 4 34562 114]
['ST19' 'Male' 'Single' 3 29342 75]
['ST19' 21 'Female' 'Partnered' 3 43214 65]
['ST19' 19 'Male' 'Single' 3 30987 84]
['ST19' 22 'Male' 'Partnered' 2 53234 46]
['ST19' 'Female' 'Partnered' 3 28345 64]
['ST19' 24 'Male' 'Partnered' 3 36432 74]
['ST19' 25 'Female' 'Single' 3 30987 86]
['ST19' 24 'Male' 'Single' 4 31234 142]]

The missing values can be computed by the methods discussed above. Here, SimpleImputer() is used for preprocessing this data to handle missing data.

```
from sklearn.impute import SimpleImputer
impute = SimpleImputer(missing_values = np.nan, strat-
egy = 'mean')
" ' Using the fit method, we apply the 'imputa' object
on the matrix of our feature x, which is AGE here. The
'fit()' method identifies the missing values and com-
putes the mean of such feature a missing value is
present" '
impute.fit(x[:, 1:2])
x[:, 1:2] = impute.transform(x[:, 1:2])
print("Imputed data (AGE feature missing values replaced
with mean of AGE) ")
print(x)
```

Output:

Imputed data (AGE feature missing values replaced with mean of AGE)

[['ST19' 32.0 'Female' 'Single' 4 34562 114]

['ST19' 23.9 'Male' 'Single' 3 29342 75]
['ST19' 21.0 'Female' 'Partnered' 3 43214 65]
['ST19' 19.0 'Male' 'Single' 3 30987 84]
['ST19' 22.0 'Male' 'Partnered' 2 53234 46]
['ST19' 23.9 'Female' 'Partnered' 3 28345 64]
['ST19' 24.0 'Male' 'Partnered' 3 36432 74]
['ST19' 25.0 'Female' 'Single' 3 30987 86]
['ST19' 24.0 'Male' 'Single' 4 31234 142]]

4.6.6.2   Categorical Data Encoding

ML algorithms work on numeric data as they are based on forming mathematical equations from the given data, so ML models require categorical data to be converted to numeric data. Encoding techniques help convert categorical or textual data into numeric data. Encoding techniques such as one-hot encoding and label encoding [10] are available in Python, which converts text data into numeric. In the Fitness. csv dataset, Gender, MaritalStatus and Fit are categorical data. One-hot encoding on the Gender feature and Label encoding on the Fit feature is applied. For our dataset, Gender has two values (Male and Female); 0 represents male and 1 represents female. Numeric order between male and female does not matter. So one-hot encoding helps as it converts the Gender column into three columns and creates a unique binary vector for male and female. Male is converted to vector [0.0 1.0], and female is converted to vector [1.0 0.0].

First, upload the .csv data file and view its contents.

```
# Data Preprocessing -- Encoding of data
import io
from google.colab import files
import pandas as pd
import numpy as np
uploaded= files.upload()
datadf=pd.read_csv(io.BytesIO(uploaded['Fitness - Fit-
ness.csv']))
print("ORIGINAL DATA")
print(datadf)
```

Output:

Fitness - Fitness.csv(text/csv) - 390 bytes, last modified: n/a - 100% done
Saving Fitness - Fitness.csv to Fitness - Fitness (4).csv
ORIGINAL DATA
ID Age Gender MaritalStatus Fitness Income MilesRun Fit
0 ST19 32 Female Single 4 34562 114 yes
1 ST19 33 Male Single 3 29342 75 no
2 ST19 21 Female Partnered 3 43214 65 yes
3 ST19 19 Male Single 3 30987 84 yes
4 ST19 22 Male Partnered 2 53234 46 yes
5 ST19 22 Female Partnered 3 28345 64 no

6 ST19 24 Male Partnered 3 36432 74 no
7 ST19 25 Female Single 3 30987 86 yes
8 ST19 24 Male Single 4 31234 142 yes

The Fit feature has "Yes" or "No" values. The label encoder (discussed above) is used to encode the Fit feature. Functions LabelEncoder() and fit_transform() are applied on the Fit attribute.

```
from sklearn.preprocessing import LabelEncoder
ylabel = datadf.iloc[:, -1].values
print(ylabel)
le = LabelEncoder()
ylabel = le.fit_transform(ylabel)
print("Label Encoded Fit Feature values")
print(ylabel)
```

Output:

['yes' 'no' 'yes' 'yes' 'yes' 'no' 'no' 'yes' 'yes']
Label Encoded Fit Feature values
[1 0 1 1 1 0 0 1 1]

A one-hot encoder (discussed above) is used to encode the Fit feature. Functions OneHotEncoder() and fit_transform() are applied on the Fit attribute.

```
# One-hot encoding on Gender Feature
from sklearn.compose import ColumnTransformer .
from sklearn.preprocessing import OneHotEncoder
xinput = datadf.iloc[:, :-1].values
colt = ColumnTransformer(transformers=[('encoder', One-
HotEncoder(), [2])], remainder= 'passthrough')
xinput = np.array(colt.fit_transform(xinput))
print("One-Hot encoding on Gender Feature")
print(xinput)
```

Output:

One-hot encoding on Gender feature

[[1.0 0.0 'ST19' 32 'Single' 4 34562 114]
 [0.0 1.0 'ST19' 33 'Single' 3 29342 75]
 [1.0 0.0 'ST19' 21 'Partnered' 3 43214 65]
 [0.0 1.0 'ST19' 19 'Single' 3 30987 84]
 [0.0 1.0 'ST19' 22 'Partnered' 2 53234 46]
 [1.0 0.0 'ST19' 22 'Partnered' 3 28345 64]
 [0.0 1.0 'ST19' 24 'Partnered' 3 36432 74]
 [1.0 0.0 'ST19' 25 'Single' 3 30987 86]
 [0.0 1.0 'ST19' 24 'Single' 4 31234 142]]

4.6.6.3   Scaling of Features

In some datasets, features have different values. Some features have very high-range values, while others have small-range values. Features scaling must be performed so that data becomes more relevant, and all the features are given the same weight and importance. If the ML model is built on unscaled data, features with high-range values will dominate those with small values and the ML model will treat the small-range value features as though they do not exist. Python has two methods that help scale data: StandardScaler() and MinMaxScaler(). StandardScaler() is applied on the Miles feature of the Fitness.csv dataset.

First, upload the .csv data file and view its contents.

```
# Data Preprocessing-Scaling of Data
import io
from google.colab import files
import pandas as pd
import numpy as np
from sklearn.preprocessing import StandardScaler
from sklearn.preprocessing import MinMaxScaler
uploaded= files.upload()
datadf=pd.read_csv(io.BytesIO(uploaded['Fitness - Fit-
ness.csv']))
print("ORIGINAL DATA")
print(datadf)
```

Output:

Fitness - **Fitness.csv**(text/csv) - 390 bytes, last modified: n/a - 100% done
Saving Fitness - Fitness.csv to Fitness - Fitness (6).csv
ORIGINAL DATA
ID Age Gender MaritalStatus Fitness Income MilesRun Fit
0 ST19 32 Female Single 4 34562 114 yes
1 ST19 33 Male Single 3 29342 75 no
2 ST19 21 Female Partnered 3 43214 65 yes
3 ST19 19 Male Single 3 30987 84 yes
4 ST19 22 Male Partnered 2 53234 46 yes
5 ST19 22 Female Partnered 3 28345 64 no
6 ST19 24 Male Partnered 3 36432 74 no
7 ST19 25 Female Single 3 30987 86 yes
8 ST19 24 Male Single 4 31234 142 yes

Next, print the values of MilesRun as we want to apply scaling on this feature.

```
datadf = datadf.iloc[:,[6]]
print("Miles column")
print(datadf)
```

Output:

Miles column
MilesRun
0 114
1 75
2 65
3 84
4 46
5 64
6 74
7 86
8 142

StandardScaler() is applied on the MilesRun column.

```
stdc = StandardScaler()
datadf = stdc.fit_transform(datadf)
print("Standard Scaled data of Miles")
print(datadf)
```

Output:

Standard-scaled data of MilesRun
[[1.12817638]
[−0.30656967]
[−0.67445327]
[0.02452557]
[−1.37343212]
[−0.71124163]
[−0.34335803]
[0.09810229]
[2.15825047]]

MinMaxScaler() is applied on MilesRun. Both scaling techniques use different formulas to scale the data.

```
minmaxdc = MinMaxScaler()
datadf = minmaxdc.fit_transform(datadf)
print("MinMax Scaled data of Miles")
print(datadf)
```

Output:

MinMax-scaled data of MilesRun
[[0.70833333]

[0.30208333]
[0.19791667]
[0.39583333]
[0.]
[0.1875]
[0.29166667]
[0.41666667]
[1.]]

4.6.6.4   Data Sampling

For sampling [11] data from population, Python uses random.choice() and random.
sample() functions, respectively, with and without replacement sampling.

```
import random
# Sample population
population = [1, 2, 3, 4, 5, 6, 7, 8, 9, 10]
# Sample size
sample_size = 5
# Random sampling without replacement
randomsample = random.sample(population, sample_size)
print("Random Sample without replacement:",
randomsample)
randomsamplewithreplacement=[random.choice(population)
for _ in range(sample_size)]
print("Random Sample with replacement:",
randomsamplewithreplacement)
```

Output:

```
Random Sample without replacement: [1, 7, 10, 2, 9]
Random Sample with replacement: [9, 5, 3, 6, 9]
```

As mentioned above, stratified sampling ensures representation from each subgroup (stratum) in the population, leading to more precise estimates for the entire population. Here dictionary data is created with two keys: "Category" and "Value." "Category" contains categorical data with three groups: "A," "B," and "C," each repeated four times. "Value" contains corresponding numerical values for each category. Groups are formed on the DataFrame by the "Category" column and then a function apply() is applied to each group to select n_samples from each group. This will select different n_samples from each category on each run.

```
import pandas as pd
# Create a sample DataFrame
data = {
  'Category': ['A', 'A', 'A', 'A', 'B', 'B', 'B', 'B',
'C', 'C', 'C', 'C'],
```

```
 'Value': [10, 20, 30, 40, 15, 25, 35, 45, 50, 60, 70,
80]
}
df = pd.DataFrame(data)
# Number of samples to draw from each stratum
n_samples = 2
# Perform stratified sampling
stratified_sample = df.groupby('Category', group_keys=-
False).apply(lambda x: x.sample(n_samples))
print("Stratified Sample:\n", stratified_sample)
```

Output:

```
Stratified Sample:
 Category Value
2 A 30
3 A 40
7 B 45
4 B 15
8 C 50
9 C 60
```

4.7 SUMMARY

This chapter serves as an introductory journey into the fundamentals of ML, equipping readers with essential knowledge and skills. Starting with an exploration of the basics of ML, readers are introduced to different types of ML paradigms. They gain insights into the importance of datasets, understanding various data types, and the foundational concepts of data preprocessing. Practical implementation using Python covers crucial tasks such as data reduction, transformation, encoding, and handling missing values, essential for preparing data for ML models. By the end of the chapter, readers will have a solid foundation in handling data effectively to support their ML endeavors.

REFERENCES

1. Aakanksha Sharaff, G. R. Sinha, *Data Science and Its Applications*, CRC Press, https://doi.org/10.1201/9781003102380
2. https://danielnhliziyoblog.files.wordpress.com/2018/07/machine-learning-with-r-2nd-edition.pdf
3. https://www.coursehero.com/file/p3qasj4d/Interpretation-For-every-additional-unit-of-spending-on-TV-and-Radio-advertising/
4. Uwe Engel, Anabel Quan-Haase, Sunny Liu, Lars E. Lyberg, *The Handbook of Computational Social Science*, CRC Press, https://doi.org/10.4324/9781003024583
5. https://sist.sathyabama.ac.in/sist_coursematerial/uploads/SIT1301.pdf
6. https://www.powershow.com/view4/83e0d2-NDA0M/Ahmed_K_Ezzat_powerpoint_ppt_presentation
7. https://www.researchgate.net/publication/359917263_Pre-processamento_de_dados

8. https://towardsdatascience.com/dimension-reduction-techniques-with-py-thon-f36ca7009e5c?gi=3d85851a8782
9. https://biapol.github.io/Quantitative_Bio_Image_Analysis_with_Python_2022/day3e_dimensionality_reduction/02_UMAP.html
10. https://www.section.io/engineering-education/data-preprocessing-python/
11. https://almarefa.net/blog/how-to-effectively-loop-within-groups-in-pandas

5 Supervised Machine Learning

5.1 SUPERVISED MACHINE LEARNING

Labeled examples are used in supervised machine learning (ML) to train algorithms to recognize patterns and make choices. This shows that each training case has an output label attached to it. In supervised learning, the objective is to build a model that can accurately map inputs to their corresponding outputs, allowing for predictions on future data. Supervised learning seeks to learn a function that can take inputs and produce accurate predictions of outputs, even for data it hasn't encountered before. Regression and classification are the two primary categories into which supervised learning tasks are typically divided. In regression, a continuous value is predicted, for instance, estimating a house's cost based on its characteristics. Classification predicts a distinct label, such as whether an email is spam.

5.2 CORRELATION AND REGRESSION ANALYSIS

We often need to understand how changes in one factor affect another. For instance, the amount of time spent studying can affect the marks obtained, or the level of rainfall can impact crop production. To analyze these relationships, we use statistical methods like correlation and regression. Regression allows us to predict the value of one variable based on another, whereas correlation assesses the strength of the relation.

5.2.1 CORRELATION ANALYSIS

The association between variables, i.e., correlation, can be studied graphically by creating a scatter plot of variables or by calculating the correlation coefficient. Both these ways of analysis are described below.

5.2.1.1 Measures of Association

In statistics, correlation denotes some form of association between two variables. For example, weight and height are correlated. The measured correlation can be positive, negative, or zero (scatterplot in Figure 5.1).

Positive Correlation: If attribute A value increases with an increase in attribute B value, and vice versa.

Negative Correlation: If attribute A value decreases with an increase in attribute B value, and vice versa.

Zero Correlation: When attribute A value varies at random with attribute B value, and vice versa.

DOI: 10.1201/9781003532170-5

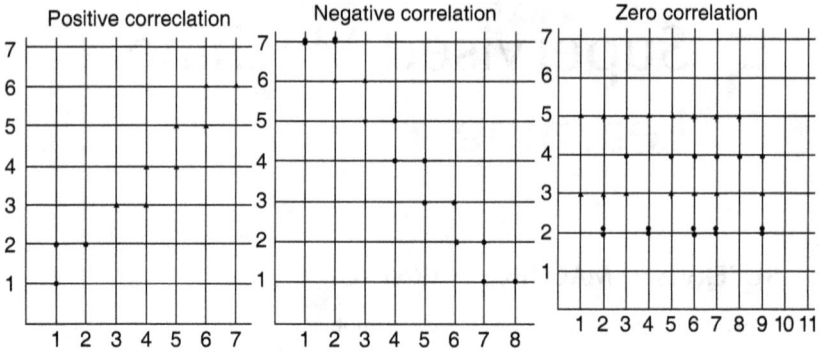

FIGURE 5.1 Scatterplot of Correlation (Types of Correlation).

5.2.1.2   Correlation Coefficient

A statistic known as correlation coefficient evaluates the linear relationship—along with its strength and direction—between numerical variables. The indications (+ and −) show the direction of the relationship, while the magnitude, which goes from 0 to 1 for a fully predicted relationship, denotes its strength. Strong positive relationships are indicated by a correlation coefficient around 1, while strong negative linear relationships are indicated by a value near −1. A coefficient of 0 denotes a weak or nonexistent linear relationship between the variables.

To calculate the correlation coefficient between two numerical attributes, Karl Pearson's method is typically employed. For ordinal attributes, Charles Spearman's rank correlation coefficient is used, where ranks are assigned to the different values of the ordinal variable.

Correlation and covariance describe the degree of a relationship. Correlation is dimensionless, while covariance is not. Its unit is obtained by multiplying the units of the two variables. To compute the correlation coefficient, a "scaleless" quantity, the product of the standard deviations of x and y divides the covariance.

Covariance is defined in terms of mean as

$$S_{xy} = \frac{1}{n-1}\sum_{i=1}^{n}(x_i - \bar{x})(y_i - \bar{y})$$

Here, x_i and y_i are observations, $(\bar{x}, \bar{y})$ represent the mean of observations, and n denotes the total number of observations.

Mathematically, the correlation coefficient is expressed as

$$\gamma_{xy} = \frac{S_{xy}}{S_x S_y}, \tag{1}$$

where S_x and S_y represent the standard deviations, and covariance is represented by S_{xy}.

5.2.1.3 Correlation and Causation

While causality indicates a cause-and-effect link between two variables, correlation identifies a relationship between two variables. It's crucial to understand that a correlation between two variables does not imply a cause-and-effect relationship. A third variable that influences both variables may be the reason for the relationship between the two. For instance, there is a correlation between temperature and ice cream sales, but not a causal relationship. In a similar vein, sales of sunglasses and ice cream may correlate, but this does not mean that one causes the other. The common factor in both cases is warm weather, which drives the sales of both ice cream and sunglasses. However, ice-cream sales does not cause warm weather, and sunglasses do not cause ice-cream sales. A cause reflects a correlation with an underlying reason. For instance, the relationship between drinking coffee and productivity is a correlation. While caffeine intake might make you feel more productive, it could also be that working at a coffee shop, away from distractions at home, increases your productivity. In this case, the cause–effect relationship is not definitive. On the other hand, the relationship between exercise and muscle growth, and between overeating and obesity are clear examples of cause–effect relationships. Exercise leads to muscle growth, and overeating leads to weight gain or obesity. In these cases, if X occurs, Y follows. Understanding cause–effect relationships is particularly valuable in business analysis, as it provides real-world context and meaning to correlations. For example, you might want to identify the factors that contributed to a successful marketing channel, understand why customers are buying your product, or determine the most appreciated feature of your product.

5.2.2 REGRESSION ANALYSIS

In order to forecast the value of a dependent variable, regression analysis analyzes the relationship between the dependent variable and one or more independent variables. This statistical modeling technique is used to establish a mathematical representation of the relationship between variables. Regression models are broadly categorized into linear and nonlinear types. Linear models can be further divided into simple and multiple regression models, as depicted in Figure 5.2.

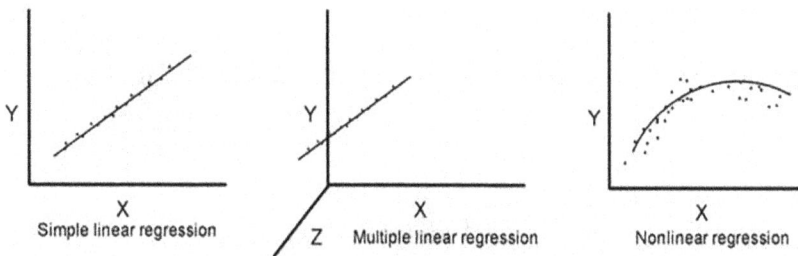

FIGURE 5.2 Regression Analysis Model.

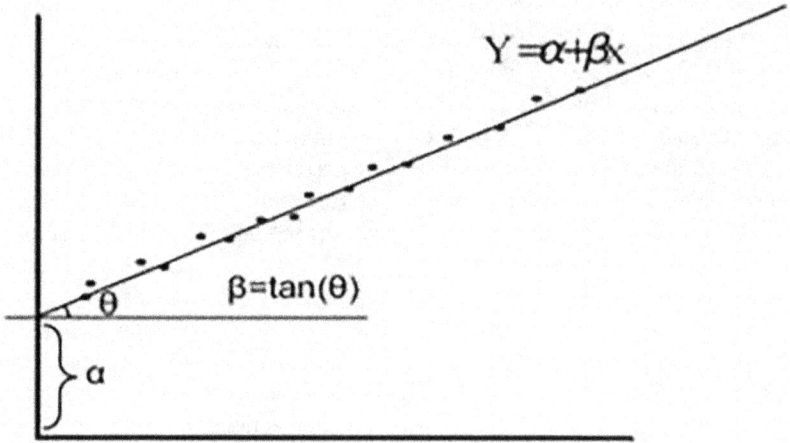

FIGURE 5.3 Simple Linear Regression.

5.2.2.1 Simple Linear Regression

Two variables are the main focus of basic linear regression: the independent variable, also known as the regressor (X), and the dependent variable, commonly known as the response (Y). Figure 5.3 shows how a linear equation expressing the relation between X and Y is expressed.

Regression analysis quantifies the strength of the relation between Y and X by finding the best fit among an infinite number of potential lines. Estimating the regression coefficients, often represented by the symbols α and β, is the aim of regression analysis. The least squares method seeks to minimize the sum of squared errors in order to determine which regression line most closely matches the data points. To accomplish this minimizing, linear regression computes the coefficients α and β.

$$e = \Sigma(Y_i - \beta - \alpha X_i)^2 \tag{2}$$

The sum of squared errors is differentiable and also positive, so it is used in linear regression. To minimize the error, the equation is differentiated with respect to the parameters and then equated to zero. The estimated values for the parameters α and β are derived from this process.

$$\alpha = \frac{(\underline{XY}) - (\underline{X})(\underline{Y})}{(\underline{Xi^2}) - (\underline{X})^2} \tag{3}$$

$$\beta = \underline{Y} - \alpha \underline{X} \tag{4}$$

Certain assumptions are necessary for drawing valid conclusions from linear regression:

1. Since they are raised to the first power and are not multiplied or divided by one another, parameters β and α are linear.
2. The independent variable is nonrandom.
3. For every observation, the error term's variance stays the same.
4. The error term, ε, follows normal distribution and shows no correlation across different observations.

5.2.2.2 Multiple Linear Regression

When there are numerous independent variables (k-independent variables, x1, x2, ..., xk), multiple regression modeling can be applied. The multiple linear regression model has linear coefficients, which may be expressed as follows:

$$y_i = \beta_0 + \beta_1 x_1 + \beta_2 x_2 + \beta_k x_k \tag{5}$$

5.2.2.3 Nonlinear Regression

When the regression equation is expressed with a degree greater than one ($r > 1$), it is referred to as a nonlinear regression model. Additionally, if there are multiple independent variables, x1, x2, . . ., xr, the model is known as a multiple nonlinear regression model, or alternatively, a polynomial regression model. Generally, it is represented as

$$y_i = \beta_0 + \beta_1 x + \beta_2 x^2 + \beta_r x^r \tag{6}$$

This approach can be useful when the relationship between the independent and dependent variables is nonlinear. The equation above illustrates how to fit the data using a polynomial regression model or you can transform the data into a linear form in order to apply a linear regression model to nonlinear data.

5.2.3 Validation of Regression Methods

Regression model evaluation involves key metrics to assess performance: mean absolute error (MAE) calculates the average magnitude of prediction errors by considering absolute differences between actual and predicted values. Mean squared error (MSE), which squares these differences, highlights larger errors, making the model sensitive to outliers. Root mean squared error (RMSE), the square root of MSE, presents errors in their original units for easier interpretation. Finally, the R^2 score (coefficient of determination) measures how well the model explains the variance in the dependent variable, with a value close to 1 indicating a strong fit and values near 0 signifying poor model performance.

$$MAE = \frac{1}{N}\sum_{i=1}^{N} |y_i - \hat{y}|,$$

$$MSE = \frac{1}{N}\sum_{i=1}^{N}(y_i - \hat{y})^2,$$

$$RMSE = \sqrt{MSC} = \sqrt{\frac{1}{N}\sum_{i=1}^{N}(y_i - \hat{y})^2},$$

$$R^2 = 1 - \frac{\Sigma(y_i - \hat{y})^2}{\Sigma(y_i - \bar{y})^2},$$

where

$\hat{y}$ – predicted value of y
$\bar{y}$ – mean value of y

Example: Let's assume the company's 5 months sales data (in thousands) is as given below. Apply the linear regression technique to predict the 8th and 12th month sales.

Xi (Month)	Yi (Sales in Thousands)
1	12
2	18
3	26
4	32
5	38

To fit the linear regression model, the parameters are calculated using the following formulas for $Y = \alpha X + \beta$.

$$\alpha = \frac{(\overline{XY}) - (\overline{X})(\overline{Y})}{(\overline{Xi2}) - (\overline{X})2}$$

$$\beta = \overline{Y} - \alpha \overline{X}$$

Xi	Yi	(Xi)²	Xi * Yi
1	12	1	12
2	18	4	36
3	26	9	78
4	32	16	128
5	37	25	185
Sum = 15	Sum = 125	Sum = 55	Sum = 439
Average of Xi = 15/5 = 3	Average of Yi = 125/5 = 25	Average of (Xi)² = 55/5 = 11	Average of (Xi*Yi) = 439/5 = 87.8

$$\alpha = ((87.8) - (3)(25)) / (11 - 3^2) = 12.8/2 = 6.4$$

$$\beta = 25 - 6.4 * 3 = 5.8$$

$$\text{Regression line } Y = 6.4 \, X + 5.8$$

$$\text{Sales of 8th month} = 6.4 * 8 + 5.8 = 57$$

$$\text{Sales of 12th month} = 6.4 * 12 + 5.8 = 82.6$$

Given the actual sales of the 8th and 12th months are 60 and 80, respectively, errors can also be calculated such as MSE, MAE, RMSE, and r2 score or R^2.

$$\text{MAE} = \tfrac{1}{2}\left((60 - 57) + \text{abs}(80 - 82.7)\right) = 2.85$$

$$\text{MSE} = \tfrac{1}{2}\left((60 - 57)^2 + (80 - 82.7)^2\right) = 8.145$$

$$\text{RMSE} = \text{sqrt}(8.145) = 2.85$$

$$\underline{Y} = 25$$

$$R^2 = 1 - \left(((60 - 57)^2 + (80 - 82.7)^2) / ((60 - 25)^2 + (80 - 25)^2)\right) = .9961$$

R^2 indicates the accuracy of the linear regression model is 99.61%.

5.2.4 SIMPLE LINEAR REGRESSION IN PYTHON

This code uses an advertising.csv file, which contains the data on TV, radio, newspaper, and sales. Here, the strongest linear relationship between data items is found out and then a linear regression model is fit for those data items. The accuracy of the model is also calculated, and the data is also represented using different graphical methods.

First, Advertising.csv file is uploaded in Google Colab.

```
# To load.csv file in colab
from google.colab import files
uploaded= files.upload()
```

```
#Simple Linear Regression
from matplotlib import pyplot
import io
import matplotlib.pyplot as plt
import pandas as pd
from sklearn.model_selection import train_test_split
from sklearn.linear_model import LinearRegression
from sklearn import metrics
import scipy.stats
```

```
dfval=pd.read_csv(io.BytesIO(uploaded['Advertising.
csv']))
```
After the csv file is uploaded, correlation coefficients between TV, radio, newspaper, and sales are calculated using Pearson's, Spearman's, and Kendall's methods.

```
#Find the correlation between variables
pearsoncorr = dfval.corr(method='pearson')
print(pearsoncorr)
spearmancorr = dfval.corr(method='spearman')
print(spearmancorr)
kendallcorr = dfval.corr(method='kendall')
print(kendallcorr)
```

Output:

	TV	Radio	Newspaper	Sales
TV	1.000000	0.054809	0.056648	0.782224
Radio	0.054809	1.000000	0.354104	0.576223
Newspaper	0.056648	0.354104	1.000000	0.228299
Sales	0.782224	0.576223	0.228299	1.000000

	TV	Radio	Newspaper	Sales
TV	1.000000	0.056123	0.050840	0.800614
Radio	0.056123	1.000000	0.316979	0.554304
Newspaper	0.050840	0.316979	1.000000	0.194922
Sales	0.800614	0.554304	0.194922	1.000000

	TV	Radio	Newspaper	Sales
TV	1.000000	0.041202	0.034156	0.621946
Radio	0.041202	1.000000	0.207077	0.419447
Newspaper	0.034156	0.207077	1.000000	0.132271
Sales	0.621946	0.419447	0.132271	1.000000

By looking at the results printed, it appears that TV and sales follow a strong linear relationship. Plot is printed on TV and sales attributes.

```
dataval1=dfval['TV']
dataval2=dfval['Sales']
# plot
pyplot.scatter(dataval1, dataval2)
pyplot.show()
```

Output:

The correlation coefficients of TV and sales can be printed using all three methods of correlation.

```
print('Using scipy, coorelation between two variables Tv
and Sales')
pearsoncorr=scipy.stats.pearsonr(dataval1,dataval2)[0]
print(pearsoncorr)
spearmancorr = scipy.stats.spearmanr(dataval1,dataval2)
[0]
```

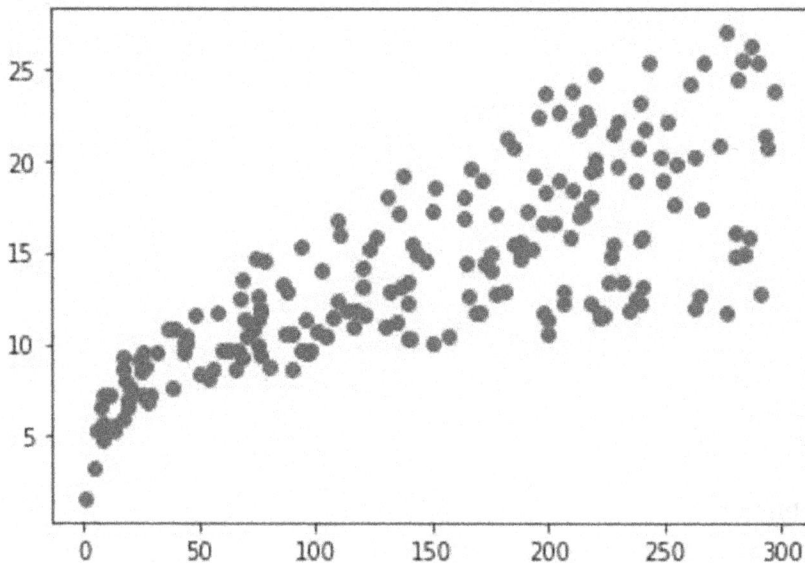

FIGURE 5.4 Scatterplot of TV and Sales (Shows Linear Relationship).

```
print(spearmancorr)
kendallcorr = scipy.stats.kendalltau(dataval1,dataval2)
[0]
print(kendallcorr)
```

Output:

```
Using scipy, coorelation between two variables TV and
Sales
0.7822244248616065
0.8006143768505688
```
0.6219463551009411

As we see a strong linear relationship between TV and
sales data, a regression model can be built for these
parameters as coded below:

```
Xval = dfval['TV'].values.reshape(-1,1)
yval = dfval['Sales'].values.reshape(-1,1)
```

```
Linear Regression model on TV and Sales data of
advertising
Xval_train, Xval_test, yval_train, yval_test = train_
test_split(Xval, yval, test_size=0.3, random_state=0)
regressorval = LinearRegression()
```

```
regressorval.fit(Xval_train, yval_train)
#To retrieve the intercept and slope of linear regres-
sion model:
print(regressorval.intercept_)
print(regressorval.coef_)
```

Output:

```
[7.31081017]
[[0.04581434]]

yval_pred = regressorval.predict(Xval_test)
df = pd.DataFrame({'Actual': yval_test.flatten(), 'Pre-
dicted': yval_pred.flatten()})
print(df)
```

Output:

```
        Actual      Predicted
0        11.3       10.481163
1         8.4        9.601527
2         8.7       11.452427
3        25.4       20.583225
4        11.7       15.108411
5         8.7        9.885576
6         7.2        7.709395
7        13.2       18.310834
8         9.2        8.401192
9        16.6       16.363724
10       24.2       19.282098
11       10.6       11.305821
12       10.5       14.485336
13       15.6       15.914744
14       11.8       10.811026
15       13.2       12.817694
  . . . . . .  . . . .
57       14.4       15.213784
58       16.6       16.588214
59        5.5        7.645255
```

This will evaluate the performance of the regression model

```
print(")
r2_score = regressorval.score(Xval_test, yval_test)
print('accuracy of model is')
print(r2_score*100,'%')
```

Output:

```
accuracy of model is
72.5606346597073 %
```

Bar graph of first 15 values to show actual and predicted values.

```
dfval1 = df.head(15)
dfval1.plot(kind='bar',figsize=(16,10))
plt.grid(which='major', linestyle=':', linewidth='0.6',
color='red')
plt.grid(which='minor', linestyle='-', linewidth='0.6',
color='green')
plt.show()
```

Output:

```
Below code to shows Predicted Y value in line, points
shows actual Y values for test data

plt.scatter(Xval_test, yval_test, color='gray')
plt.plot(Xval_test, yval_pred, color='red', linewidth=2)
plt.show()
```

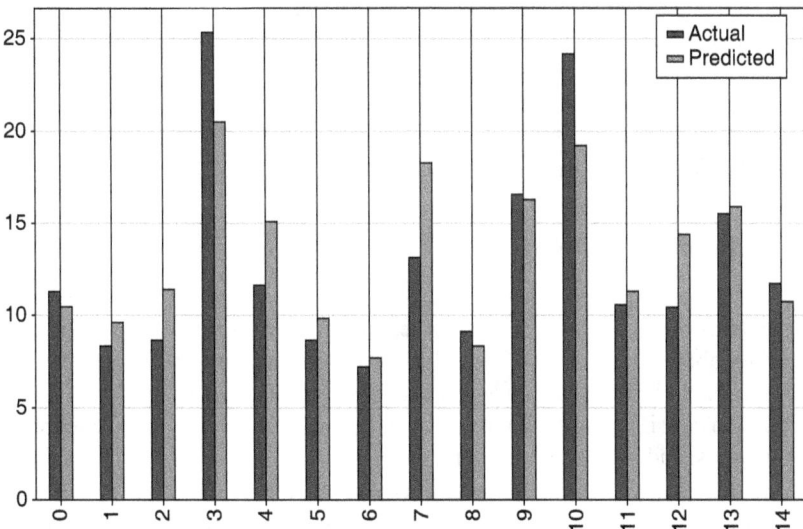

FIGURE 5.5   Actual and Predicted Values of Simple Linear Regression on Advertising Data.

#output

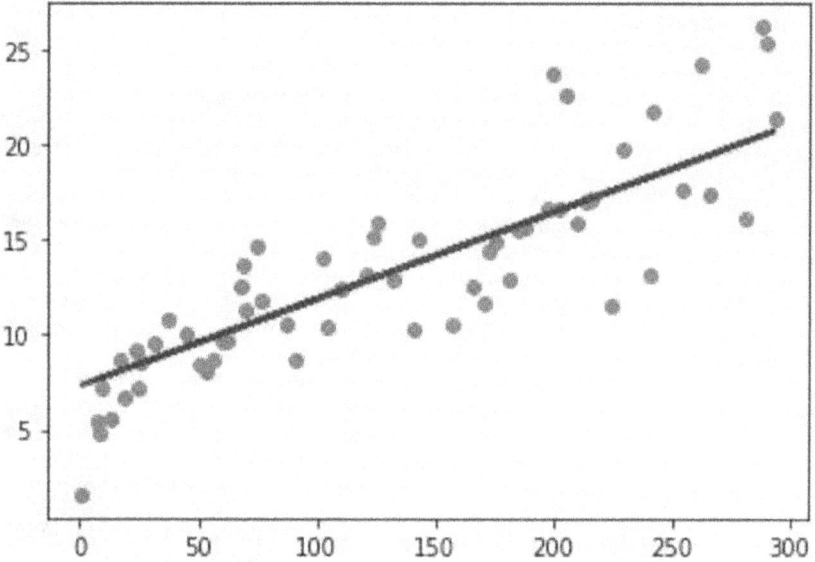

FIGURE 5.6   Regression Line of Advertising Data.

From the Advertising.csv file, which contains the data on TV, radio, newspaper, and sales, multiple linear regression can also be fitted. "Sales" data items are considered as a dependent variable, whereas TV, newspaper, and radio are considered as independent variables. Using this model, sales is predicted based on TV, newspaper, and radio. The accuracy of the multiple linear regression model is 86%, while that of the simple linear regression model is 72% only, as discussed above. Here results shows that the sales prediction is better considering those of TV, radio, and newspaper together instead of considering only TV data.

5.3   CLASSIFICATION

Statistical ML methods, particularly classification techniques, are employed to categorize items based on specific traits or features. For example, classification can be applied to label documents as "Secret" or "Confidential," or to recognize handwritten characters in languages such as Gujarati, Bengali, and Devanagari.

Common classification algorithms include Naive Bayes, k-NN, logistic regression, decision trees, and support vector machines.

Classification problems are generally divided into two primary types: binary classification and multiclass classification. Binary classification focuses on distinguishing between two groups, such as determining whether cancer is present or classifying an email as spam. In contrast, multiclass classification addresses scenarios with more than two categories, such as identifying different faces, categorizing various plant species, or recognizing distinct characters.

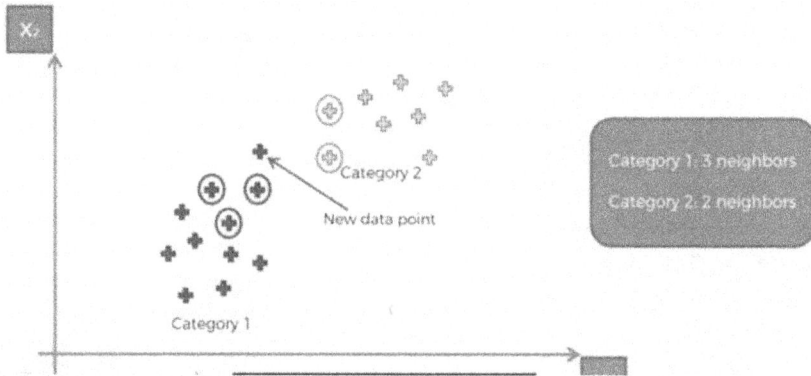

FIGURE 5.7   k-NN Classification.

To adapt binary classification algorithms for multiclass scenarios, strategies like one-versus-one and one-versus-rest can be employed. The one-versus-rest approach involves training a separate binary classifier for each category against all other categories, while the one-versus-one method trains binary classifiers for every possible pair of categories. These techniques can be effectively utilized by algorithms such as support vector machines and logistic regression for multiclass classification tasks.

5.3.1   k-NN Classification

k-NN is a straightforward, nonparametric ML method that doesn't make any assumptions about the underlying data. Unlike many other algorithms that need a training phase, k-NN classifies [1] incoming data points based on how similar they are to preexisting data points. The effectiveness of k-NN is dependent on the choice of k or the number of nearest neighbors considered. To classify a new data point, the algorithm calculates its distance from the current data points (using methods such as the Euclidean distance). k-NNs are estimated using these calculated distances. In Figure 5.7, a new data point is classified in category 1 as of five neighbors, three nearest neighbors are from category 1. As a constant, k has an odd value.

5.3.1.1   k-NN Classification Using Python

Breast cancer data is used here to classify test data points as "malignant" or "benign." The k-value taken here is 5. The distance measure used here is Euclidean distance. These parameters are specified in the KNeighborsClassifier() function of the sklearn library. Data is split into training and test sets. The dataset contains a total of 570 data points, and 114 data points are considered as test data points. The k-NN classifier classifies 109 points correctly, and the accuracy of the model is 95.61%.

```
#K-nn Classification
import numpy as np
import pandas as pd
```

```
from sklearn import datasets, metrics
from sklearn.preprocessing import StandardScaler
from sklearn.metrics import confusion_matrix
from sklearn.neighbors import KNeighborsClassifier
from sklearn.model_selection import train_test_split
cancer = datasets.load_breast_cancer()
Xval = cancer.data
yval = cancer.target
scaler = StandardScaler()
X_scaledval = scaler.fit_transform(Xval)
X_trainval, X_testval, y_trainval, y_testval = train_
test_split(X_scaledval, yval, test_size = 0.2, random_
state = 1)

#K nearest neighbor classifier is built, which is using
euclidean distance measure to find 5 nearest points.
Prediction and accuracy is also calculated here.
knnclassifier = KNeighborsClassifier(n_neighbors=5,
metric='euclidean')
knnclassifier.fit(X_trainval, y_trainval)
y_pred = knnclassifier.predict(X_testval)
print(confusion_matrix(y_testval, y_pred))

r2_score = knnclassifier.score(X_testval, y_testval)
print('accuracy of model is ')
print(r2_score*100,'%')
```

Output:
```
[[37  5]
 [ 0 72]]
accuracy of model is 95.6140350877193 %
```

5.3.2 DECISION TREE

A decision tree is a flowchart-like graphic that shows the various possible outcomes depending on a series of choices. It serves various purposes, including decision-making, research analysis, and strategic planning. Tree-based algorithms are widely employed in supervised learning tasks due to their versatility. Decision trees are capable of processing numerical and categorical input, and they are valued for their ease of interpretation and visualization. Typically, decision trees consist of three main components:

Root Node: Represents the ultimate objective or the big decision you're trying to make.
Branches: Represent the options that are available when making a decision.
Leaf Node: Represents possible outcomes for each action.

Advantages of Decision Tree:

➤ Minimal effort is needed for data preparation or cleaning during the prepro-cessing phase.
➤ Decision trees do not require data normalization or scaling.
➤ Missing data does not significantly impact the decision tree building process.
➤ Decision trees are valued for their simplicity and clarity, making them easy to explain to both technical teams and stakeholders.

Disadvantages of Decision Tree:

➤ The tree structure can alter significantly even with little changes in the data.
➤ In comparison to other methods, the necessary computations can get more complicated.
➤ The training process may be time-consuming, particularly with numerous class labels and deeper tree structures.
➤ Decision trees are less effective for regression tasks.

Working of Decision Tree Algorithm:

1. Splitting: It is the procedure for dividing data into smaller groups.
2. Pruning or Information Gain: It is the process of shortening the branches of a decision tree to limit the tree depth. To keep the decision tree simple, you need to ensure that the tree is small. To measure the information cor-responding to each feature, information gain is calculated using entropy. Entropy is a measure of the uncertainty, quantifying the amount of infor-mation or disorder present in data.
3. Tree Selection: This is the process of determining which tree, in terms of size, best matches the data. To keep the decision tree simple, the informa-tion present must be pure. Tree selection mainly deals with selecting the best attribute for the root and other internal nodes. There are two techniques that help in selecting the best attributes:
   - Information gain
   - Gini index

5.3.2.1   Information Gain

Information gain tells about how much information that feature or attribute provided about a class. Information gain can be calculated as

```
Informatio_ Gain (A)= Entropy_Info(T)- Entropy_Info(T,A)
```

Here T is the training dataset, A is the set of attributes $\{A_1, A_2, \ldots, A_n\}$, and m is the number of classes in the training dataset. Let P_i be the probability that a data instance "d" belongs to class C_i. It is calculated as: dC_i

$$P_i = \frac{|dCi|}{|T|}$$

P_i = Total number of data instances that belongs to class C_i in T/Total number of tuples in training set T.

Entropy specifies randomness in data. It measures the impurity in a given attribute or feature. Entropy can be calculated as

$$\texttt{Entropy\_Info}(T) = -\sum_{i=1}^{m} P_i \log_2 P_i$$

$$\texttt{Entropy\_Info}(T,A) = \sum_{i=1}^{v} \frac{|Ai|}{|T|} \star \texttt{Entropy\_Info}(A_i)$$

Here, attribute A has got "v" distinct values $\{a_1, a_2, \ldots, a_v\}$, $|Ai|$ is the number of instances for distinct value "" in attribute A, and Entropy_Info(Ai) is the entropy for that set of instances. Entropy and information gain are inversely related; i.e., as entropy increases, information gain decreases.

Example: To assess a student's performance during his course of study and predict whether the student will get a job offer or not. The training dataset contains 10 instances with attributes CGPA, interactiveness, practical knowledge, and job offer. The target class is a job offer. Let's create a decision tree to solve this problem.

First, calculate the Entropy of the target class "job offer."

$$\text{Entropy\_Info(target attribute = job offer)} =$$

$$\text{Entropy\_Info}(7,3) = -\left[\frac{7}{10}\log_2\frac{7}{10} + \frac{3}{10}\log_2\frac{3}{10}\right]$$

$$= -(-.3599 + -.5208) = .8807$$

TABLE 5.1
Student Data

SN	CGPA	Interactiveness	Practical Knowledge	Job Offer
1	≥ 9	Yes	Very good	Yes
2	≥ 8	No	Good	Yes
3	≥ 9	No	Average	No
4	< 8	No	Average	No
5	≥ 8	Yes	Good	Yes
6	≥ 9	Yes	Good	Yes
7	< 8	Yes	Good	No
8	≥ 9	No	Very good	Yes
9	≥ 8	Yes	Good	Yes
10	≥ 8	Yes	Average	Yes

TABLE 5.2

Entropy Information for CGPA

CGPA	Job Offer = Yes	Job Offer = No	Total
≥ 9	3	1	4
≥ 8	4	0	4
< 8	0	2	2

TABLE 5.3

Entropy Information for Interactiveness

Interactiveness	Job Offer = Yes	Job Offer = No	Total
Yes	5	1	6
No	2	2	4

Now calculate the Entropy_Info and information gain for each attribute. First, let's calculate for the CGPA attribute, as shown in Table 5.2.

$$\text{Entropy\_Info}\,(\text{T, CGPA}) = \frac{4}{10}\left[-\frac{3}{4}log_2\frac{3}{4}-\frac{1}{4}log_2\frac{1}{4}\right]$$
$$+\frac{4}{10}\left[-\frac{4}{4}log_2\frac{4}{4}-\frac{0}{4}log_2\frac{0}{4}\right]+\frac{2}{10}$$
$$\left[-\frac{0}{2}log_2\frac{0}{2}-\frac{2}{2}log_2\frac{2}{2}\right]$$
$$= .3243$$

$$\text{Gain(CGPA)} = .8807 - .3243 = \textbf{.5564}$$

Next calculate the entropy and information gain for attribute Interactiveness as shown in Table 5.3.

$$\text{Entropy\_Info(T, Interactiveness)t} = \frac{6}{10}\left[-\frac{5}{6}log_2\frac{5}{6}-\frac{1}{6}log_2\frac{1}{6}\right]+\frac{4}{10}$$
$$\left[-\frac{2}{4}log_2\frac{2}{4}-\frac{2}{4}log_2\frac{2}{4}\right]= .3898+.3998 = .7896$$

Gain(Interactiveness) = .8807 − .7896 = **.0911**

Likewise calculate entropy for practical knowledge. It is **0.2246**. So the best split is using CGPA as its information gain is highest among all attributes. The CGPA attribute will become the root of the decision tree.

In the next step, the gain of the remaining attributes is calculated, and a decision is made on the next level root node from the remaining attributes.

TABLE 5.4

Data for CGPA $\geq$ 9

Interactiveness	Practical Knowledge	Job Offer
Yes	Very good	Yes
No	Average	No
Yes	Good	Yes
No	Very good	Yes

CGPA <8 has job offer = "No" only, and CGPA $\geq$ 8 also has job offer = "No" only. But CGPA $\geq$ 9 has job offer "Yes" and "No" both for the following data, as shown in Table 5.4.

So in this step, the same process of computing Entropy_Info and Gain are repeated with the above subset of data. This subset has only four data items. Of these four data, three has job offer "Yes" and only one has job offer "No."

$$\text{Entropy\_Info(target attribute = job offer)} =$$

$$\text{Entropy\_Info}(3,1) = -\left[\frac{3}{4}log_2\frac{3}{4} + \frac{1}{4}log_2\frac{1}{4}\right]$$

$$= .8108$$

$$\text{Entropy\_Info(T, Interactiveness)} = \frac{2}{4}\left[-\frac{2}{2}log_2\frac{2}{2} - \frac{0}{2}log_2\frac{0}{2}\right] + \frac{2}{4}$$

$$\left[-\frac{1}{2}log_2\frac{1}{2} - \frac{1}{2}log_2\frac{1}{2}\right] = 0 + .4997 = .4997$$

$$\text{Gain(Interactiveness)} = .8108 - .4497 = \mathbf{.3111}$$

$$\text{Entropy\_Info(T, Practical knowledge)} = \frac{2}{4}\left[-\frac{2}{2}log_2\frac{2}{2} - \frac{0}{2}log_2\frac{0}{2}\right] + \frac{1}{4}$$

$$\left[-\frac{0}{1}log_2\frac{0}{1} - \frac{1}{1}log_2\frac{1}{1}\right] + \frac{1}{4}\left[-\frac{1}{1}log_2\frac{1}{1} - \frac{0}{1}log_2\frac{0}{1}\right] = 0$$

$$\text{Gain(Interactiveness)} = .8108$$

Gain of practical knowledge is high compared to that of Interactiveness, so it becomes the next level root node. The final decision tree is shown in Figure 5.8.

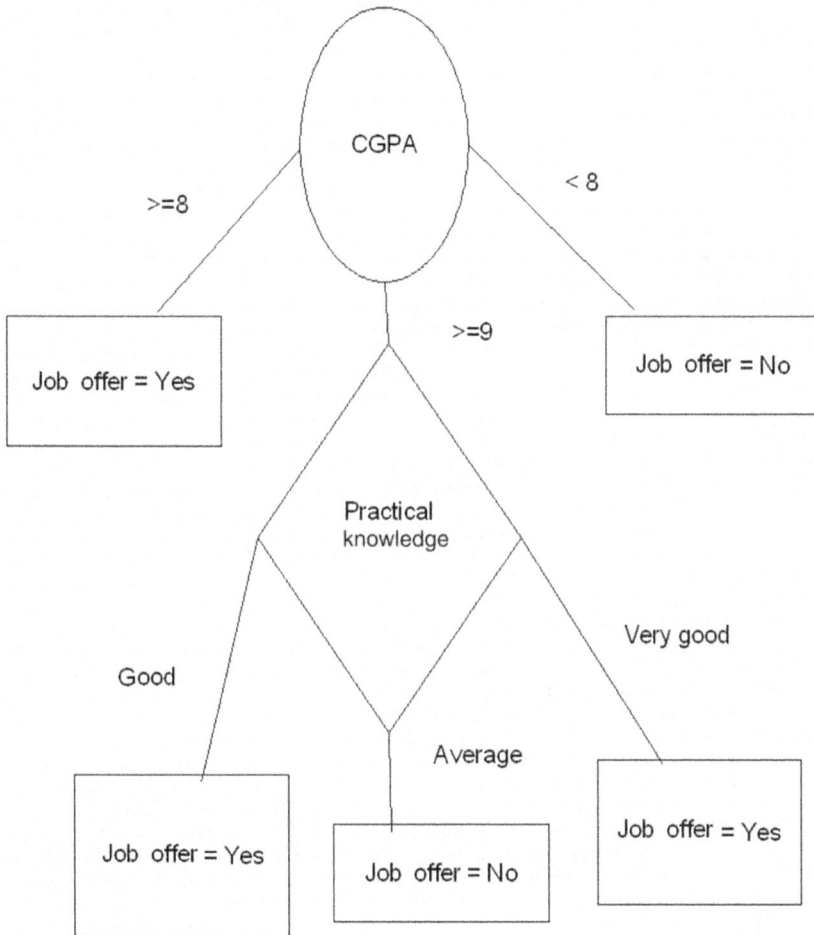

FIGURE 5.8   Final Decision Tree for Student Dataset Using Entropy and Information Gain.

Gini Impurity:

When there are many class labels in the data, this measure of misclassification metric is applied. Gini is comparable to entropy, but it computes significantly more quickly. Gini is used as an impurity parameter in algorithms such as CART (Classification and Regression Tree) algorithms. Python, by default, uses the Gini index for identifying the best attributes for decision-making.

   Example: You want to find whether a person is married or not based on the data collected on the age, income, and gender of different persons, as shown in Table 5.5. A ML algorithm to construct a decision tree is required that best selects the branches

TABLE 5.5

Personal Data

Married	Age		Income		Gender	
	<30	>30	<50000	>50000	Male	Female
Yes	43	90	59	102	83	96
No	77	30	61	18	37	24

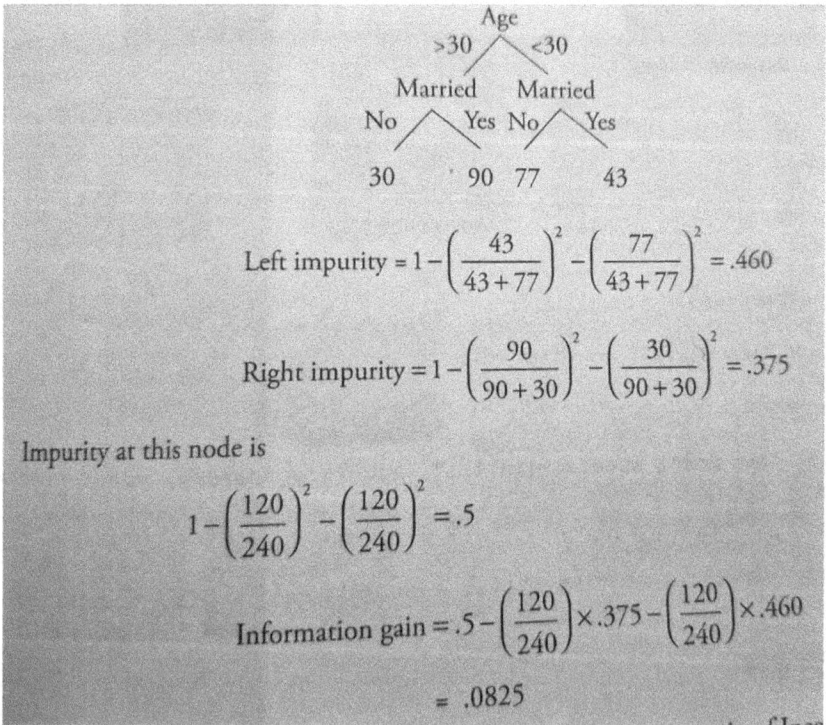

Left impurity $= 1 - \left(\dfrac{43}{43+77}\right)^2 - \left(\dfrac{77}{43+77}\right)^2 = .460$

Right impurity $= 1 - \left(\dfrac{90}{90+30}\right)^2 - \left(\dfrac{30}{90+30}\right)^2 = .375$

Impurity at this node is

$$1 - \left(\frac{120}{240}\right)^2 - \left(\frac{120}{240}\right)^2 = .5$$

$$\text{Information gain} = .5 - \left(\frac{120}{240}\right) \times .375 - \left(\frac{120}{240}\right) \times .460$$

$$= .0825$$

FIGURE 5.9   Impurity Calculation Example.

automatically considering each feature (here age, salary, and gender) to find how well each feature separates people who are married and who are not.

In order to find out which split is better, information gain is calculated for each feature, and the feature with the highest information gain is selected for decision tree-making. Here in this case, there is impurity in each feature as none is saying 100% yes in any case. So the Gini impurity of the left and right leaves is calculated. To do this, it is required to subtract the square of the fraction of people who are married and the square of the fraction of people who are not married from 1 for that feature. For example, Age feature Gini impurity can be calculated as

The age information gain calculated above is .0825, as shown in Figure 5.9. Likewise, the information gain of income and gender features can also be calculated. In this case, the information gain of the income feature is 0.1375 and the gender feature is 0.1265. So in this case, root splitting will be best on the income feature, rather than splitting on age and gender features. This process goes on for all next subsequent nodes until a value below the threshold level is reached.

5.3.2.2 Decision Tree Using Python

An "Iris" dataset is used here. The dataset contains three classes (Setosa, Versicolour, and Virginica) and four features, i.e., petal width, petal length, sepal width, and sepal length. Python, by default, uses the Gini index for decision tree.

```
import numpy as np
import seaborn as sns
from sklearn.metrics import classification_report, con-
fusion_matrix,acc uracy_score
from sklearn.preprocessing import LabelEncoder
from sklearn.tree import DecisionTreeClassifier
from sklearn.model_selection import train_test_split
import matplotlib.pyplot as plt
from sklearn.tree import plot_tree
```

Load the Iris dataset on Google Colab. Some preprocessing operations such as isnull() checking and applying labelencoder are performed on the target variable. After preprocessing, a decision tree ML model is built on the dataset. The accuracy of the model is 100%. The decision tree is also printed.

```
dfd = sns.load_dataset('iris')
dfd.isnull().any()
target = dfd['species']
dfd1 = dfd.copy()
dfd1 = dfd1.shape
X = dfd1
lee = LabelEncoder()
tar = lee.fit_transform(target)
y = tar
dectree=DecisionTreeClassifier()
dectree.fit(X,y)
print('Decision Tree Classifier Created')
ydpred=dectree.predict(X)
cma = confusion_matrix(y, ydpred)
print(cma)
print("Decision tree model accuracy(in %):", accuracy_
score(y, ydpred)*100)

# Visualising the graph without the use of graphviz
plt.figure(figsize = (20,20))
dec_tree = plot_tree(decision_tree=dectree, feature_
names = dfd1.columns,
```

```
class_names =["setosa", "vercicolor", "verginica"],
filled = True, precision = 4, rounded = True)
plt.savefig("one.png")
```

Output:

Decision Tree Classifier Created
[[50 0 0]
[0 50 0]
[0 0 50]]
Decision tree model accuracy(in %): 100.0

5.3.3 Support Vector Machine

Support vector machine (SVM) [2] is widely used for classification problems, but it can also be used for regression problems. It is a supervised ML algorithm that finds the separating line for two-dimensional and hyper planes for multidimensional data.

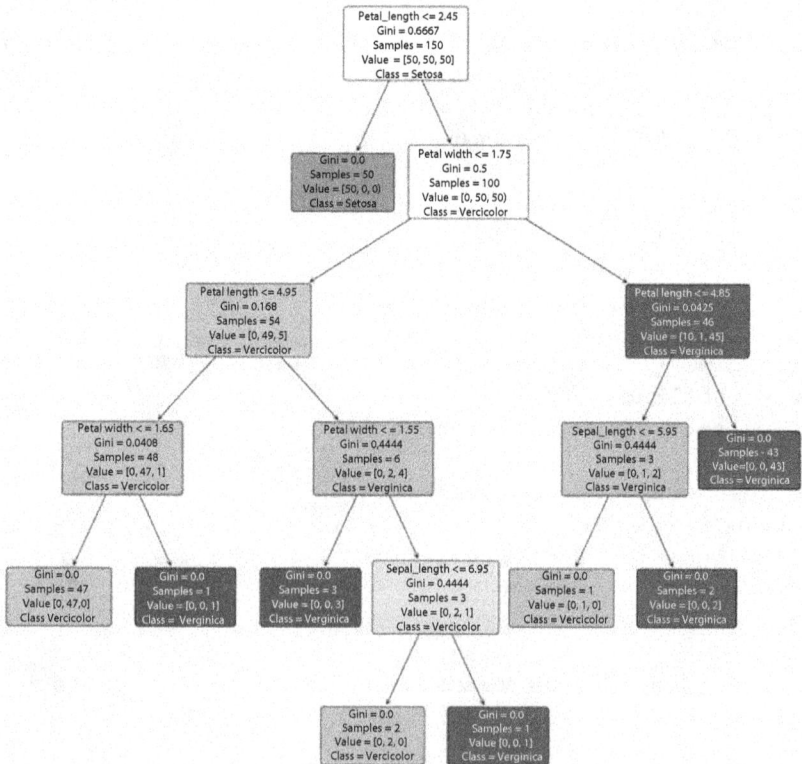

FIGURE 5.10   Decision Tree on Iris Data.

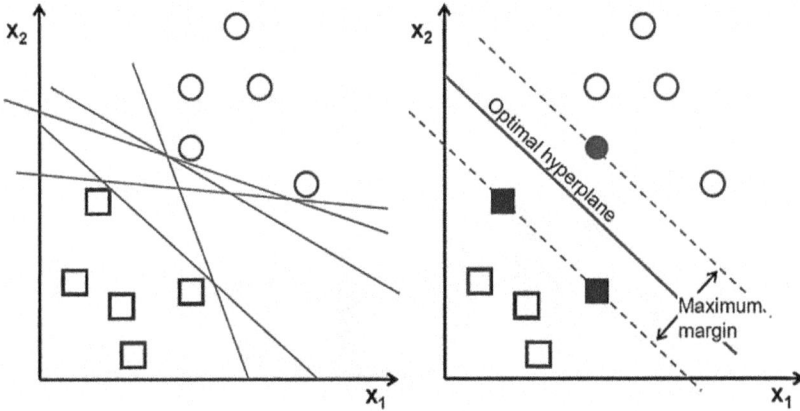

FIGURE 5.11   Possible Hyperplanes and SVM.

In two-dimensional data, there can be many separating lines, which helps separate the data well. But the accuracy of these lines for real-life test data is not good. The separating line calculated by the SVM has the maximum margin between the nearest data points of the training data. As this line has the maximum margin, it gives better accuracy for real-life test data points. Figure 5.11 shows the possible hyperplanes and the hyperplane by supporting a vector machine of linearly separable data. SVM performs well even if data points are not linearly separable [2], as shown in Figure 5.12. SVM applies a kernel trick, which converts non-separable data points to separable data points. SVM kernel is a function applied on low dimension space to convert them to higher dimensional space. For Figure 5.12 data points, one more dimension is added, i.e., z-axis along with x- and y-axes with $z = x^2 + y^2$. After adding this dimension to the data points in Figure 5.12, there is a clear separation of plotted data points in the x- and z-axes. The plot is shown in Figure 5.13. Polynomial, linear, nonlinear, radial basis function, etc., are some of the kernel functions used in the SVM algorithm.

The following are important concepts in SVM:

Support Vectors: These are the data points nearest to the hyperplane. They are crucial in defining the position and orientation of the separating line.

Hyperplane: As illustrated in Figure 5.11, it is a decision boundary that separates different classes in the dataset.

Margin: This is the distance between two lines drawn parallel to the hyperplane, passing through the closest data points from each class (the support vectors). A larger margin is preferable as it indicates better separation between the classes, whereas a smaller margin is less desirable.

The primary objective of SVM is to categorize the data points into classes by identifying a hyperplane that maximizes the margin (maximum marginal hyperplane or

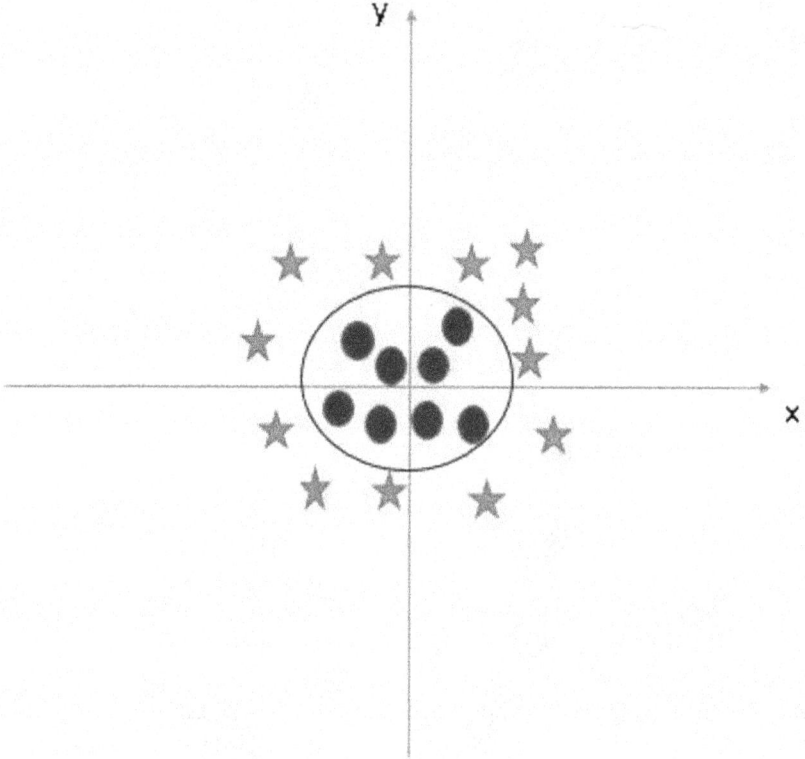

FIGURE 5.12 Nonlinearly Separable Data Points.

MMH). In contrast to the decision theoretic minimum distance classifier that uses only one decision boundary, SVM uses a reference hyperplane and two decision boundaries to classify the points. This is the major difference between SVM and all other classifiers. This shown in Figure 5.11, where there is a reference hyperplane shown with a dark line and two parallel boundaries in dotted lines. The decision boundary should be far away from the data points; hence, the distance should be maximized between the line and the nearest data point.

As of now, let us consider a SVM that implements a binary classifier. This means that there are only two classes, say +1 and −1. A multiclass SVM can also be implemented. Let us consider a dataset:

$$D = \left\{(x_1, y_1), (x_2, y_2), (x_n, y_n)\right\}, x \in R^n \text{ and } y = \left\{-1, +1\right\}$$

The aim of hard margin SVM is to find a hyperplane that maximally separates the classes. Hyperplane equation:

$$h(x) = b + w_1 x_1 + w_2 x_2 + \ldots\ldots\ldots + w_n x_n = 0$$

$$\text{or } b + w^T x = 0$$

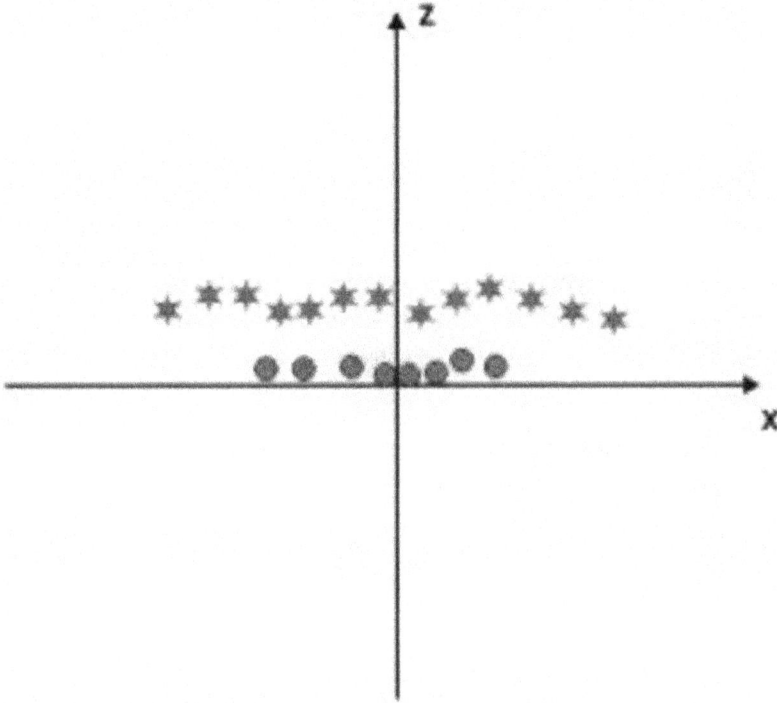

FIGURE 5.13   Kernel Trick Applied on Data Points Mentioned in Figure 5.12.

Here, b is the intercept; $w_1, w_2, \ldots, w_n$ are coefficients; and n is the dimension of data points. For a simple two-dimension, the hyperplane equation can be written as wx + b = 0.

   The hyperplane equation separates the data points x into two classes −1 and +1. This hyperplane equation can also be written as $w^T x = 0$. Here, w is the weight vector and b is the bias or offset from origin. SVM uses two decision lines constructed using the reference hyperplane. The two lines act as two classifiers. This is written as follows:

$$H_1: w. x_i + b \geq 0 \text{ for } y = +1 \text{ and}$$
$$H_2: w. x_i + b < 0 \text{ for } y = -1$$

This classifier is suitable for two class problems. One can also bring the output y into the above equation, and that changes to equation to

$$h(x) = y_i (w.x_i + b) \geq 1 \text{ for } I = 1, 2, 3 \ldots, n,$$
or one can alternatively find predictions as
$$h(x_i) = \text{sign}(w.x_i + b)$$

The sign of h(x) is always positive if it is correctly classified. Its value is negative if it is wrongly classified.

Kernel Trick: In real-world classification problems, nonlinear hyperplanes are required to separate the data as the data can be text, image, video, or sequence. Kernel provides a solution to this problem. One solution to this problem is to map the data into higher dimensional space and define a separating hyperplane. The mapping process, i.e., $\phi(x)$, is the vector representation of the feature x. In short, the mapping function transforms the data point in the input space and maps to another point in space called feature space. Usually, mapping functions are used to map data from a lower dimension to a higher dimension. When the data is mapped from two dimension to another feature space, the data points are nicely segregated in different planes and hence can be separated by a plane. While mapping functions play a major role here, it makes the computation time high and also there is no generalized thumb rule describing which transformation should be applied. Kernels are useful in this context as it computes similar values without transforming the data. Kernels are a set of functions used to transform data from low dimension to high dimension and to manipulate data using dot products at a higher dimension.

Kernels are of different types as given below:

Linear Kernel: $k(x,y) = \phi(x)\phi(y) = \left(x^T.y\right)^{q}$ q

defines the degree of polynomial.

RBF (Gaussian) Kernel: $k(x,y) = exp\left(\dfrac{(x-y)2}{2\sigma2}\right)$

5.3.3.1 SVM Using Python

SVM is implemented here on the breast cancer dataset. It has 31 features. These features are used to classify data into M or B class of the diagnosis feature.

First, upload the dataset. It has 31 features. The last column is used as the target variable, which is stored in yval here. All the remaining features are in xval. Data is preprocessed by applying standard scalar, and transforming data is done by using the transform function.

```
import numpy as np
import pandas as pd
from sklearn.metrics import accuracy_score
from sklearn.model_selection import train_test_split
from sklearn import datasets
from sklearn import svm
from sklearn.preprocessing import StandardScaler
cancerdata = datasets.load_breast_cancer()
df = pd.DataFrame(np.c_[cancerdata['data'], cancer-
data['target']], columns = np.append(cancerdata['fea-
ture_names'], ['target']))
```

```
df.head()
Xval = df.iloc[:, 0:-1]
yval = df.iloc[:, -1]
x_trainval, x_testval, y_trainval, y_testval= train_
test_split(Xval, yval, test_size= 0.25, random_state=3)
scs = StandardScaler()
x_trainval = scs.fit_transform(x_trainval)
x_testval = scs.transform(x_testval)

#Create a svm Classifier
clfsvm = svm.SVC(kernel='linear') # Linear Kernel
#Train the model using the training sets
clfsvm.fit(x_trainval, y_trainval)
#Predict the response for test dataset
y_predval = clfsvm.predict(x_testval)
from sklearn.metrics import confusion_matrix
cm= confusion_matrix(y_testval, y_predval)
print(cm)
print('Accuracy of SVM is :', accuracy_score(y_testval,
y_predval))
```

Output:

```
[[51  2]
 [ 1 89]]
Accuracy of SVM is : 0.979020979020979
```

SVC() function is used to build SVM for the breast cancer dataset. As data is linearly separable, linear kernel is used here. The SVM accuracy achieved is 97.9%.

5.3.4 NAIVE BAYES CLASSIFICATION

It is a classification algorithm based on supervised learning. Its foundation is the Bayes theorem, which is employed in the computation of conditional probabilities.

$$P(A/B) = \frac{P(B/A)P(A)}{P(B)},$$

where P(A/B), also known as posterior probability, is the chance that event A will occur given that event B has already occurred.

P(B/A) is the probability that event B will occur in the event that event A has already happened.

P(A) is the probability that event A will occur.

P(B) is the probability that event B will occur.

$$P(A/y_1, y_2, y_3, \ldots y_n) = \left[P(y_1/A) P(y_2/A) \ldots P(y_n/A) * P(A) \right] / \left[P(y_1) \ P(y_2) \ldots P(y_n) \right]$$

$$= \left[P(A) \prod_{i=1}^{n} P(y_i/A) \right] / \left[P(y_1) \ P(y_2) \ldots P(y_n) \right]$$

$$A = \text{Argmax } P(A) \prod_{i=1}^{n} P(y_i/A)$$

P(A) = Class probability

$P(y_i/A)$ = Conditional probability

Given below is an example of Naive Bayes. Here, the data used is of stolen cars that is presented in Table 6, which includes features such as color, type of car, and origin of car and is classified as stolen or not.

Probabilities are calculated as given in the above formula. New data points, which need to be classified as stolen (yes or no) will be based on the calculated maximum probability of the class. The new data points given as (Red, Domestic, and SUV) can be classified as "No" stolen class based on the given data.

P(Yes) = Probability of "Yes" class = 5/10 = .5
P(No) = Probability of "No" class = 5/10 = .5

The probability of color, type, and origin feature is shown in Tables 5.7, 5.8, and 5.9, respectively.

P(Red/Yes, Domestic/Yes, SUV/Yes) = ⅗ * ⅖ * ⅕ = 6/125
P(Red/No, Domestic/No, SUV/No) = ⅖ * ⅗ * ⅗ = 18/125
So P(Red, Domestic, SUV) will be classified as "No," as the probability of this class is higher.

TABLE 5.6
Stolen Cars Data

SN	Color	Type	Origin	Stolen
1	Red	Sports	Imported	Yes
2	Red	SUV	Imported	No
3	Yellow	SUV	Domestic	No
4	Yellow	SUV	Domestic	Yes
5	Yellow	SUV	Domestic	No
6	Yellow	Sports	Imported	Yes
7	Yellow	Sports	Domestic	No
8	Red	Sports	Domestic	Yes
9	Red	Sports	Domestic	No
10	Red	Sports	Domestic	Yes

TABLE 5.7
Probability of Color Feature

Color Feature	Yes	No	P(Yes)	P(No)
Red	3	2	3/5	2/5
Yellow	2	3	2/5	3/5
Total	5	5		

TABLE 5.8
Probability of Type Feature

Type Feature	Yes	No	P(Yes)	P(No)
Domestic	2	3	2/5	3/5
Imported	3	2	3/5	2/5
Total	5	5		

TABLE 5.9
Probability of Origin Feature

Origin Feature	Yes	No	P(Yes)	P(No)
SUV	1	3	1/5	3/5
Sport	4	2	4/5	2/5
Total	5	5		

All variations of Naive Bayes classifiers operate on the same principle: the assumption that feature values are independent of each other, given the class variable. Naive Bayes requires minimal training data to estimate the necessary parameters for classification. Different types of data, such as categorical, binary, and numerical, require different methods to estimate probability distribution parameters. For numerical data, Gaussian distribution is used, while binary data (e.g., 0/1 or yes/no) relies on binomial distribution, and categorical data uses multinomial distribution. These distributions are so commonly applied that Naive Bayes classifiers are often named after them.

5.3.4.1 Gaussian Naive Bayes

The assumption made here is that the data values associated with each class follow a normal or Gaussian distribution. This works best with continuous data. The bell-shaped normal distribution curve is symmetrical around the feature/attribute value mean. It is assumed that the feature likelihood value is

$$P(x_i \mid y) = \frac{1}{\sqrt{2\pi\sigma_y^2}} \exp - \left(\frac{(x_i - \mu_y)^2}{2\pi\sigma_y^2} \right)$$

Python function GaussianNB() can be used to build the ML model.

5.3.4.2 Multinomial Naive Bayes

This is mostly utilized in the field of natural language processing (NLP) for document classification and where the categorical data values are used for classification. Frequencies of generation of events are represented in the feature vector, which follows a multinomial distribution, i.e., it considers the feature vector that represents the number of times it appears in text or data.

$$\log p(C_k \mid X) \infty \log p(C_k) \prod_{i=1}^{n} pki^{xi})$$
$$= \log p(C_k) \sum_{i=1}^{n} x_i \cdot \log pki$$
$$= b + W_k^T X$$

The example for multinomial Naive Bayes here considers the following data shown in Table 5.10, and the test data is classified using multinomial Naive Bayes.

Probabilities cannot be zero, but in the given data some words do not occur in all documents, so their probabilities will be calculated as zero. To avoid this, Laplace smoothing can be used with value as

$$P = (X_i + \alpha) / (N + \alpha d), \text{ where } \alpha = 1 \tag{1}$$

d = Total different words = 6

d = [India, Beijing, Shanghai, Macao, Tokyo, Japan]

$N_{yes} = 8$

N_{yes} = [India Beijing India India India Shanghai India Macao]

$N_{no} = 3$

N_{no} = [Tokyo Japan India]

P(I) = P(India) = 3/4

P($\underline{I}$) = 1/4

TABLE 5.10

Text Data of Documents

	Doc No	Words in Document	In I = India??
Training data	1	India Beijing India	yes
	2	India India Shanghai	yes
	3	India Macao	yes
	4	Tokyo Japan India	no
Test Data		India India India Tokyo Japan	??

P(India/I) = (5 + 1)/(8 + 6) = 6/14 = 3/7 as India occurs five times in I = India yes category. So applying equation (1) will give this probability

P(Tokyo/I) = (0 + 1)/(8 + 6) = 1/14   P(Japan/I) = (0 + 1)/(8 + 6) =1/14

P(India/ $\underline{I}$) = (1 + 1)/(3 + 6) = 2/9 as India occurs once in I = India no category. So applying equation (1) will give this probability

P(Tokyo/ $\underline{I}$) = (1 + 1)/(3 + 6) = 2/9   P(Japan/ $\underline{I}$) = (1 + 1)/(3 + 6) = 2/9

So the test data (India India India Tokyo Japan) to be categorized in India = Yes or no will be determined by the calculated probability as follows:

P(India India India Tokyo Japan/I) = ¾ *(3/7 *3/7 *3/7* 1/14 * 1/14)

= .0003

P(India India India Tokyo Japan/ $\underline{I}$) = ¼ *(2/9 * 2/9 *2/9 * 2/9* 2/9)

= .0001

The probability of the test data occurring in I India = yes class is higher than the probability of it occurring in I India = no class, so the test data will be categorized in **India = yes**.

5.3.4.3 Bernoulli Naive Bayes

Bernoulli distribution [3] is used for binary data, i.e., where the data values take the form of true/false, yes/no, 0/1, success/failure, presence/absence, etc. Bernoulli Naive Bayes uses Bernoulli distribution, so feature values are binary in this case, and the distribution works best on discrete data. This model is also popular for document classification, but here binary term occurrences are used as features rather than the frequencies of a word in the document.

The Bernoulli Distribution

$$p(x) = p[X = x] = \begin{cases} q = 1 - p & x = 0 \\ p & x = 0 \end{cases}$$

The example demonstrates the Bernoulli Naive Bayes for document classification. The data given is related to either Sports(S) or Informatics(I). The training set has 11 documents, and the aim here is to estimate a Bernoulli document model to classify the unlabeled document as S or I. Documents have eight feature words, i.e., w_1 = goal, w_2 = tutor, w_3 = variance, w_4 = speed, w_5 = drink, w_6 = defense, w_7 = performance, and w_8 = field. We have six documents of the Sports(S) category and five documents of the Informatics(I) category. B(Sports) has eight feature occurrences (1/0) in six documents, so it has a dimension of 6 x 8, and B(Informatics) has eight feature occurrences (1/0) in five documents, so it has a dimension of 5 x 8.

B(Sports) =

Goal	Tutor	Variance	Speed	Drink	Defense	Performance	Field
1	0	0	0	1	1	1	1
0	0	1	0	1	1	0	0
0	1	0	1	0	1	1	0
1	0	0	1	0	1	0	1
1	0	0	0	1	0	1	1
0	0	1	1	0	0	1	1

B(Informatics) =

Goal	Tutor	Variance	Speed	Drink	Defense	Performance	Field
0	1	1	0	0	0	1	0
1	1	0	1	0	0	1	1
0	1	1	0	0	1	0	0
0	0	0	0	0	0	0	0
0	0	1	0	1	0	1	0

Using the given data, if our aim is to classify b_1 (1 0 0 1 1 1 0 1) and b_2 (0 1 1 0 1 0 1 0) using Bernaulli Naive Bayes, calculating the probabilities is required as follows:

$$N = \text{Total number of documents} = 11$$

N_S = Number of documents in sports = 6
N_I = Number of documents in informatics = 5, so P(S) = 6/11 and P(T) = 5/11.

Feature	N_S (feature)	P(feature/S) Probability of Feature in Sports Document	Probability of Not Occurring That Feature	N_I (feature)	P(feature/I) Probability of Feature in Informatics Document	Probability of Not Occurring That Feature
Goal	3	3/6	1−3/6 = 3/6	1	1/5	1−1/5 = 4/5
Tutor	1	1/6	1− 1/6 = 5/6	3	3/5	1−3/5 = 2/5
Variance	2	2/6	1− 2/6 = 4/6	3	3/5	1−3/5 = 2/5
Speed	3	3/6	1−3/6 = 3/6	1	1/5	1−1/5 = 4/5
Drink	3	3/6	1−3/6 = 3/6	1	1/5	1−1/5 = 4/5
Defense	4	4/6	1−4/6 = 2/6	1	1/5	1−1/5 = 4/5
Performance	4	4/6	1−4/6 = 2/6	3	3/5	1−3/5 = 2/5
Field	4	4/6	1−4/6 = 2/6	1	1/5	1−1/5 = 4/5

$P(S/b_1)$ = Probability of b_1 occurring in S

$\quad b_1 = (1\ 0\ 0\ 1\ 1\ 1\ 0\ 1)$

$P(S/b_1) = 6/11 * (3/6 * \frac{5}{6} * 4/6 * 3/6 * 3/6 * 4/6 * 2/6 * 4/6)$

$P(S/b_1) = 5.6 * 10^{-3}$

$P(I/b_1)$ = Probability of b_1 occurring in I

$\quad b_1 = (1\ 0\ 0\ 1\ 1\ 1\ 0\ 1)$

$P(I/b_1) = 5/11 * (\frac{1}{5} * \frac{2}{5} * \frac{2}{5} * \frac{1}{5} * \frac{1}{5} * \frac{1}{5} * \frac{2}{5} * \frac{1}{5})$

$P(I/b_1) = 9.3 * 10^{-6}$

$P(S/b_1)$ is higher, so b_1 will be classified in the Sports category.

$P(S/b_2)$ = Probability of b_2 occurring in S

$\quad b_2 = (0\ 1\ 1\ 0\ 1\ 0\ 1\ 0)$

$P(S/b_2) = 6/11 * (3/6 * 1/6 * 2/6 * 3/6 * 3/6 * 2/6 * 4/6 * 2/6)$

$P(S/b_2) = 2.8 * 10^{-4}$

$P(I/b_2)$ = Probability of b_1 occurring in I

$\quad b_2 = (0\ 1\ 1\ 0\ 1\ 0\ 1\ 0)$

$P(I/b_2) = 5/11 * (4/5 * 3/5 * 3/5 * 4/5 * 1/5 * 4/5 * 3/5 * 4/5)$

$P(I/b_2) = 8.0 * 10^{-3}$

$P(I/b_2)$ is higher, so b_2 will be classified in the informatics category.

5.4   METRICS FOR EVALUATING CLASSIFIER PERFORMANCE

Evaluating classifier performance is an excellent way of getting feedback whether what you are doing is correct or not. It is a tool for comparing the performance of ML models. Ultimately, it is required to build a model of high-performance accuracy, which can help us make better decisions in real-world scenarios. The most commonly used classification evaluation metric is to calculate its accuracy. But measuring accuracy is not the correct measure of evaluating performance as data is not balanced in real-life scenarios such as in spam email detection, financial cases (credit card, fraud, etc.), and medical diagnosis. So, only measuring accuracy will not give the correct picture of the constructed model: other measures are required to evaluate the performance of classifiers. The confusion matrix shown [4] in Figure 5.14 is the performance measure that gives the details of accuracy, recall, and precision. F1-score and area under the ROC curve (AUC)-Receiver Operating Characteristic (ROC) curve are also used as performance metrics [4].

		Actual Value	
		Positive	Negative
Predicted Value	Positive	TP (True Positive)	FP (False Negative)
	Negative	FN (False Negative)	TN (True Negative)

- True Positive (TP): Observation is positive and is predicted to be positive.
- False Negative (FN): Observation is positive but is predicted to be negative.
- True Negative (TN): Observation is negative and is predicted to be negative.
- False Positive (FP): Observation is negative but is predicted to be positive.

FIGURE 5.14 Confusion Matrix.

Accuracy:

$$ACC = \frac{TP + TN}{TP + TN + FP + FN}$$

Recall:

$$Recall = \frac{TP}{TP + FN}$$

Precision:

$$Precision = \frac{TP}{TP + FP}$$

F_1 score:

$$F_1 = \frac{2}{\frac{1}{Recall} + \frac{1}{Precision}}$$

FIGURE 5.15 Key Classification Metrics.

Confusion matrix not only gives the correct picture of the model, which classes are wrongly and correctly predicted or classified, but also tells what type of errors are being made by the model. Here, TP, FP, FN, and TN are calculated for the model as shown in Figure 5.15, which are useful for measuring precision, recall or sensitivity, specificity, accuracy, and AUC-ROC curve of the model. The relevance of calculating precision, recall, accuracy, or specificity depends on the application. F1 score is useful when the optimal blend of precision and recall is required. A good F1 score (perfect model when the F1 score is 1 and model failure when the F1 score value is 0) indicates low false negatives and low false positives, so the model is not disturbed by false alarms. Classifiers can be characterized based on various performance metrics. When every instance is correctly classified, it's a perfect classifier; i.e., when its TP = P and TN = N, accuracy will be 1. When every instance is wrongly classified, it's a worst classifier; i.e., when its TP = 0 and TN = 0, accuracy will be 0. When the classifier always predicts the positive class correctly, it's a ultra-liberal classifier, i.e., its FN = 0 and TN = 0. When the classifier always predicts the negative class correctly, it's a ultra-conservative classifier, i.e., its TP = 0 and FP = 0.

$$True\ positive\ rate = \frac{True\ positives}{True\ positives + False\ negatives} False\ negatives\ rate$$
$$= \frac{False\ positives}{False\ positives + True\ negatives}$$

True Positive (TP):	**False Positive (FP):**
Actuals are positive and are predicted as positive	Type 1 error
Example: You predicted that a woman is pregnant and she actually is	Actuals are negative and are predicted as positive
	Example: You predicted that a man is pregnant, but he actually is not
False Negative (FN):	**True Negative (TN):**
Type 2 error	Actuals are negative and are predicted as positive
Actuals are positive and are predicted as negative	Example: You predicted that a man is not pregnant, and he actually is not
Example: You predicted that a woman is not pregnant, and she actually is	

FIGURE 5.16 TPR and FPR.

ROC curve [4] is a visualization method that summarizes the true positive rate (TPR) and false positive rate (FPR) of the model. It plots tpr versus fpr data, shown in Figure 5.17. Performance of the model is assessed by the AUC. If it is less than 0.6, the model is considered a failure; if the value is between 0.9 and 1, the model is excellent; if the value is between 0.8 and 0.9, the model is good; if the value is 0.7–0.8, the model is fair; and if the value is 0.6–0.7, the model is poor.

5.5 MODEL TRAINING AND CROSS-VALIDATION

ML models can be trained in different ways based on chosen algorithms. Two important methods to mention here are batch and gradient descent.

Gradient Descent:

Gradient descent is a first-order optimization algorithm used to find the minimum of a function. By calculating the gradient (slope) of the function at a given point, it adjusts the parameters in the opposite direction to minimize the function. This process is commonly applied to loss functions in ML to optimize model parameters. There are two primary methods for gradient descent:

- **Batch Gradient Descent:** All training data is used to calculate the average gradient, and the parameters are updated based on this average. It is suitable for convex or relatively smooth error surfaces but can be inefficient for large datasets.
- **Stochastic Gradient Descent (SGD):** A single training example is used to calculate the gradient, and the parameters are updated immediately. This method is more efficient for large datasets but can be noisy due to fluctuations in gradients.

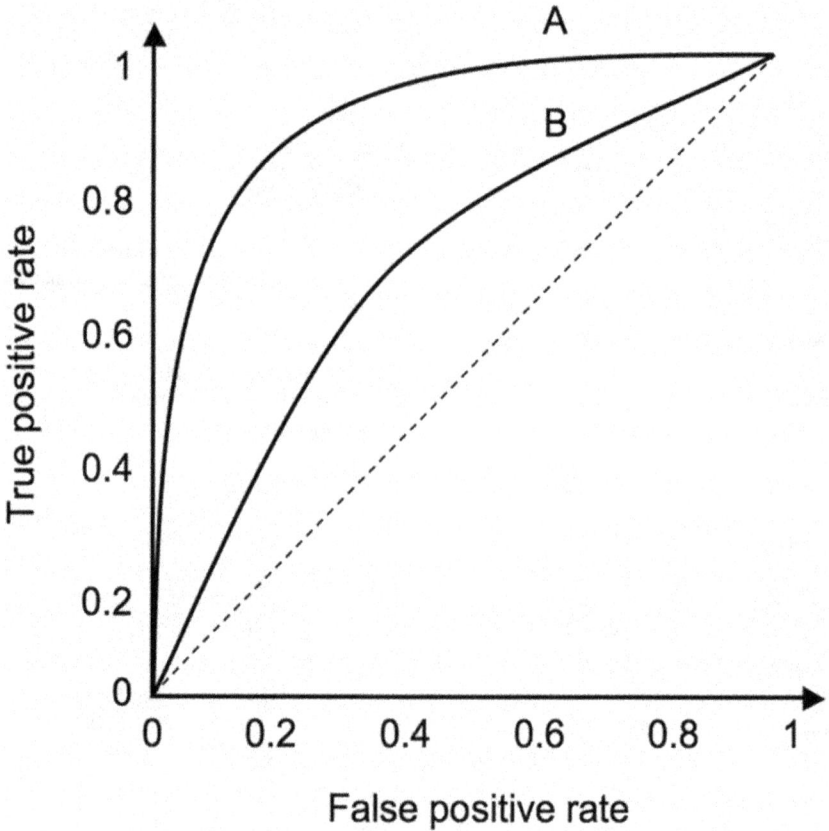

FIGURE 5.17 ROC Curve.

Some examples where gradient descent can applied are as follows:

   Example 1: Consider that you are attempting to fit a dataset of points to a straight line. $y = mx + b$ is the equation of the line. The objective is to determine the values of b (intercept) and m (slope) that minimize the separation between the data points and the line. Iteratively adjusting m and b via gradient descent can be done until the line best fits the data.

   Example 2: The weights and biases of the neurons in a neural network control the network's output. To reduce the network's error on a particular dataset, these weights and biases are adjusted via gradient descent. This is often accomplished by computing the gradient of the loss function with respect to the weights and biases and then updating the parameters in the opposite direction as the gradient.

One method for evaluating a ML model's performance on a small dataset is cross-validation [5]. It entails breaking up the dataset into smaller subsets, using few of those subsets to train the model, and then testing the model's performance on the remaining subsets. To provide a more accurate estimate of the generalization performance of the model, this step is performed several times. You can choose the best method for your particular problem by utilizing cross-validation to compare the performance of various models. Let's say you have 100 samples in your dataset. Five subsets of the dataset are created for five-fold cross-validation. The remaining four subsets are utilized for training, while one subset is used for testing. This procedure is carried out five times, with a different subset being tested each time. The model's generalization ability is determined by averaging performance across all folds. Two cross-validation approaches exist: exhaustive and non-exhaustive.

5.5.1   NON-EXHAUSTIVE METHODS

Non-exhaustive cross-validation methods do not consider all ways of splitting the original data. Holdout method and k-fold cross-validation methods [6] are non-exhaustive methods, as discussed below.

5.5.1.1   Holdout Method

In this method, the entire dataset is divided into training set and test set. Usually data is divided into ratios of 80:20 or 70:30, and data is shuffled randomly before splitting. Model training is done using a training set, and the model accuracy is evaluated using a test set. There are some disadvantages of this method. Model can give different results every time it is trained, and test it as data is shuffled randomly so the model is trained on different data points every time. And we are never sure about the train set that we picked to represent the whole dataset. Also, when the dataset is small, there are high chances that the test data contain some important information that is not present in the train set.

5.5.1.2   k-Fold Cross-Validation

k-fold validation method shown in Figure 5.18 is an improvement on the holdout method, as this method is not dependent on the way our training and testing dataset is picked. In the k-fold cross-validation method, k subsets of the dataset are formed and a holdout method is applied on each subset. So eventually the holdout method is repeated k number of times as shown in Figure 5.18. Entire dataset is randomly split into k subsets. For each fold, the model is trained on k–1 folds of the dataset and test on the kth fold. And this process is repeated k times, so each fold will have different training and testing sets. The overall accuracy of the model is calculated as the average of k recorded accuracies. This method helps in increasing the accuracy of the model.

The disadvantage of this method is that it requires k times more computation as the training algorithm has to be rerun from scratch k times. And at times it is possible to get imbalanced folds; i.e., one fold might have the majority of data belonging to one class and few of other classes. This can affect the accuracy of the model,

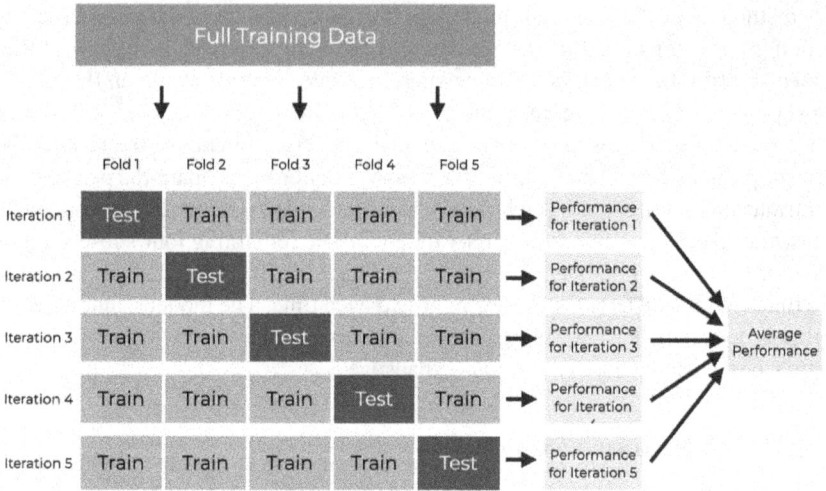

FIGURE 5.18   k-Fold Cross-Validation.

and training will also get affected. Stratified k-fold cross-validation helps avoid this imbalance process by using stratification.

5.5.1.3   Non-Exhaustive Cross-Validation Using Python

```
Python code to implement k-fold cross-validation method
#Importing required libraries
from matplotlib import pyplot
import io
import matplotlib.pyplot as plt
import pandas as pd
from sklearn.model_selection import train_test_split
from sklearn.linear_model import LinearRegression
from sklearn import metrics
import scipy.stats
from sklearn.model_selection import KFold
from sklearn.metrics import accuracy_score

from google.colab import files
uploaded= files.upload()

dfval=pd.read_csv(io.BytesIO(uploaded['Advertising.
csv']))
#Loading the dataset
Xval = dfval.iloc[:,0:3]
yval = dfval['Sales'].values.reshape(-1,1)
```

```
#Implementing cross validation. Five-fold cross-
validation is done here. In each fold, i.e., in each
iteration, one fold is used as the testing set. Overall
accuracy is the average of all classifiers' accuracy.
k = 5
kfd = KFold(n_splits=k, random_state=None)
model = LinearRegression()
accuracy_score = []
for train_index, test_index in kfd.split(Xval):
    Xval_train, Xval_test=Xval.iloc[train_index,:],
Xval.iloc[test_index,:]
    yval_train, yval_test = yval[train_index],
yval[test_index]
    model.fit(Xval_train,yval_train)
    pred_values = model.predict(Xval_test)
    r2_score = model.score(Xval_test, yval_test)
    print('accuracy of model is')
    print(r2_score*100,'%')
    accuracy_score.append(r2_score)

avg_accuracy_score = sum(accuracy_score)/k
print('accuracy of each fold - {}'.
format(accuracy_score))
print('Avg accuracy : {}'.format(avg_accuracy_score))
```

Output:

```
accuracy of model is
87.8651980483134 %
accuracy of model is
91.7632116561446 %
accuracy of model is
92.93303235799652 %
accuracy of model is
81.44390391722337 %
accuracy of model is
89.54782879224385 %
accuracy of each fold - [0.878651980483134,
0.917632116561446, 0.9293303235799653,
0.8144390391722337, 0.8954782879224386]
Avg accuracy : 0.8871063495438435
```

Here, the linear regression is performed on Advertising.csv file, which contains sales, TV, newspaper, and radio fields. Details of this linear regression is discussed in the previous chapter. k-fold cross-validation with k = 5 is implemented here. The dataset is divided into five subsets. For each iteration, four subsets are used for training and one for testing. Calculate the accuracy of all five iterations, which is different for different iterations, i.e., 87.86%, 91.76%, 92.93%, 81.44%, and 89.54%. Overall accuracy is the average accuracy of all iterations, which comes out to be 88.71%.

5.5.2   EXHAUSTIVE METHODS

Exhaustive cross-validation methods consider all ways of splitting the original data into training and testing sets. Leave-one-out and leave-p-out cross-validation methods are exhaustive methods.

5.5.2.1   Leave-p-Out Cross-Validation

In this method, p number of points are taken out from the whole dataset of total n points. The (n-p) points are used for training the model, and the remaining p points are used for testing the model. This process is iterated for all possible combinations of p points. Overall accuracy of the model is the average of all iterations. Here, training is done for every possible combination of data points.

5.5.2.2   Leave-One-Out Cross-Validation

If we set the value of p as one, the method is called leave-one-out cross-validation. Taking p = 1 makes the method less exhaustive.

5.5.2.3   Exhaustive Cross-Validation Using Python

First, import libraries in Google Colab. Cross-validation need not be implemented manually, Scikit-learn library in Python provides a simple implementation that will split the data accordingly. An array of few numbers are taken here and printed as an independent variable and dependent variable, i.e., x and y, respectively. The function LeaveOneOut() is used, and data is split using a for loop, and the splits are enumerated and iterated through the training index and test index. And finally, the training set and validation set are printed.

```
# importing libraries
import numpy as np
from sklearn.model_selection import LeaveOneOut
# creating the data
X = np.array([[1, 2], [3, 4]])
y = np.array([1, 2])
# Independent variable
print("\nIndependent variable:")
print(X)
# Dependent variable
print("\nDependent variable:")
print(y)
# creating the leave one out function
loo = LeaveOneOut()
loo.get_n_splits(X)
```

```
# printing the training and validation data
for train_index, test_index in loo.split(X):
X_train, X_test = X[train_index], X[test_index]
y_train, y_test = y[train_index], y[test_index]
print("\nTraining set:", X_train, y_train)
print("\nValidation set:", X_test, y_test)
```

Output:

```
Independent variable:
[[1 2]
[3 4]]
Dependent variable:
[1 2]
Training set: [[1 2]] [1]
Validation set: [[3 4]] [2]
```

5.6   REGULARIZATION

Let's understand regularization and its importance with a very simple example of learning animal drawing. You practice drawing a lot of different animals. You might draw dogs, cats, elephants, and birds. If you only practice drawing dogs over and over, you'll get really good at drawing dogs, but you might not be as good at drawing other animals like cats or elephants. Now think of regularization applied in learning to draw animals. Regularization is like balanced drawing practice. This is like your art teacher giving you rules to follow so you become a better all-around artist, not just an expert at drawing dogs. L1 regularization is where your teacher tells you to only draw the most important parts of each animal. So, you might focus on the dog's ears and tail but keep the drawing simple. L2 regularization is when your teacher tells you to draw every animal with light, smooth lines, not pressing too hard with your pencil. This way, your drawings don't have any overly dark, heavy lines that stand out too much. So with regularization you become a better artist overall, able to draw any animal you see, not just the ones you practiced the most. So in simple terms, regularization is like having drawing rules from your art teacher to help you become good at drawing all sorts of animals. Instead of just drawing dogs really well, you learn to draw all animals nicely and clearly. This way, when you need to draw a new animal you've never seen before, you can do it easily because you practiced drawing in a balanced way.

In ML models, regularization is a technique used to stop overfitting. When a model learns the noise in the training data instead of the underlying pattern, it is said to be overfitting and has poor generalization to new, unseen data. Regularization encourages simpler, more broadly applicable models by introducing more constraints or penalties into the model. Regularization introduces bias into the model but reduces variance, leading to a lower overall error on unseen data. It encourages simpler models by penalizing large coefficients, thus reducing the risk of overfitting.

5.6.1 Types of Regularization

1. **L1 Regularization (Lasso):**
   o Imposes a penalty equivalent to the amount of the coefficients' absolute value.
   o Encourages sparsity, leading to models where some feature weights become exactly zero, effectively performing feature selection.
   o Loss function with L1 regularization: $L(\theta)+\lambda\Sigma_i|\theta_i|$.
2. **L2 Regularization (Ridge):**
   o Applies a penalty that is the square of the coefficients' magnitude.
   o Helps in reducing the impact of correlated features and spreads out the weights more evenly.
   o Loss function with L2 regularization: $L(\theta)+\lambda\Sigma_i\theta_i^2$.
3. **Elastic Net:**
   o Combines L1 and L2 regularization.
   o Useful when there are multiple features with high collinearity.
   o Loss function: $L(\theta)+\lambda_1\Sigma_i|\theta_i|+\lambda_2\Sigma_i\theta_i^2$.

5.7 HYPERPARAMETER TUNING

The settings made to an ML model prior to the start of the learning process are known as hyperparameters. They serve to regulate the learning process rather than being acquired from the data. An ML model's performance and accuracy can be greatly impacted by the selection of hyperparameters [7]. Improved model performance, decreased overfitting, and increased efficiency all depend on hyperparameter adjustment. Some common hyperparameters for various types of ML models are as follows:

- ➤ **Learning Rate:** Regulates the gradient descent optimization process's step size.
- ➤ **Batch Size:** Number of training cases used in a single iteration.
- ➤ **Number of Epochs:** Number of complete passes through the training dataset.

However, specific models have specific hyperparameters. Some ML models' hyperparameters are detailed in Table 5.11.

5.7.1 Methods for Hyperparameter Tuning

1. **Grid Search:** Determines which combination of parameter values yields the best performance by methodically going through several permutations and cross-validating along the way.
2. **Random Search:** In order to determine the ideal set of parameters, hyperparameters are sampled from specified distributions and evaluated using the random search technique for hyperparameter tuning [6] in ML. It is frequently compared to grid search, which does a thorough search over a predetermined set of hyperparameters. Random search is more efficient in

TABLE 5.11
Hyperparameters of ML Models

Model	Hyperparameters
Linear models	*Regularization strength (α or λ) for L1, L2 regularization*
k-NN	**n_neighbors**: Number of neighbors
	Weights: Indicates if the impact of each neighbor is the same or if those who are closer have a bigger say
	Metric: The measurement of distance that is utilized to determine the separation of data points
	Algorithm: The algorithm that calculates the closest neighbors
	leaf_size: Size of leaf
	Metric parameters: Additional parameters for the chosen distance metric
Decision Trees	**Max depth:** The tree's maximum depth
	Minimum sample split: The smallest quantity of samples needed to split an internal node
	Minimum example leaf: The bare minimum of samples needed at each leaf node
	Max features: The greatest number of features to take into account when choosing a split
	Bootstrap: Using bootstrap samples in tree construction
SVMs	**C (regularization parameter):** Manages the trade-off between minimizing the weights' norm and obtaining a low error on the training set
	Kernel type: Indicates the kind of kernel that will be applied to the method (e.g., RBF, polynomial, or linear).
	Gamma: The kernel coefficient for "sigmoid," "poly," and "rbf"
Naive Bayes	Gaussian Naive Bayes
	➢ var_smoothing: The highest variance of all features added to variances for stability
	Multinomial Naive Bayes
	➢ **Alpha:** Additive smoothing parameter (Laplace/Lidstone)
	➢ **fit_prior:** The decision to learn or not learn class prior probabilities
	Bernoulli Naive Bayes
	➢ **Alpha:** Additive smoothing parameter (Laplace/Lidstone)
	➢ **Binarize:** The threshold at which sample features are binarized (mapped to Booleans)
	➢ **fit_prior:** The decision to learn or not learn class prior probabilities
Neural Networks	**Number of layers:** The total number of the network's hidden layers
	Number of units per layer: Neurons in each hidden layer
	Activation function: Rectified Linear Unit (ReLU), Sigmoid, Tanh, and other similar activation functions to be employed
	Optimizer: Algorithm for optimization (such as SGD and Adam)
	Dropout rate: Ratio of input units to be dropped in order to avoid overfitting

high-dimensional spaces because it does not evaluate all possible combinations but rather a random subset.

3. **Bayesian Optimization:** For hyperparameter tuning, Bayesian optimization is a more effective method than grid search, particularly in cases involving vast search spaces. It makes use of probabilistic models to intelligently explore the parameter space, concentrating on areas that have a higher chance of producing ideal outcomes.

4. **Hyperband:** Hyperband is a powerful hyperparameter optimization algorithm that uses adaptive resource allocation and early stopping to efficiently search for the best hyperparameters. It is particularly effective for models like SVMs, where training can be computationally expensive. It can significantly enhance the performance of your ML model.

The code given below explains the random search for hyperparameter tuning of the Decision Tree Classifier. Other methods like hyperband, Bayesian optimization, and grid search can also be implemented on similar lines.

```
import numpy as np
from sklearn.tree import DecisionTreeClassifier
from sklearn.datasets import load_iris
from sklearn.model_selection import RandomizedSearchCV,
train_test_split
from scipy.stats import randint

# Load the Iris dataset
data = load_iris()
X = data.data
y = data.target

# Split the dataset into training and testing subsets
X_train, X_test, y_train, y_test = train_test_split(X,
y, test_size=0.2, random_state=42)

# Initialize the Decision Tree Classifier model
decision_tree = DecisionTreeClassifier()

# Define the hyperparameter search space with random
distributions
hyperparameter_space = {
    'max_depth': randint(1, 20),
    'min_samples_split': randint(2, 20),
    'min_samples_leaf': randint(1, 20),
    'criterion': ['gini', 'entropy']
}

# Set the number of iterations for Randomized Search
iterations = 110

# Perform Randomized Search with cross-validation
random_search = RandomizedSearchCV(
    estimator=decision_tree,
    param_distributions=hyperparameter_space,
```

```
    n_iter=iterations,
    cv=5, # Cross-validation strategy
    verbose=2, # Display detailed output
    random_state=42, # For reproducibility
    n_jobs=-1 # Utilize all available cores
)

# Fit the Randomized Search to the training data
random_search.fit(X_train, y_train)

# Output the best hyperparameters found
print("Optimal hyperparameters: ", random_search.
best_params_)

# Evaluate the optimized model on the test set
best_decision_tree = random_search.best_estimator_
accuracy = best_decision_tree.score(X_test, y_test)
print("Test set accuracy: ", accuracy)
```

Output:

```
Fitting 5 folds for each of 100 candidates, totaling 500
fits
Best parameters found: {'criterion': 'entropy', 'max_
depth': 15, 'min_samples_leaf': 3, 'min_samples_split':
9}
Test set accuracy: 1.0
```

Selecting and tuning the right hyperparameters is often an iterative process and essential for building effective and efficient ML models. Different methods can give different results for the same model and dataset as their underlying principle of working is different.

5.8 SUMMARY

In this chapter, readers delve into the foundational aspects of supervised ML, beginning with an exploration of classification, correlation, and regression analysis. They gain practical insights into applying simple and multiple linear regression techniques, as well as understanding nearest neighbor learning through the k-NN algorithm. The chapter covers essential concepts such as entropy, Gini index, and information gain, which are pivotal in decision tree construction. Readers also grasp the basics of probability theory and Bayes' theorem, followed by a detailed study of Naive Bayes classifiers—Bernoulli, multinomial, and Gaussian—for handling discrete and continuous attributes. Introducing SVMs, the chapter elucidates the concepts of hyperplanes, margins, and the kernel trick. Furthermore, readers learn to evaluate classifier performance using a confusion matrix and explore both exhaustive and non-exhaustive methods of cross-validation to ensure robust model assessment. The chapter concludes by imparting an understanding of regularization techniques and hyperparameter tuning methods to optimize model performance effectively. All concepts are detailed with their implementation using Python.

REFERENCES

1. https://towardsdatascience.com/knn-algorithm-what-when-why-how-41405c16c36f
2. https://www.analyticsvidhya.com/support-vector-machine/
3. https://mafiadoc.com/text-classification-using-naive-bayes_597a5c7c1723dd91e-8e52ac6.html
4. https://www.kdnuggets.com/2020/04/performance-evaluation-metrics-classification.html
5. https://www.turing.com/kb/different-types-of-cross-validations-in-machine-learning-and-their-explanations
6. https://www.mygreatlearning.com/blog/cross-validation/
7. https://www.analyticsvidhya.com/blog/2022/02/a-comprehensive-guide-on-hyperparameter-tuning-and-its-techniques/

6 Unsupervised Machine Learning

6.1 INTRODUCTION

When a model is trained on data without predetermined labels or results, it is referred to as unsupervised machine learning (ML). Finding patterns, structures, and relationships in data is the aim of this ML; however, there is no predetermined guidance on what to look for. Unsupervised ML approaches include dimensionality reduction, association rule mining, and clustering. This chapter will cover two main methods for unsupervised learning: association rule mining and clustering. Few applications where unsupervised ML techniques can be used are custom segmentation, anomaly detection, recommendation systems, and identifying patterns in biological data.

Unsupervised learning provides powerful tools for making sense of data when labels are not available, enabling the discovery of meaningful patterns and insights that might not be evident through manual analysis.

6.2 CLUSTERING

An unsupervised ML method called clustering is used to put related objects in one group. This method of learning involves observation rather than examples. Minimum and maximum intra-class and inter-class distances will be present in clustered data. Data points in one group will have similar properties, while data points in another group will have different properties. Data points are unlabeled for unsupervised learning, and they help in finding hidden structures within data. The optimal grouping is determined by the data's structure. For instance, four distinct groupings based on an individual's salary might be created:

- Earning less than $10,000
- Earning between $10,000 and $30,000
- Earning between $30,000 and $60,000
- Earning more than $60,000

Here, income is used for grouping a person. Income, however, is not a reliable indicator of how a group's members relate to one another. In other words, there's no intrinsic reason to think that someone making $80,000 will act any differently than someone making $10,000 or $120,000 [1]. Groupings of income are determined by simple points of differentiation. If more variables are added such as qualification, house size, age, experience, and expenditure, the grouping will change altogether. Thus, as more dimensions are added to data, grouping becomes more meaningful and complex.

Clustering techniques help us find natural grouping of persons by considering many dimensions. Instead of making any predictions, it organizes comparable data by identifying similarities between data points based on data properties.

Different clustering methods [2, 3] use different distance measures. K-means utilizes Euclidean/Manhattan/city block distance between points; DBSCAN uses distance between the nearest points; affinity propagation and spectral clustering are based on graph distances; Gaussian mixtures are based on Mahalanobis distance. Clustering techniques have numerous applications in marketing, economics, biology, city planning, real estate, and various branches of science.

6.3   DISTANCE MEASURES

Distance measure is the building block of clustering algorithms. It is the measure of similarity and dissimilarity of data. Similarity is a numerical measure that defines how alike the data points are. If similarity is high, data is more alike. Dissimilarity is a numerical measure that defines how different the data points are. If dissimilarity is high, data are more different. Different data types such as numerical, binary, ordinal, and categorical have different distance measure metrics [4, 5].

Numeric Data Distance Measures:

- **Euclidean Distance:** It is among the most often applied distance metrics to numerical data. Below is the Euclidean distance between the data points x and y with n features:

$$d(x, y) = \sqrt{\sum_{i=1}^{n}(y_i - x_i)^2}$$

- **Manhattan Distance:** This is also called city block distance, absolute value distance, L1 norm, and boxcar. The Manhattan distance between x and y data points with n features is given below:

$$d(x, y) = \sum_{i=1}^{n} |x_i - y_i|$$

- **Minkowski Distance:** In general, all distances formulated above can be generalized as given below. Here p is a parameter. The distance measure is known as Euclidean distance when p is equal to 2 and as Manhattan distance when p is equal to 1. With n features, the Minkowski distance between x and y points is as follows:

$$D(x, y) = \left(\sum_{i=1}^{n} |x_i - y_{il}|^p \right)^{\frac{1}{p}}$$

- **Chebyshev Distance:** This is often referred to as the maximum value distance or supremum distance. Given two points x and y and n features, the Chebyshev distance between them is as follows:

$$D_{Chebyshev}(x, y) = \max_{i}(|x_i, y_i|)$$

Binary Data Distance Measures: Binay data can have only two values. The distance measures discussed above cannot be applied for binary data. To find the distance between binary attributes, a contingency table needs to be created. The entries in the contingency table can be constructed by counting the number of matching transactions: 0–0, 0–1, 1–0, 1–1.

Attributes matching	0	1
0	a	b
1	c	d

In this case, a = total number of attributes, where both x and y attributes are 0.

b = Total number of attributes where x and y attributes are 0 and 1, respectively.
c = Total number of attributes where x and y attributes are 1 and 0, respectively.
d = Total number of attributes where x and y both attributes are 1.

- **Jaccard Coefficient:** This is calculated for binary attributes as follows:
  - $J = d/(b + c + d)$
- **Simple Matching Coefficient (SMC):** This is defined as the ratio of the number of matching attributes and the number of attributes.
  - $SMC = (a + d)/(a + b + c + d)$
- **Hammond Distance:** This indicates the number of positions at which the characters or binary attributes are different. For example, the Hammond distance between (1 0 1) and (1 1 0) is 2 as both differ in two positions. The distance between "hood" and "wood" is 1 as both differ in just one position.
- **Symmetric Data Distance:** If both attribute values are equally valuable and carry the same weight, for example, gender attribute is symmetric (male, female) as both are equally valuable. the distance for these attributes is calculated as
  - $Distance = (b + c)/(a + b + c + d)$
- **Asymmetric Data Distance:** If both attribute values are not equally valuable and do not carry the same weight, for example, positive and negative outcomes of a disease test or examination. The distance for these attributes is calculated as
  - $Distance = (b + c)/(b + c + d)$

Categorical Data Distance Measures: Categorical data is a symbol or code to represent a value, for example, gender attribute, where code 0 can represent male and 1 can represent female. To find the distance between categorical attributes, we need to check if they are equal or not. If they are equal, the distance will be 0; otherwise, the distance will be 1.

Ordinal Data Distance Measures: Ordinal attributes are similar to categorical attributes, but they have an inherent order. For example, qualification and job designation have an order. Job designation can be 1, 2, or 3, where 1 is higher than 2 and 2 is higher than 3. The distance between x and y can be calculated as

$$Distance\ (X,Y) = |position(X) - position(Y)| / n - 1$$

Here, *position* refers to the attribute position in the order and n is the total number of orders.

6.4 K-MEANS CLUSTERING

The k-means is the most popularly used clustering algorithm [6]. This is an iterative partitioning algorithm that finds k groups in the data. Here, k denotes the requested non-overlapping clusters or groups that must be established as stated. Two clusters are indicated by the value k = 2, three clusters are indicated by the value k = 3, and so on. Based on feature similarity, which is determined using Euclidean distance, data points are clustered. The first step in k-means clustering is to use k distinct randomly generated centroid points; each data point is matched to the closest centroid. The centroid is computed as the average of all the points assigned to it once each point has been assigned. Until the centroids are stabilized or a defined number of iterations have been reached, this process is repeated.

The k-means algorithm steps are as follows:

1. Choose a k value and select k random points from the data as centroids. (It can be different from the input dataset).
2. Assign each data point to its closest centroid by computing the Euclidean distance. Here, x, y are data points of n dimension.

$$d(x, y) = \sqrt{\sum_{i=1}^{n} (y_i - x_i)^2}$$

3. Recompute the centroids of newly formed clusters by averaging (arithmetic mean) the points assigned to that cluster.
4. Repeat steps 2 and 3 till the centroids are stabilized or a defined number of iterations have been reached.

6.4.1 K-MEANS CLUSTERING USING PYTHON

Example 1: The grades_km_input.csv file contains data of the marks of 619 students in maths, science, and English. This data needs to be grouped into three groups. The results shown here are group 1 has 207 students, group 2 has 210 students, and group 3 has 202 students. The notations used for group 1, group 2, and group 3 are 0, 1, and 2, respectively . It takes 300 iterations to reach the three-group formation.

```
from matplotlib import pyplot
import io
import pandas as pd
from sklearn.cluster import KMeans
import numpy as np
from google.colab import files
uploaded= files.upload()
```

```
dfval=pd.read_csv(io.BytesIO(uploaded['grades_km_input.
csv']))

kmeans = KMeans(n_clusters=3, random_state=0).fit(dfval)
print("Cluster parameterrs are ",kmeans)
print("Cluster centers are ",kmeans.cluster_centers_)
kmeans.predict(dfval)
```

Output:

Cluster parameterrs are KMeans(algorithm='auto', copy_x=True, init='k-means++', max_iter=300,
n_clusters=3, n_init=10, n_jobs=None, precompute_distances='auto',
random_state=0, tol=0.0001, verbose=0)
Cluster centers are [[306.5 85.04326923 77.26442308 79.11538462]
[515.42857143 72.8 66.61904762 66.04285714]
[101.5 95.5 90.21287129 93.59405941]]
array([2, 2, 2, 2, 2, 2, 2, 2, 2, 2, 2, 2, 2, 2, 2, 2, 2, 2, 2, 2, 2, 2,
2, 2, 2, 2, 2, 2, 2, 2, 2, 2, 2, 2, 2, 2, 2, 2, 2, 2, 2, 2, 2, 2,
2, 2, 2, 2, 2, 2, 2, 2, 2, 2, 2, 2, 2, 2, 2, 2, 2, 2, 2, 2, 2, 2,
2, 2, 2, 2, 2, 2, 2, 2, 2, 2, 2, 2, 2, 2, 2, 2, 2, 2, 2, 2, 2, 2,
2, 2, 2, 2, 2, 2, 2, 2, 2, 2, 2, 2, 2, 2, 2, 2, 2, 2, 2, 2, 2, 2,
2, 2, 2, 2, 2, 2, 2, 2, 2, 2, 2, 2, 2, 2, 2, 2, 2, 2, 2, 2, 2, 2,
2, 2, 2, 2, 2, 2, 2, 2, 2, 2, 2, 2, 2, 2, 2, 2, 2, 2, 2, 2, 2, 2,
2, 2, 2, 2, 2, 2, 2, 2, 2, 2, 2, 2, 2, 2, 2, 2, 2, 2, 2, 2, 2, 2,
2, 2, 2, 2, 2, 2, 2, 2, 2, 2, 2, 2, 2, 2, 2, 2, 2, 2, 2, 2, 2, 2,
2, 2, 2, 2, 0, 0, 0, 0, 0, 0, 0, 0, 0, 0, 0, 0, 0, 0, 0, 0, 0, 0,
0, 0, 0, 0, 0, 0, 0, 0, 0, 0, 0, 0, 0, 0, 0, 0, 0, 0, 0, 0, 0, 0,
0, 0, 0, 0, 0, 0, 0, 0, 0, 0, 0, 0, 0, 0, 0, 0, 0, 0, 0, 0, 0, 0,
0, 0, 0, 0, 0, 0, 0, 0, 0, 0, 0, 0, 0, 0, 0, 0, 0, 0, 0, 0, 0, 0,
0, 0, 0, 0, 0, 0, 0, 0, 0, 0, 0, 0, 0, 0, 0, 0, 0, 0, 0, 0, 0, 0,
0, 0, 0, 0, 0, 0, 0, 0, 0, 0, 0, 0, 0, 0, 0, 0, 0, 0, 0, 0, 0, 0,
0, 0, 0, 0, 0, 0, 0, 0, 0, 0, 0, 0, 0, 0, 0, 0, 0, 0, 0, 0, 0, 0,
0, 0, 0, 0, 0, 0, 0, 0, 0, 0, 0, 0, 0, 0, 0, 0, 0, 0, 0, 0, 0, 0,
0, 0, 0, 0, 0, 0, 0, 0, 0, 0, 0, 0, 0, 0, 1, 1, 1, 1, 1, 1, 1, 1,
1, 1, 1, 1, 1, 1, 1, 1, 1, 1, 1, 1, 1, 1, 1, 1, 1, 1, 1, 1, 1, 1,
1, 1, 1, 1, 1, 1, 1, 1, 1, 1, 1, 1, 1, 1, 1, 1, 1, 1, 1, 1, 1, 1,
1, 1, 1, 1, 1, 1, 1, 1, 1, 1, 1, 1, 1, 1, 1, 1, 1, 1, 1, 1, 1, 1,
1, 1, 1, 1, 1, 1, 1, 1, 1, 1, 1, 1, 1, 1, 1, 1, 1, 1, 1, 1, 1, 1,
1, 1, 1, 1, 1, 1, 1, 1, 1, 1, 1, 1, 1, 1, 1, 1, 1, 1, 1, 1, 1, 1,
1, 1, 1, 1, 1, 1, 1, 1, 1, 1, 1, 1, 1, 1, 1, 1, 1, 1, 1, 1, 1, 1,
1, 1, 1, 1, 1, 1, 1, 1, 1, 1, 1, 1, 1, 1, 1, 1, 1, 1, 1, 1, 1, 1,
1, 1, 1, 1, 1, 1, 1, 1, 1, 1, 1, 1, 1, 1, 1, 1, 1, 1, 1, 1, 1,
1, 1, 1, 1], dtype=int32)

If multidimensional data needs to be visualized in 2D, it must be reduced to 2D. If the centroids and groups of data need to be visualized, the following code is modified. Dimension reduction can be performed using principal component analysis (PCA).

```
from matplotlib import pyplot
import io
import pandas as pd
from sklearn.cluster import KMeans
import numpy as np
import matplotlib.pyplot as plt
from google.colab import files
uploaded= files.upload()
dfval=pd.read_csv(io.BytesIO(uploaded['grades_km_input.
csv']))


#plotting data
from sklearn.decomposition import PCA
pca = PCA(2)
#Transform the data
datadf = pca.fit_transform(dfval)
kmeans = KMeans(n_clusters= 3)
#predict the labels of clusters.
label = kmeans.fit_predict(datadf)
print(label)
#Getting unique labels
u_labels = np.unique(label)
#plotting the results:
#Getting the Centroids
centroids = kmeans.cluster_centers_
u_labels = np.unique(label)

#plotting the results:

for i in u_labels:
    plt.scatter(datadf[label == i, 0], datadf[la-
bel == i, 1], label
 = i)
plt.scatter(centroids[:,0], centroids[:,1], s = 80,
color = 'k')
plt.legend()
plt.show()
```

Output:

```
[0 0 0 0 0 0 0 0 0 0 0 0 0 0 0 0 0 0 0 0 0 0 0 0 0 0 0 0 0 0 0 0 0 0 0 0 0 0 0
 0 0 0 0 0 0 0 0 0 0 0 0 0 0 0 0 0 0 0 0 0 0 0 0 0 0 0 0 0 0 0 0 0 0 0 0 0 0 0
 0 0 0 0 0 0 0 0 0 0 0 0 0 0 0 0 0 0 0 0 0 0 0 0 0 0 0 0 0 0 0 0 0 0 0 0 0 0 0
 0 0 0 0 0 0 0 0 0 0 0 0 0 0 0 0 0 0 0 0 0 0 0 0 0 0 0 0 0 0 0 0 0 0 0 0 0 0 0
 0 0 0 0 0 0 0 0 0 0 0 0 0 0 0 0 0 0 0 0 0 0 0 0 0 0 0 0 0 0 0 0 0 0 0 0 0 0 0
 0 0 0 0 0 0 0 0 0 0 0 0 0 0 0 0 0 2 2 2 2 2 2 2 2 2 2 2 2 2 2 2 2 2 2 2 2 2 2
 2 2 2 2 2 2 2 2 2 2 2 2 2 2 2 2 2 2 2 2 2 2 2 2 2 2 2 2 2 2 2 2 2 2 2 2 2 2 2
 2 2 2 2 2 2 2 2 2 2 2 2 2 2 2 2 2 2 2 2 2 2 2 2 2 2 2 2 2 2 2 2 2 2 2 2 2 2 2
 2 2 2 2 2 2 2 2 2 2 2 2 2 2 2 2 2 2 2 2 2 2 2 2 2 2 2 2 2 2 2 2 2 2 2 2 2 2 2
 2 2 2 2 2 2 2 2 2 2 2 2 2 2 2 2 2 2 2 2 2 2 2 2 2 2 2 2 2 2 2 2 2 2 2 2 2 2 2
 2 2 2 2 2 2 2 2 2 2 2 2 2 2 2 2 2 2 2 2 2 2 2 2 2 2 2 2 2 2 2 2 2 2 2 2 2 2 2
 2 2 2 1 1 1 1 1 1 1 1 1 1 1 1 1 1 1 1 1 1 1 1 1 1 1 1 1 1 1 1 1 1 1 1 1 1 1 1
 1 1 1 1 1 1 1 1 1 1 1 1 1 1 1 1 1 1 1 1 1 1 1 1 1 1 1 1 1 1 1 1 1 1 1 1 1 1 1
 1 1 1 1 1 1 1 1 1 1 1 1 1 1 1 1 1 1 1 1 1 1 1 1 1 1 1 1 1 1 1 1 1 1 1 1 1 1 1
 1 1 1 1 1 1 1 1 1 1 1 1 1 1 1 1 1 1 1 1 1 1 1 1 1 1 1 1 1 1 1 1 1 1 1 1 1 1 1
 1 1 1 1 1 1 1 1 1 1 1 1 1 1 1 1 1 1 1 1 1 1 1 1 1 1 1 1 1 1 1 1 1 1 1 1 1 1 1
 1 1 1 1 1 1 1 1 1 1 1 1 1 1 1 1 1 1 1 1 1 1 1 1 1 1 1 1 1 1 1 1]
```

Example 2: A healthcare chain wants to open a series of hospitals in a region. It has data about the location of highly accident-prone areas in the region. The chain needs to decide the number of the hospitals to be opened and the location of these

FIGURE 6.1   k-Means Clustering for k = 3 on Marks Data.

hospitals so that all the accident-prone areas are covered. The k-means clustering algorithm is the most appropriate to determine the location of these hospitals to cover that region. Here, the km_data.csv file contains the location latitude and number of accidents for that location.

```python
import pandas as pd
import numpy as np
import matplotlib.pyplot as plt
from sklearn.preprocessing import MinMaxScaler
from sklearn.cluster import KMeans
from math import sqrt

df = pd.read_csv("km_data.csv",encoding='latin-1')
#read the location data
#add a column for no. of accidents using randomly gener-
ated numbers
#dataset is randomly sampled 3 times and each sample is
provided with #randomly generated numbers
df1=df.sample(100, random_state=30)
df2=df.drop(df1.index).sample(80, random_state=30)
df3 = df.drop(df1.index)
df3 = df3.drop(df2.index)
np.random.seed(99999999)
df1['No. of Accidents'] = np.random.randint(0, 40000,
df1.shape[0])
df2['No.of Accidents'] = np.random.randint(50000,
100000, df2.shape[0])
df3['No.of Accidents'] = np.random.randint(80000,
150000, df3.shape[0])
data = pd.concat([df1,df2,df3])
#scale the data
scaler = MinMaxScaler()
data[['latitude','No.ofAccidents']]= scaler.fit_trans-
form(data[['latitude','No. of Accidents']])
#applying k-means clustering to group data into 4
clusters
k=4
km = KMeans(n_clusters=k)
y_pred = km.fit_predict(data[['latitude', 'No. of
Accidents']])
data['cluster']=y_pred #add the predicted cluster values
as a column to the dataset
#plot each cluster as a scatter plot
for i in range(k):
```

```
plt.scatter(data[data.cluster==i]['latitude'],data[-
data.cluster==i]['No. of Accidents'])
plt.xlabel("Latitude")
plt.ylabel("No. of Accidents")
print("Centroid values using inbuilt KMeans are: ")
sno=1
for i in km.cluster_centers_:
plt.scatter(i[0],i[1],marker="*",s=100,label="centroid
{}".format(sno))
 sno=sno+1
 print(i)

plt.legend()
plt.show()
```

Output:

Centroid values using inbuilt KMeans are:

[0.39613256 0.30321862]
[0.50697146 0.83881822]
[0.67967907 0.14859177]
[0.71794245 0.5813726]

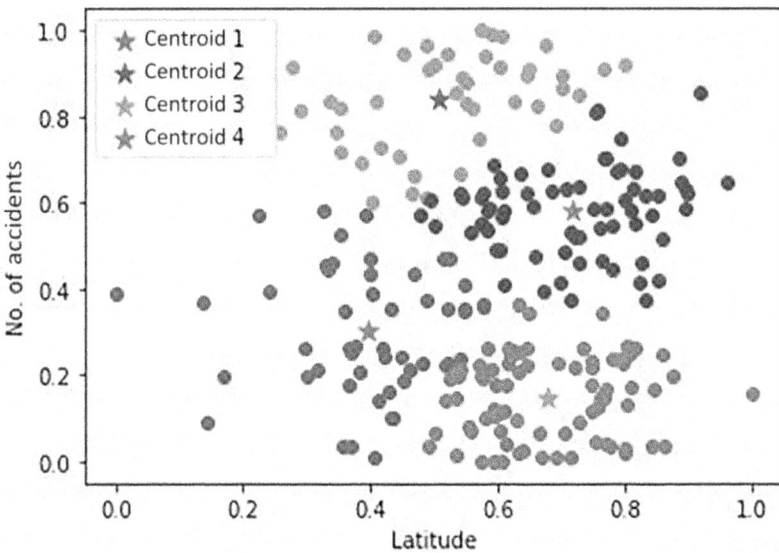

FIGURE 6.2 k-Means Clustering for k = 4 on Healthcare Chain Data Using Built-in Function.

User-defined functions for k-means clustering for the km_data.csv file

```
#creating an array of the datapoints
user_data = []
for x,y in zip(data['latitude'],data['No. of
Accidents']):
 user_data.append([x,y])


#function which randomly chooses the centroids (required
initially)
def choose_centroids(X,k):
 #X is an array with each element of type [latitude, no.
of accidents]
  np.random.seed(90)
 positions = np.random.choice(range(len(X)), size=k,
replace=False) #randomly sample k no. of index values
  centroids=[]
 #choose the datapoints at the indices sampled above,
they will be the #centroids
 for i in positions:
   centroids.append(X[i])
 return centroids


#function which creates the initial clusters using the
centroids chosen by choose_centroids()
def initiate_cluster(X,k):
 #X is an array with each element of type [latitude, no.
of accidents]
 centroids = choose_centroids(X,k)
 clusters = [] #will store the clusters as lists, so
data points in one list belong to one cluster
 #create k no. of empty sub-lists for k no. of clusters
 for i in range(k):
   clusters.append([])


 #find distance of each datapoint from each cluster
centroid
 for dpoint in X:
   distances=[] #store the distances from each centroid
   for point in centroids:
     dist = sqrt((point[0]-dpoint[0])**2 +
(point[1]-dpoint[1])**2)
     distances.append(dist)
   #find the index of the cluster for which minimum dis-
tance is #obtained
   cluster_index = distances.index(min(distances))
```

```
    clusters[cluster_index].append(dpoint) #assign the
datapoint to that list(i.e. cluster) whose index is
obtained above
 return clusters


#function which continues clustering after initial clus-
tering has been performed
def calculate_cluster(X,og_data,k):
 #here X is a list of clusters
 #X is of form [ [[x1,y1],[x2,y2],...],
[[a1,b1],[a2,b2]], [datapoints of cluster 3],... ]


 new_centroids=[] #to store newly calculated centroids
of each cluster
 #below i is a list of datapoints [x,y] in an individual
cluster
 for i in X:
   x = [a[0] for a in i]
   y = [a[1] for a in i]
   centroid = [np.mean(x),np.mean(y)]
   new_centroids.append(centroid)
 clusters = [] #will store clusters as lists, so data-
points in one list #belong to one cluster
 #creating k no. of empty sublists to store datapoints
of k no. of #clusters
 for i in range(k):
   clusters.append([])
 #find distance of each datapoint from each cluster
centroid and assign the point to cluster with minimum
distance
 for dpoint in og_data:
   distances=[]
   for point in new_centroids:
     dist = sqrt((point[0]-dpoint[0])**2 +
(point[1]-dpoint[1])**2)
     distances.append(dist)
   cluster_index = distances.index(min(distances))
   clusters[cluster_index].append(dpoint)
 return clusters


#function to check if two clustered datasets are equal
def equality(cluster_1, cluster_2):
 for x,y in zip(cluster_1, cluster_2):
   if not ((((len(x) == len(y)) and (all(i in x for i in
y))))):
 return False
```

```
 return True

#function for performing the whole process of kmeans
clustering using the above functions
def fit_kmeans(X,k):
 clusters = initiate_cluster(X,k) #creating initial clusters
   old_clusters = calculate_cluster(clusters,X,k) #per-
form clustering on initially created clusters
 new_clusters = calculate_cluster(old_clusters,X,k)
#recluster again
 #keep reclustering until the datapoints stop changing
clusters
 while not(equality(old_clusters,new_clusters)):
   old_clusters = calculate_cluster(old_clusters,X,k)
   new_clusters = calculate_cluster(old_clusters,X,k)
 #plot each cluster as a scatter plot
 for i in new_clusters:
   plt.scatter([a[0] for a in i],[a[1] for a in i])
 plt.xlabel("Latitude")
 plt.ylabel("No. of Accidents")
 print("cluster centroids are: ")
 global new_centroids
 new_centroids=[]
 for i in new_clusters:
   x = [a[0] for a in i]
   y = [a[1] for a in i]
   centroid = [np.mean(x),np.mean(y)]
   new_centroids.append(centroid)
 sno=1
 for i in new_centroids:
   plt.scatter(i[0],i[1],marker="*", s=100, label="cen-
troid {}".format(sno))
   sno = sno+1
   print(i)
 plt.legend()
 plt.show()
 return

fit_kmeans(user_data,k)
```

Output:

Cluster centroids are

[0.3975908984795953, 0.28642034239739017]
[0.7180242213722119, 0.5822410919925798]
[0.4967087261507008, 0.8242655976854173]
[0.6817238823525831, 0.14801280894564953]

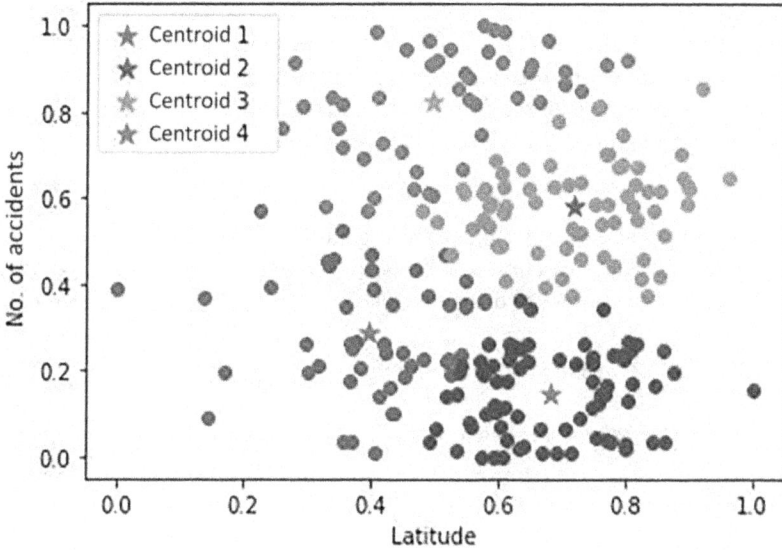

FIGURE 6.3 k-Means Clustering for k = 4 on Healthcare Chain Data Using User-Defined Function.

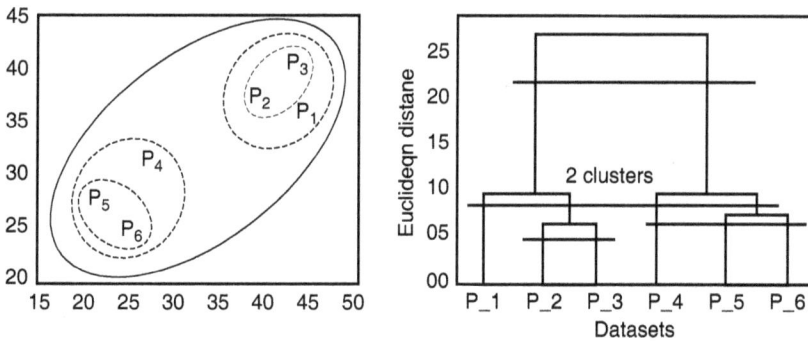

FIGURE 6.4 Dendrogram.

It can be observed that the results of the built-in function and user-defined function are exactly the same.

6.5 HIERARCHICAL CLUSTERING

Hierarchical methods produce nested partitions of data with hierarchical relationships among them. Hierarchical relationships are generally shown in the form of dendrograms (Figure 6.4).

Hierarchical methods include agglomerative methods and divisive methods. Agglomerative clustering uses a bottom-up approach, whereas divisive clustering uses a top-down approach for grouping samples. In agglomerative methods, initially all the individual samples are considered as a separate cluster, that is, a cluster with a single element. They are merged subsequently, and the process continues to obtain a single cluster or desired number of clusters. Divisive methods consider all the samples in a single cluster and then partition it. This partition process is continued until the cluster is split into smaller clusters or the desired number of clusters.

Agglomerative clustering [7] can be performed using the following three methods:

- **Single Linkage or MIN Slgorithm:** In this algorithm, the distance (x,y), where x is from one cluster and y is from another cluster, is the smallest distance of two points in different clusters.

$$D_{SL}\left(c_i, c_j\right) = \text{minimum}_{a \in \ ci, \ b \in \ cj} d(a,b)$$

- **Complete Linkage or MAX Algorithm:** In this algorithm, the distance (x,y), where x is from one cluster and y is from another cluster, is the largest distance of two points in different clusters.

$$D_{SL}\left(c_i, c_j\right) = \text{maximum}_{a \in \ ci, \ b \in \ cj} d(a,b)$$

- **Average Linkage or MIN Algorithm:** In this algorithm, the average distance of all pairs of points across the clusters is used to form a cluster. The average value computed between cluster c_i and c_j is given as follows:

$$D_{AL}\left(c_i, c_j\right) = \text{avg}_{a \in \ ci, \ b \in \ cj} d(a,b)$$

  – **or**

$$D_{AL}\left(c_i, c_j\right) = \frac{1}{mi \, mj} \cdots \sum_{a \in \ ci, b \in \ cj} d(a,b)$$

Here mi and mj are the sizes of clusters.

Example 1: Five data points of two dimensions are considered. We apply the single linkage algorithm, complete linkage algorithm, and average linkage algorithm on the given data to form two clusters.

Data Points:

Data Point No.	x	y
1	4	4
2	8	4
3	15	8
4	24	4
5	24	12

A table is computed considering the Euclidean distance among the given data points:

	{1}	{2}	{3}	{4}	{5}
{1}	0	4	11.7	20	21.5
{2}		0	8.1	16	17.9
{3}			0	9.8	9.8
{4}				0	8.0
{5}					0

Here, the minimum distance is 4, which is between data points 1 and 2. So data points 1 and 2 form a single cluster {1,2}, and the distances are modified based on the algorithm chosen. If the single linkage algorithm is applied, distances will be modified as follows:

$$D_{SL}\left(c_i, c_j\right) = \text{minimum}_{a \in c_i, b \in c_j} d\left(a, b\right)$$

The distance between groups {1,2} and {3} is computed using the following formula:

Minimum ({1,3},{2,3}) = Minimum {11.7, 8.1} = 8.1.
Thus, the distance between {1,2} and {4} is
Minimum ({1,4},{2,4}) = Minimum {20, 16} = 16.
Thus, the distance between {1,2} and {5} is
Minimum ({1,5},{2,5}) = Minimum {21.5, 17.9} = 17.9.

	{1,2}	{3}	{4}	{5}
{1,2}	0	8.1	16	17.9
{3}		0	9.8	9.8
{4}			0	8.0
{5}				0

The similarity matrix is modified, and there are still four different clusters. So the minimum distance is found again in the modified similarity matrix, and the clusters are formed. {4} and {5} will be combined in a single cluster now as the minimum distance is 8. The distances will be modified according to the formula as follows:

	{1,2}	{3}	{4,5}
{1,2}	0	8.1	16
{3}		0	9.8
{4,5}			0

The distance of {1,2} with {4,5} will be calculated as
Minimum (({1,2},{4}), ({1,2},{5})) = Minimum {16, 17.9} = 16.

There are still three clusters, so one more iteration of the process can be applied on the data. The next minimum distance in the similarity matrix is 8.1, which is between {3} and {1,2}. So they are combined from a single cluster as {1,2,3}. After applying the single linkage algorithm on the given data points, the two clusters formed are {1,2,3} and {4,5}.

Complete linkage algorithm can also be applied on the same data. Here, initially {1} and {2} clusters are combined as they have a minimum distance of 4 between them. The distances are modified using the following formula:

$$D_{CL}\left(c_i, c_j\right) = \text{maximum}_{a \in c_i, b \in c_j} d\left(a, b\right)$$

The distance between groups {1,2} and {3} is computed using the formula:
Maximum ({1,3},{2,3}) = Maximum {11.7, 8.1} = 11.7.

Thus, the distance between {1,2} and {4} is
Maximum ({1,4},{2,4}) = Maximum {20, 16} = 20.

Thus, the distance between {1,2} and {5} is
Maximum ({1,5},{2,5}) = Maximum {21.5, 17.9} = 21.5.

	{1,2}	{3}	{4}	{5}
{1,2}	0	11.7	20	21.5
{3}		0	9.8	9.8
{4}			0	8.0
{5}				0

The minimum distance between {4} and {5} is 8. So they form one cluster and the distances are modified again considering the formula given above.

	{1,2}	{3}	{4,5}
{1,2}	0	11.7	21.5
{3}		0	9.8
{4,5}			0

The distance of {1,2} with {4,5} will be calculated as
Maximum (({1,2},{4}), ({1,2},{5})) = Maximum {20, 21.5} = 21.5.

There are still three clusters, so one more iteration of the process can be applied on the data. The next minimum distance in the similarity matrix is 9.8, which is between {3} and {4,5}. So they are combined from a single cluster as {3,4,5}. After applying the complete linkage algorithm on the given data points, the two clusters formed are {1,2} and {3,4,5}.

Similarly, the **average linkage algorithm** can be applied on the same data. Here, initially {1} and {2} clusters are combined as they have a minimum distance of 4 between them. The distances are modified using the formula

$$D_{AL}(c_i, c_j) = avg_{a \in ci, b \in cj} d(a,b)$$

or

$$D_{AL}(c_i, c_j) = \frac{1}{mi \, mj} \ldots\ldots \sum_{a \in ci, b \in cj} d(a,b)$$

The distance between groups {1,2} and {3} is computed using the formula

Average (({1,3},{2,3}) = Average {11.7, 8.1} = 9.9.
Thus, the distance between {1,2} and {4} is

Average (({1,4},{2,4}) = Average {20, 16} = 18.
Thus, the distance between {1,2} and {5} is

Average (({1,5},{2,5}) = Average {21.5, 17.9} = 19.7.

	{1,2}	{3}	{4}	{5}
{1,2}	0	9.9	18	19.7
{3}		0	9.8	9.8
{4}			0	8.0
{5}				0

The minimum distance is 8 between {4} and {5}. So they form one cluster, and the distances are modified again considering the formula given above.

	{1,2}	{3}	{4,5}
{1,2}	0	9.9	18.9
{3}		0	9.8
{4,5}			0

The distance of {1,2} with {4,5} will be calculated as
Average ((({1,2},{4}), ({1,2},{5})) = Average {18, 19.7} = 18.9.

There are still three clusters, so one more iteration of the process can be applied. The next minimum distance in the similarity matrix is 9.8, which is between {3} and {4,5}. So they are combined from a single cluster as {3,4,5}. After applying the average linkage algorithm on the given data points, the two clusters formed are {1,2} and {3,4,5}.

6.5.1 Hierarchical Clustering Using Python

The agglomerative clustering algorithm is implemented for the data given in the example above. The data needs to be clustered into two groups.

```python
# Agglomerative clustering
import numpy as np
import matplotlib.pyplot as plt
import pandas as pd
import scipy.cluster.hierarchy as sch
from sklearn.cluster import AgglomerativeClustering

d = {"x": [4, 8, 15, 24, 24], "y": [4, 4, 8, 4, 12]}
df = pd.DataFrame(d)
print(df)
dendro = sch.dendrogram(sch.linkage(df, method =
'ward'))
plt.title('Dendrogram')
plt.xlabel('data points')
plt.ylabel('Euclidean-distances')
plt.show()

AC = AgglomerativeClustering(n_clusters = 2, affinity =
'euclidean', linkage = 'ward')
cluster = AC.fit_predict(df)
print (cluster)
```

Output:

```
x y
0 4 4
1 8 4
2 15 8
3 24 4
4 24 12
[1 1 0 0 0]
```

The given data is clustered into two groups, where data points 1 and 2 are in one cluster and data points 3, 4, and 5 are in another cluster.

6.6   DBSCAN CLUSTERING

The k-means clustering algorithm has some challenges to address. First, it may cluster loosely related data together. It clusters every data point; that is, even if the data point is very far in vector space, it will cluster the point. Using a very far point to make clusters may affect the outcome of the whole cluster. DBSCAN clustering

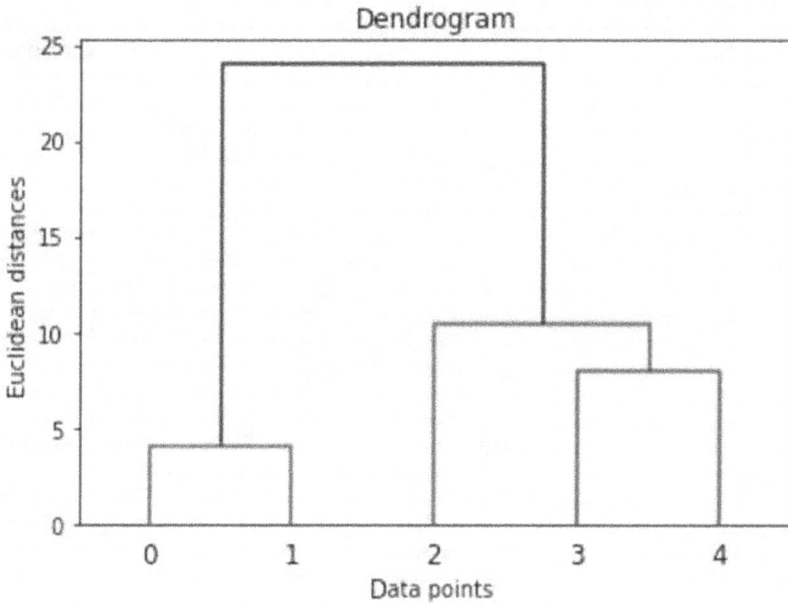

FIGURE 6.5   Dendogram of above Data.

algorithm [8] addresses this problem. Another challenge in k-means clustering is that it works on the value of k; that is, the value of k should be known a priori or a number of clusters beforehand. Many a times, the k value is not known a priori. In DBSCAN, it is not required that the number of clusters must be specified, that is, the value of k. DBSCAN only needs a function to calculate the distance between data points and some information for defining closeness. The distance that will be considered as close needs to be specified. DBSCAN produces reasonably good results. It produces good results for arbitrary shape clusters also.

DBSCAN is a clustering algorithm based on density, which defines clusters through density and connectivity. The central concept is that a cluster represents a region of high density, distinguished from other clusters by regions of lower density. The algorithm operates with two main parameters: the neighborhood radius (ε) and the minimum number of points required (minPts) (see Figure 6.6).

A core point is identified if it has at least the minimum number of points (minPts) within its ε-neighborhood. A border point has fewer than minPts within its neighborhood but is adjacent to a core point. Points that are neither core nor border points are classified as noise. The algorithm requires that each data point must have a minimum number of neighbors within its ε-neighborhood, which must contain at least minPts points.

The algorithm's effectiveness relies on the concept of density connectivity. A point X is considered densely reachable from point Y if X is within the ε-neighborhood of Y, and Y is a core point. Additionally, X is densely reachable from Y if there is a

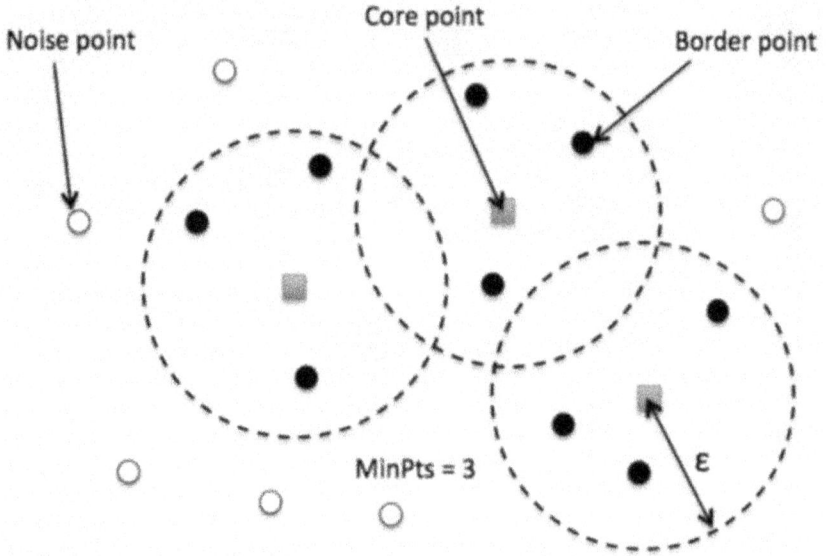

FIGURE 6.6   DBSCAN Points.

sequence of core points connecting Y to X. Points X and Y are densely connected if there is a core point Z such that both X and Y are densely reachable from Z.

Steps in DBSCAN Clustering:

1. Arbitrarily pick a point p in the data set and proceed till all the points are visited. Compute the distance between p and all the other data points.
2. Mark it as a core point by finding all the points from p with respect to its neighborhood, and check if it has a minimum number of points m.
3. A new cluster is formed if it is a core point or an existing cluster is enlarged.
4. Move to the next point if it is a border point.
5. Remove the point if it is a noise point.
6. Merge the mergeable cluster dist $(c_i, c_j) < \varepsilon$.
7. Repeat steps 3–6 for all data points.

6.6.1   DBSCAN CLUSTERING USING PYTHON

Let's use DBSCAN to cluster spherical data for better visualization. We'll generate a dataset with just two features to simplify the process. We will use a function called PointsInCircum(), which accepts the radius and the number of data points as inputs and returns an array of points that form a circle when plotted. To effectively observe DBSCAN's clustering capability, we will create three concentric circles with varying radii, as a single circle alone may not demonstrate the clustering performance sufficiently. Additionally, we will introduce some noise into the dataset to evaluate how well the algorithm handles noisy data.

About 2,300 spherical training data points are generated with corresponding labels. The plotted data points in the output show that it forms a circle. After that, the features of the training data need to be standardized, and DBSCAN is applied from the sklearn library.

The optimum value of epsilon is 30 in this case, and the minPts value is 6. These optimum values can be found out using the k-distance graph method. The DBSCAN algorithm is trained using these parameters. The results shown here indicate three clusters are formed with values 0, 1, and 2 as their labels. −1 indicates noisy data. About 2,300 points are created in total: 1,030 points are in cluster 0, 730 points are in cluster 1, 318 points are in cluster 2, and 222 are noise points.

```
#DBSCAN Algorithm
import numpy as np
import pandas as pd
import math
import matplotlib.pyplot as plt
import matplotlib
from sklearn.cluster import DBSCAN
np.random.seed(42)


# Function for creating datapoints in the form of a
circle
def PointsInCircle(r,n=100):
    return [(math.cos(2*math.pi/n*x)*r+np.random.nor-
mal(-30,30),math.sin(2*math.pi/n*x)*r+np.random.nor-
mal(-30,30)) for x in range(1,n+1)]
# Creating data points in the form of a circle

df=pd.DataFrame(PointsInCircum(500,1000))
df=df.append(PointsInCircum(300,700))
df=df.append(PointsInCircum(100,300))

# Adding noise to the dataset
df=df.append([(np.random.randint(-600,600),np.random.
randint(-600,600)) for i in range(300)])

plt.figure(figsize=(10,10))
plt.scatter(df[0],df[1],s=15,color='red')
plt.title('Whole Dataset',fontsize=22)
plt.xlabel('Feature 1 values',fontsize=16)
plt.ylabel('Feature 2 values',fontsize=16)
plt.show()
#DBSCAN and its plot
dbscan_optclus=DBSCAN(eps=30,min_samples=6)
dbscan_optclus.fit(df[[0,1]])
df['DBSCAN_opt_labels']=dbscan_optclus.labels_
print(df['DBSCAN_opt_labels'].value_counts())
```

```
# Plotting the resulting clusters
plt.figure(figsize=(10,10))
plt.scatter(df[0],df[1],c=df['DBSCAN_opt_labels'],c-
map=matplotlib.colors.ListedColormap(colors),s=14)
plt.title('DBSCAN Clustering on whole
dataset',fontsize=22)
plt.xlabel('Feature 1 values',fontsize=16)
plt.ylabel('Feature 2 values',fontsize=16)
plt.show()
```

Output:

0 1,030
1 730
2 318
-1 222
Name: DBSCAN_opt_labels, dtype: int64

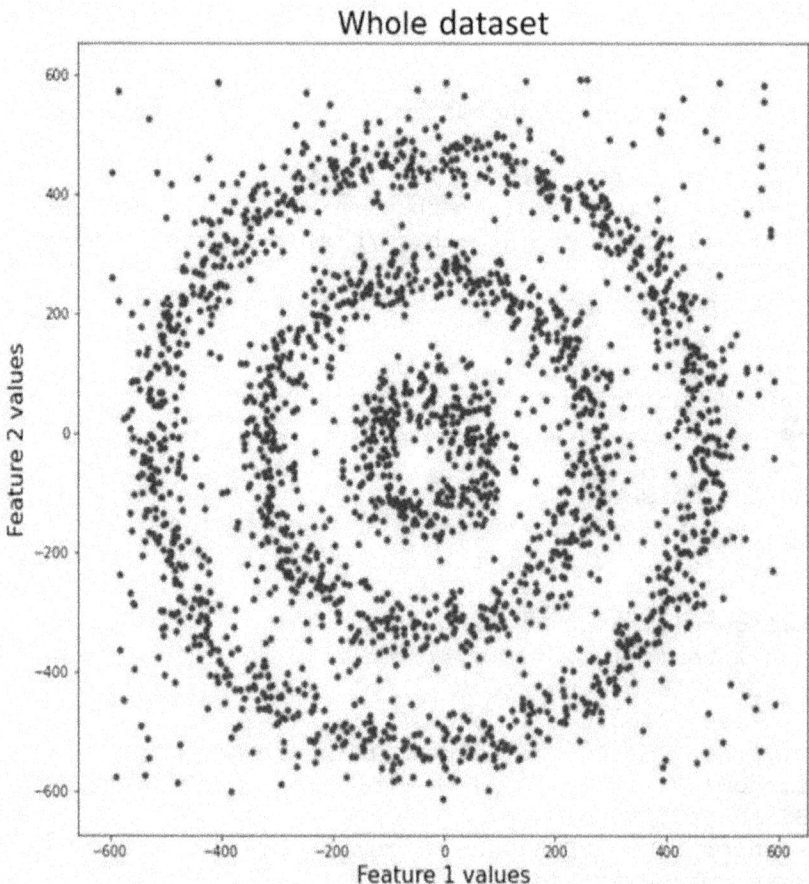

FIGURE 6.7 Generated Data Points for DBSCAN Clustering.

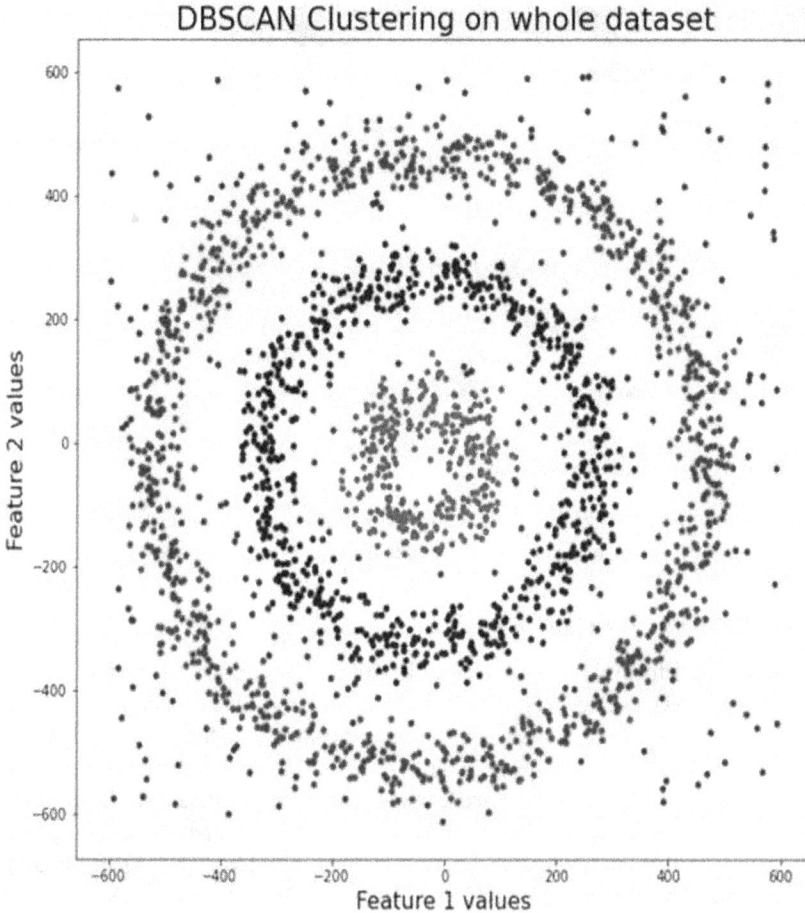

FIGURE 6.8 DBSCAN Clustering Results on Generated Data Samples.

6.7 ASSOCIATION RULE MINING

Association rule mining helps us find patterns in data. Market basket analysis, which tries to find patterns in user purchases, is its primary application. An example of a pattern can be that customers who purchase bread also purchase butter. So a store owner could place bread and butter together in his/her store to increase sales. In 2004, Walmart observed that people tend to stock up or buy strawberry pop-tarts before a hurricane struck. There did not seem to be any relation between hurricanes and strawberry pop-tarts, but Walmart mined their data and found this correlation. Later, it was discovered that strawberry pop-tarts require no cooking and they last long, making them the most purchased item in a disaster. One more example where association rule mining helped find the business strategy was in combo meal offers in fast food chains. They learnt that because of the high salt content in fast food, people feel thirsty. Thus customers bought food and drinks together.

Therefore, finding patterns using data mining is very helpful for companies' decision-making. The ultimate aim of association rules is to discover interesting patterns and relationships among items from a given transaction. They help identify the items

ID	Items
1	{Bread, Milk}
2	{Bread, Diapers, Beer, Eggs}
3	{Milk, Diapers, Beer, Cola}
4	{Bread, Milk, Diapers, Beer}
5	{Bread, Milk, Diapers, Cola}
...	...

Market basket transactions

{Diapers, Beer}   Example of a frequent itemset

{Diapers} → {Beer}   Example of an association rule

FIGURE 6.9   Association Rule Mining.

that are frequently bought together. Association rules give an idea of user purchasing behavior as well. Figure 6.9 shows the general idea behind association rules.

6.7.1 THE A PRIORI ALGORITHM

The a priori algorithm [9] is the most basic algorithm of association rule finding. "a priori" means "using previous knowledge." So, this algorithm finds frequent items using an iterative approach. First, it finds 1-frequent item sets, and using this, it finds 2-frequent item sets and continues to do so until no more frequent item sets can be found. The 1-frequent item sets could be {bread}{milk}{butter} and 2-frequent item sets could be {bread, milk} {milk, butter}. The a priori property of the item set helps reduce the search space. This property states that if {milk, butter} is a frequent item set, then {milk} and {butter} should also be frequent items. This property tells us that all subsets of frequent items must also be frequent.

This algorithm needs values for minimum support and confidence threshold too. The formulas are given as shown in Figure 6.10.

The support parameter indicates how frequently that item appears in transactions. Specifying minimum support value in a priori helps prune the transactions. If the data item does not match the minimum support value, that particular data item is not considered further for finding association rules. Support indicates the popularity of the item.

Confidence indicates the likelihood of occurrence of both data items A and B. The a priori algorithm takes an iterative approach to find frequent item sets, using "join" and "prune." The algorithm says that if the P(I) value is less than the minimum support value, that is, threshold value, then item I is not frequent. All those item sets and supersets can be pruned or ignored when the support value is below the minimum threshold value. The steps in the a priori algorithm (Figure 6.11) are as follows:

1. Join: This deals with the generation of (k + 1) item sets using the k-item set by joining items.
2. Prune: In this step, reduction of the size of the candidate item set occurs. Scanning of the count of each item set is performed and cross-checked with minimum support value. Based on the count value and the minimum support threshold value, the item is regarded as frequent or infrequent.

$$\text{Support}(A) = \frac{\text{Number of transaction in which A appears}}{\text{Total unmber of transactions}}$$

$$\text{Confidence}(A \rightarrow B) = \frac{\text{Support}(A \cup B)}{\text{Support}(A)}$$

$$\text{Lift}(A \Rightarrow B) = \frac{\text{Confidence}(A \Rightarrow B)}{P(B)}$$
$$= \frac{P(A \cup B)}{P(A)P(B)}$$

FIGURE 6.10   Support, Confidence, and Lift in a priori Algorithm.

```
Algorithm a priori(T, min_support; mm confidence)
Input:
  T → Transaction dataset
  min_support → Minimum support threshold
  min_confidence → Minimum confidence threshold
Output:
Frequent itemsets L
Strong association rules

1. C1 ← Generate all umque items from dataset T
2. LI ← Prune(Cl) //Remove items with support <
   min_support
3. k ← 2
4. While L(k-1) # 0 do:
     a. Ck ←Jom(L(k-1))
         // Generate candidate itemsets by combining
(k-1)-size frequent itemsets
     b. For each transaction t m T do:
          If Ck c t then:
             Increment support count of Ck
     c. Lk ←Prune(Ck)
        fi Remove itemsets with support < mm_support
     d. k ← k + 1
5. Frequent itemsets L ← u Lk
6. Generate Association Rules:
     For each frequent itemset X m L do:
       For each subset A c X do:
         B ← X - A
         If Confidence(A → B) > min_confidence then:
            Add rule A → B
7. Return Frequent Itemsets L and Association Rules.
```

FIGURE 6.11   A priori Algorithm.

TABLE 6.1
Transactions

Transaction	List of Items
T1	Milk, butter, jam
T2	Butter, jam, bread
T3	Bread, paneer
T4	Milk, butter, bread
T5	Milk, butter, jam, paneer
T6	Milk, butter, jam, bread

6.7.2   EXAMPLE OF A PRIORI ALGORITHM

Here, a table of six transactions of purchasing of milk, butter, jam, bread, and paneer are shown. Using these transactions, the association rules can be found. Here, the support threshold = 50% and confidence = 60%.

Solution: Here, the threshold value for support is 50%, that is, 0.5 x 6 = 3. So, the minimum support is 3.

6.7.2.1   Step 1: Counting Each Item

TABLE 6.2
Item Count

Item	Count
Milk	4
Butter	5
Jam	4
Bread	4
Paneer	2

6.7.2.2   Step 2: Prune

We can see from Table 6.2 that paneer does not meet the minimum support value criterion. So this item will not be considered further. Only milk, butter, jam, and bread meet min_sup count as their count values are more than 3.

6.7.2.3   Step 3: Join

The two-item set can be formed from Table 6.3. Occurrences of the two-item set can be found from the transactions given in Table 6.1.

6.7.2.4   Step 4: Prune

From Table 6.4, we can see that the item sets {milk, bread} and {jam, bread} do not meet the minimum support value; thus, these transactions are deleted or pruned and not considered for further processing.

TABLE 6.3
Data after Pruning

Item	Count
Milk	4
Butter	5
Jam	4
Bread	4

TABLE 6.4
Two-Item Sets

Item	Count
Milk, butter	4
Milk, jam	3
Milk, bread	2
Butter, jam	4
Butter, bread	3
Jam, bread	2

TABLE 6.5
Pruning of Two-Item Sets

Item	Count
Milk, butter	4
Milk, jam	3
Butter, jam	4
Butter, bread	3

6.7.2.5   Step 5: Join and Prune

Using Table 6.1, the three-item set can be formed and their occurrences can be found. For the item set {milk, butter, jam}, subsets {milk, butter}, {milk, jam}, and {butter, jam} meet the minimum support criterion, and they occur in Table 6.5. So {milk, butter, jam} is considered as frequent.

For the item set {milk, butter, bread}, subsets {milk, butter}, {milk, bread}, {butter, bread}, and {milk, bread} are not frequent, as they do not meet the minimum support criterion and do not occur in Table 6.5. Hence, {milk, butter, bread} is not frequent, and it is pruned and not considered for further processing.

Only {milk, butter, jam} is frequent.

TABLE 6.6
Three-Item Sets

Item

Milk, butter, jam
Milk, butter, bread
Milk, jam, bread
Butter, jam, bread

6.7.2.6   Step 6: Generate Association Rules

We can form the association rule by using the frequent item set discovered above, as follows:

```
{milk, butter} => {jam}
confidence = support {milk, butter, jam} / support
{milk, butter} = (3/ 4)* 100 = 75%
lift = confidence / support {jam} =.75 / (4/6) = 1.12

{milk, jam} => {butter}
confidence = support {milk, butter, jam} / support
{milk, jam} = (3/ 3)* 100 = 100%
lift = confidence / support {butter} = 1 / (5/6) = 1.2

{butter, jam} => {milk}
confidence = support {milk, butter, jam} / support {but-
ter, jam} = (3/ 4)* 100 = 75%
lift = confidence / support {milk} =.75 / (4/6) = 1.12

{milk} => {butter, jam}
confidence = support {milk, butter, jam} / support
{milk} = (3/ 4)* 100 = 75%
lift = confidence / support {butter, jam} =.75 / (4/6) =
1.12

{butter} => {milk, jam}
confidence = support {milk, butter, jam} / support {but-
ter} = (3/ 5)* 100 = 60%
lift = confidence / support {milk, jam} =.60 / (3/6) =
1.2

{jam} => {milk, butter}
confidence = support {milk, butter, jam} / support
{jam} = (3/ 4)* 100 = 75%
lift = confidence / support {milk, butter} =.75 /
(4/6) = 1.12
```

All of the above association rules are strong as the minimum confidence threshold here is 60%.

6.7.3 CASE STUDY: TRANSACTIONS IN A GROCERY STORE

The example above illustrates the application of the a priori algorithm in a relatively simple case that generalizes to those used in practice. Companies like Walmart have made great use of the a priori algorithm in suggesting products bought by its customers.

Here, the sample data is of six transactions of five items: milk, butter, jam, bread, and paneer. Data is inserted in a .csv file as shown:

Milk	Butter	Jam		
	Butter	Jam		Paneer
			Bread	Paneer
Milk	Butter		Bread	
Milk	Butter	Jam		Paneer
Milk	Butter	Jam	Bread	

The a priori() function from the apyori package implements the a priori algorithm to create frequent item sets and association rules. The apyori package can be installed using the command:

```
pip install apyori
```

Here, the minimum support value is set as 0.5 and confidence value as 0.6. In output, only {milk, butter, jam} is considered as frequent. All the subsets of {milk, butter, jam} have confidence greater than 60%.

```
import io
import numpy as np
import pandas as pd
from apyori import a priori
from google.colab import files
uploaded= files.upload()

dfval=pd.read_csv(io.BytesIO(uploaded['a priorifile1.
csv']))
dfval.head()
print(dfval.shape)
listrecordset = []
for i in range(0, 6):
    listrecordset.append([str(dfval.values[i,j]) for j
in range(0, 5)])

print(listrecordset)
```

```
rulesofassociation = a priori(listrecordset, min_
support=0.5, min_confidence=0.6, min_lift=1.2,
min_length=2)
resultsofassociation = list(rulesofassociation)
print(resultsofassociation)
```

Output:

```
(6, 5)

[['nan', 'Butter', 'Jam', 'nan', 'Paneer'], ['nan',
'nan', 'nan', 'Bread', 'Paneer'], ['Milk', 'Butter',
'nan', 'Bread', 'nan'], ['Milk', 'Butter', 'Jam', 'nan',
'Paneer'], ['Milk', 'Butter', 'Jam', 'Bread', 'nan'],
['Milk', 'Butter', 'Jam', 'nan', 'nan']]

[ RelationRecord(items=frozenset({'Jam', 'Milk',
'Butter'}), support=0.5, ordered_statistics=[Or-
deredStatistic(items_base=frozenset({'Butter'}),
items_add=frozenset({'Jam', 'Milk'}), confidence=0.6,
lift=1.2), OrderedStatistic(items_base=frozenset({'Jam',
'Milk'}), items_add=frozenset({'Butter'}), confi-
dence=1.0, lift=1.2)])........................
```

It displays all the subsets of {milk, butter, jam} with their support and confidence. All the subsets have confidence values greater than 60.

6.8   SUMMARY

A thorough review of unsupervised ML algorithms is given in this chapter, with an emphasis on association rule mining and clustering methods. Investigating the data's underlying structure or distribution is the main objective. A crucial method in unsupervised learning is clustering, which groups related data points into clusters. This technique helps in identifying natural groupings within datasets. Distance measures define the similarity between data points and significantly impact the clustering results. Different distance measures and taxonomy of clustering algorithms are also discussed in detail. Association rule mining is used to identify interesting relationships between variables in large datasets, commonly applied in market basket analysis. The chapter is accompanied by practical Python implementations to reinforce all the concepts.

REFERENCES

1. https://archive.org/stream/big-data-collection-pdf/Data%20Science%20and%20 Big%20Data%20Analytics_%20Discovering%2C%20Analyzing%2C%20Visualizing%20and%20Presenting%20Data_djvu.txt
2. https://www.kdnuggets.com/2018/06/5-clustering-algorithms-data-scientists-need-know.html

3. https://www.analyticsvidhya.com/blog/2016/11/an-introduction-to-clustering-and-different-methods-of-clustering/

4. "A concise guide to market research", *The Process, Data and Methods Using IBMSPSS Statistics*, Springer, https://doi.org/10.1007/978-3-662-56707-4

5. Krawczak, M., & Szkatuła, G. (2015). On asymmetric matching between sets. *Information Sciences, 312*, 89–103, https://doi.org/10.1016/j.ins.2015.03.037

6. Bisong, E. (2019). *Clustering. In: Building Machine Learning and Deep Learning Models on Google Cloud Platform*, Apress, Berkeley, CA, https://doi.org/10.1007/978-1-4842-4470-8_25

7. https://www.coursehero.com/sitemap/schools/1475-Stevens-Institute-Of-Technology/courses/6556972-CS513/

8. www.analyticsvidhya.com/blog/2020/09/how-dbscan-clustering-works/

9. https://www.slideshare.net/search?utf8=%E2%9C%93&searchfrom=header&q=apriori+algorithm

7 Neural Networks and Deep Learning

7.1 INTRODUCTION

The human brain is an interesting phenomenon, so little when looked at physically yet incomprehensible when studied about. The working of the human mind has been studied since the 17th century, and yet there exist certain phenomena we cannot find an explanation for. Neurons are special cells that send messages all over one's body to enable one to do everything from breathing to talking to eating and thinking. These neurons form what is called a neural network in our minds that light up when one is thinking. Similarly, to make a computer algorithm "think", we must recreate this neural network to enable artificial intelligence (AI), similar to our own. The following paragraphs shall explore various concepts and methods related to such neural networks.

With the goal of transforming how robots or algorithms see, comprehend, and interact with the environment, neural networks have emerged as revolutionary forces in the field of AI in recent years. Neural networks are computer models made up of neurons, which are interconnected nodes that analyze and learn from data. They are inspired by the intricate workings of the human brain. A kind of machine learning (ML) called "deep learning" uses multilayered neural networks (hence the term "deep") to simulate intricate correlations and patterns [1] in big datasets that haven't been well examined before.

The power of deep learning and neural networks lies in their ability to automatically identify and extract meaningful patterns from raw data, eliminating the need for human feature engineering, which has become synonymous with ML applications. This has resulted in notable advancements in a variety of fields, including speech and picture recognition, natural language processing, and gaming, frequently surpassing human skills in these applications.

The structures, learning techniques, and applications of neural networks and deep learning are examined in this chapter, which dives into their fundamentals. We will look at the fundamental ideas that make them successful, like gradient descent and backpropagation, as well as the difficulties and constraints they encounter. We can use these potent tools to solve challenging issues and push the boundaries of AI research if we comprehend their complexities.

A foundational aspect of neural networks is ML. Now, the basic concept behind ML is that computer algorithms cannot comprehend data like images or audio or video like the human mind does; rather it can be trained to observe patterns in data. If we "train" a computer algorithm by providing it with some data and the observed characteristics and repeat this process a reasonable number of times, we can accomplish an algorithm capable of finding patterns or "learning" from the data.

DOI: 10.1201/9781003532170-7

Think about the task of recognizing faces—something we perform effortlessly every day. Whether it's identifying family members or friends from their faces or photographs, we can do so despite changes in pose, lighting, hairstyle, and other variations. However, this process happens unconsciously, and we struggle to explain exactly how we accomplish it. This makes it difficult to manually program a computer to perform the same task. Yet, we know that a face is more than a random assortment of pixels—it has a well-defined structure. Faces are symmetrical, with key features like eyes, a nose, and a mouth arranged in specific positions. Every face is characterized by a unique combination of these features. By analyzing sample images of a person's face, a learning algorithm can identify the distinctive pattern associated with that individual. It then uses this pattern to recognize the person in new images. This illustrates how pattern recognition works in practice.

ML builds mathematical models using statistical principles, as its main objective is to infer patterns from sampled data. Computer science plays a critical role in two main areas: first, during the training phase, it provides efficient algorithms to address optimization problems and manage large datasets. Second, both the model's representation and the inference algorithms must be computationally efficient once the model has been trained. In some scenarios, the computational efficiency of these algorithms, measured by their space and time complexity, can be as important as the model's ability to make accurate predictions.

If a linear model falls short, one option is to generate new features by applying nonlinear transformations to the input, such as higher-order terms, and then develop a linear model in the resulting feature space. However, this requires prior knowledge of effective basis functions. Another option is to leverage feature extraction techniques like PCA or Isomap, which are advantageous because they are trained directly on the data.

PCA is a common technique for reducing data complexity and can be very useful when working with neural networks. PCA aims to identify the most significant features or principal components in a dataset, allowing for the reduction of the input dimensionality without losing too much of the original information. In the context of neural networks, PCA can be employed in several ways:

1. Feature Extraction and Preprocessing:

    Prior to being fed into a neural network, PCA can be used as a preprocessing step to extract the most pertinent characteristics from the input data. Through the reduction of the input's dimensionality, PCA can enhance the neural network's efficiency and overall performance, as it focuses on the most informative features and reduces the risk of overfitting.

2. Visualization and Interpretation:

    PCA can simplify high-dimensional data by visualizing it in a lower-dimensional space, typically two or three dimensions. This can offer important insights into the patterns and connections within the data, which can aid in the interpretation and understanding of the neural network's behavior.

3. Regularization and Dimensionality Reduction:

   PCA can be integrated directly into the neural network architecture as a form of regularization. Projecting input data onto the principal components encourages the network to focus on learning representations that align with the data's most significant features, which improves generalization and prevents overfitting.

4. Initialization and Weight Optimization:

   PCA can also be used to initialize the weights of a neural network, especially for the connections between the first hidden layer and the input layer. Aligning the initial weights with the principal components can help the network train faster and improve its performance. Overall, the integration of PCA into neural network architectures and training processes can enhance the performance, interpretability, and robustness of these powerful ML models.

Still, the best approach is to use a Multilayer Perceptron (MLP). It extracts these features in its hidden layer, with the benefit that both the feature extraction in the first layer and the combination of those features to predict the output in the second layer are learned together in a connected and supervised way.

The goal of deep learning is to automatically learn features at various abstraction levels with minimal human involvement. These methods are appealing because they require less manual effort and there's no need to design specific features, basis functions, or even the network architecture manually. With enough data and computational power, we let the learning algorithm independently uncover what it needs. The concept of multiple layers capturing progressively abstract features, which forms the foundation of deep learning, is straightforward and intuitive. The concept of abstraction layers extends beyond visual tasks such as identifying handwritten digits or faces and applies to many other fields. Discovering these abstract representations can provide valuable insights, improve visualization, and offer a clearer description of the problem at hand.

7.2   INTRODUCTION TO NEURAL NETWORKS

A neural network is a computational model inspired by the structure and function of the human brain. It is used in ML and AI to solve complex problems by learning patterns from data. Neural networks are particularly effective for tasks like image recognition, natural language processing, and time-series prediction.

Neural networks, as previously mentioned, are made up of interconnected nodes or "neurons" arranged in layers. They learn to perform tasks by adapting the strengths of connections between neurons based on input data and feedback signals. This ability to adjust enables neural networks to approximate complex functions and uncover intricate patterns in data without the need for explicitly programmed rules.

The growing focus on neural networks in recent years, often described as the "deep learning revolution," has been driven by several key factors.

1. Increased computational power, particularly through advancements in graphics processing units (GPUs);

2. Availability of large-scale datasets for training;
3. Advancements in network architectures and training algorithms;
4. Improved regularization techniques to prevent overfitting.

These advancements have facilitated the development of deep neural networks with multiple layers, capable of learning hierarchical data representations and delivering state-of-the-art performance across various tasks.

7.3 FUNDAMENTALS OF NEURAL NETWORKS

1. **Biological Inspiration:**
   Neural networks draw inspiration from the structure and function of biological nervous systems. In the human brain, neurons communicate through electrical and chemical signals, forming complex networks capable of processing and storing information. Artificial neural networks aim to mimic this biological architecture in a simplified form, with artificial neurons (nodes) connected by weighted edges that represent synaptic strengths.

2. **Basic Structure:**
   Neurons (Nodes):
   - The building blocks of a neural network.
   - Each neuron receives input, processes it (via an activation function), and produces output.

   Layers:
   - Input Layer: Accepts raw data features.
   - Hidden Layers: Perform computations to extract patterns and relationships.
   - Output Layer: Produces the final predictions or classifications.

   Weights and Biases:
   - Weights determine the importance of inputs.
   - Bias shifts the activation function to help the network fit the data better.

   Activation Functions:
   - Functions like Rectified Linear Unit (ReLU), Sigmoid, and Softmax introduce nonlinearity, enabling the network to model complex relationships.

3. **Activation Functions:**
   An activation function in a neural network determines whether a neuron should be activated or not. It introduces nonlinearity into the network, enabling it to learn and model complex patterns in the data. Without activation functions, a neural network would simply perform linear transformations, severely limiting its capability. Common activation functions include the following:

   a. Sigmoid: $f(x) = \dfrac{1}{1+e^{-x}}$

   b. Hyperbolic Tangent (tanh): $f(x) = \dfrac{e^x - e^{-x}}{e^x + e^{-x}}$

c. ReLU: $f(x) = (0, x)$

d. Leaky ReLU: $f(x) = (\alpha x, x)$, where α is a small constant.

The selection of an activation function plays a crucial role in determining the network's performance and training behavior.

4. **Learning Process:**

Neural networks undergo an iterative learning process where weights are adjusted to reduce the error between predicted and actual outputs. This process usually includes the following:

a. **Forward Propagation:** It is the process in which input data flows through the layers of a neural network to generate predictions. Each layer transforms the input data by applying numerical parameters called weights and biases, which determine the strength and influence of connections between neurons. These transformations are further enhanced by activation functions, which introduce nonlinearity, enabling the network to learn and model complex patterns in the data. The final layer processes the transformed data to produce predictions, which may represent probabilities for classification tasks or numeric values for regression tasks. This step is essential for the network to make decisions based on the input it receives.

b. **Loss Calculation:** The purpose of loss calculation is to measure the difference between the neural network's predicted outputs and the actual target values, providing a way to evaluate the network's performance. This is achieved using a loss function, a mathematical formula that quantifies the error. Common loss functions include mean squared error (MSE), which is used for regression tasks to measure the average squared differences between predictions and targets, and cross-entropy loss, which is commonly applied in classification tasks to assess how well the predicted probability distribution matches the actual labels. The loss function outputs a single scalar value, with lower values indicating better performance of the network. This loss value serves as the basis for improving the network through backpropagation and weight adjustment.

c. **Backpropagation:** The purpose of backpropagation is to determine how to adjust the weights and biases of a neural network to minimize the loss, thereby improving its predictions. This is achieved by calculating the gradient of the loss with respect to each weight and bias using the chain rule of calculus. Gradients provide information on how much a small change in a parameter will impact the loss, guiding the network on how to update these parameters effectively. The calculations flow backward through the network, starting from the output layer and moving to the input layer, hence the name "backpropagation." This process identifies which weights and biases contributed most to the error, enabling the network to focus its adjustments where they are needed most.

d. **Weight Adjustment:** Weight adjustment is the process of updating a neural network's weights to reduce the loss and improve future predictions. This is done using optimization algorithms like gradient descent or its variants (e.g., Adam and RMSProp), which adjust the weights by taking small steps in the direction of the negative gradient of the loss. This iterative process involves repeating forward propagation, loss calculation, backpropagation, and weight adjustment over multiple iterations (epochs) until the loss reaches an acceptable level or stops improving, enabling the network to effectively learn from the data. This iterative process enables neural networks to achieve the accuracy required for practical, production-level applications.

The code provided below demonstrates building and training a simple neural network using TensorFlow to classify handwritten digit images from the digits dataset. First, the dataset is loaded [2], normalized, and its labels are converted to one-hot encoded format for multiclass classification. The data is then split into training and testing sets. The neural network consists of an input layer, a single hidden layer with 64 neurons using ReLU activation, and an output layer with softmax activation to predict the probability of each digit class (0–9). The model is compiled using the Adam optimizer and categorical cross-entropy loss and then trained for ten epochs with a batch size of 32. Finally, the model's performance is evaluated on the test set, displaying the loss and accuracy metrics.

```python
import tensorflow as tf
from tensorflow.keras import layers, models
from sklearn.datasets import load_digits
from sklearn.model_selection import train_test_split
from sklearn.preprocessing import OneHotEncoder
import numpy as np

# Load the digits dataset
digits = load_digits()
X = digits.data
y = digits.target

# Normalize the input data
X = X / 16.0

# One-hot encode the labels
encoder = OneHotEncoder(sparse_output=False)
y = encoder.fit_transform(y.reshape(-1, 1))

# Split the data into training and testing sets
train_X, test_X, train_y, test_y = train_test_split(X,
y, test_size=0.2, random_state=42)

# Build the neural network model with one hidden layer
model = models.Sequential([
```

```
    layers.InputLayer(input_shape=(X.shape[1],)), #
Input layer
    layers.Dense(64, activation='relu'), # Single hidden
layer
    layers.Dense(y.shape[1], activation='softmax') #
Output layer
])

# Compile the model
model.compile(optimizer='adam',loss='categorical_cros-
sentropy',
              metrics=['accuracy'])

# Train the model
model.fit(train_X, train_y, epochs=10, batch_size=32,
validation_split=0.2)

# Evaluate the model on the test set
loss, accuracy = model.evaluate(test_X,test_y)
print(f"Test Loss: {loss:.4f}, Test Accuracy:
{accuracy:.4f}")
```

This example illustrates how to preprocess data, construct a neural network, and train it for classification tasks.

5. Types of Learning:

Neural networks can adapt and learn in various ways, based on the characteristics of the data and the specific problem being addressed.

The three main types of learning are as follows:

Supervised Learning: In supervised learning, the network is trained using a labeled dataset, where each input is matched with a specific target or output. The aim is to develop a mapping function capable of accurately predicting outputs for previously unseen inputs.

Key Characteristics:

- Requires paired input–output data
- Widely applied in tasks like classification and regression
- Examples include image classification, speech recognition, and price prediction

Challenges:

- Acquiring large, precisely labeled datasets often requires significant time and expense
- Risk of overfitting to the training data

Unsupervised Learning: Unsupervised learning involves training on unlabeled data, where the network attempts to discover inherent patterns or structures within the data.

Key Characteristics:

- No predefined output or labels
- Applied in clustering, dimensionality reduction, and feature extraction tasks
- Examples include customer segmentation, anomaly detection, and generative models

Challenges:

- Difficulty in evaluating the quality of learned representations
- Interpretability of discovered patterns

Reinforcement Learning: Reinforcement learning is a process where an agent learns to make decisions through interactions with its environment. The agent gets feedback in the form of rewards or punishments depending on the actions it takes.

Key Characteristics:

- Learning through trial and error
- Maintains a balance between exploring new possibilities and utilizing actions proven to be effective
- Used in game playing, robotics, and autonomous systems

Challenges:

- Designing appropriate reward functions
- Handling large state and action spaces
- Sample efficiency in learning

Semi-Supervised Learning: A combined method incorporating aspects of supervised and unsupervised learning, utilizing a small quantity of labeled data alongside a substantial amount of unlabeled data.

Key Characteristics:

- Leverages both labeled and unlabeled data
- Can improve performance when labeled data is scarce
- Examples include text classification with limited annotations

Challenges:

- Balancing the influence of labeled and unlabeled data
- Designing effective algorithms to leverage unlabeled data

7.4   NEURAL NETWORK ARCHITECTURES

This section will brief about various architectures of neural network.

1. Feedforward Neural Networks:

A feedforward neural network is a type of artificial neural network where data flows in one direction, from the input layer through one or more hidden layers to the output layer. It does not have loops or feedback connections, making it simple and efficient for tasks like classification and regression. The network learns by adjusting weights during training to minimize the error between predicted and actual outputs.

Key Features:

- Fully connected layers
- Suitable for tabular data and simple pattern recognition tasks
- Limited in capturing spatial or temporal dependencies

2. Convolutional Neural Networks:

These are specialized for handling grid-based data, such as images, and employ convolutional layers to learn spatial hierarchies of features automatically. It uses convolutional layers to automatically extract spatial features, making it highly effective for tasks like image recognition, object detection, and video analysis.

Key Features:

- Local connectivity and parameter sharing
- Pooling layers for down-sampling
- Highly effective for image and video processing tasks

3. Recurrent Neural Networks:

It is a type of neural network designed to process sequential data by retaining information about previous inputs through hidden states. It is widely used in tasks like time-series analysis, language modeling, and speech recognition, where understanding temporal dependencies is crucial.

Key Features:

- Feedback connections
- Gated recurrent units (GRU) and long short-term memory (LSTM) are two variants that are intended to solve the vanishing gradient issue.

4. Transformer Networks:

Transformer networks, a recent introduction, rely entirely on self-attention mechanisms to process sequential data.

Key Features:

- Parallelizable computation
- Well-suited for modeling long-range dependencies
- Forms the foundation for numerous cutting-edge models in natural language processing

5. Generative Adversarial Networks:

Generative adversarial networks (GANs) are composed of two neural networks—a generator and a discriminator—trained together using adversarial learning.

Key Features:

- Can generate new, synthetic data samples
- Applied in tasks such as image generation, style transfer, and data augmentation
- Challenging to train due to instability issues

7.5 CONVOLUTIONAL NEURAL NETWORKS

Convolutional neural networks (CNNs) are a class of deep learning models primarily designed for processing data that has a grid-like topology, such as images. They are highly effective for tasks like image recognition, object detection, and segmentation but are also applied to other domains like video processing, speech recognition, and natural language processing.

Convolutional layers provide the basis of CNNs; the term "convolution" describes the mathematical process of combining two functions to create a third. The input image is processed by these layers using learnable filters. These filters, also called as kernels, are employed to identify discrete characteristics including textures, forms, and edges. Moving the filters across the image enables them to detect and localize features while constructing a hierarchical representation of the input data. One of the main features of CNNs is their ability to handle the spatial and local dependencies within images.

CNNs differ from traditional ML algorithms by automatically learning key features from the data, reducing the necessity of manual feature engineering. This is accomplished using shared weights and local connectivity, which minimize the number of parameters and enable the network to efficiently handle large-scale images. A standard CNN architecture is composed of several convolutional layers, pooling layers, and fully connected layers as shown in Figure 7.1.

Convolutional layers capture features from the input image, while pooling layers shrink the spatial dimensions of the feature maps, improving the network's resilience to small changes in the input. The ultimate classification or prediction is made by the completely connected layers at the end of the network. CNN training relies on extensive datasets and significant computational resources. Through backpropagation, the network's parameters are adjusted iteratively to minimize the discrepancy between its predictions and the ground truth data. This process enables the network

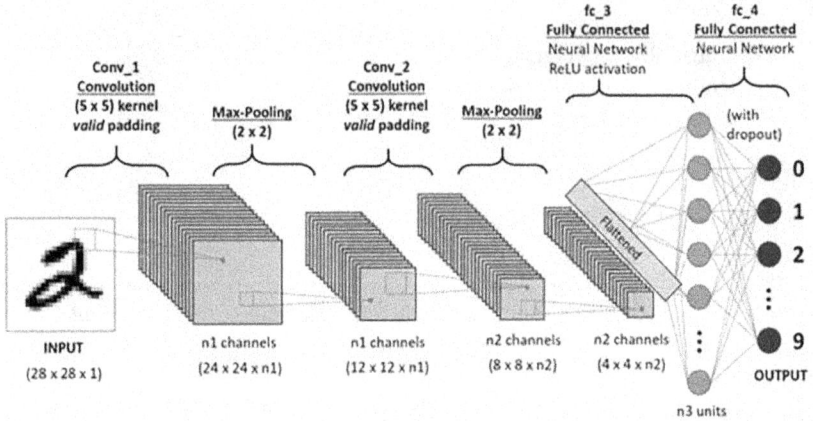

FIGURE 7.1 CNN Architecture.

to uncover patterns and relationships within the image data, allowing it to make accurate predictions on previously unseen images.

In recent years, CNNs have attained cutting-edge performance on various image recognition benchmarks, like ImageNet and CIFAR-10. These advancements have led to numerous applications and breakthroughs, from autonomous driving and medical image analysis to facial recognition and object detection in surveillance systems. Despite their success, CNNs are not without their challenges.

One of the main challenges is the interpretability of the learned features, as the complex interactions between the convolutional filters can make it difficult to understand how the network arrives at its predictions. Additionally, CNNs can be sensitive to the quality and quantity of training data and may struggle with tasks that require reasoning or abstraction beyond the patterns present in the images. As the field of CNNs continues to evolve, researchers are exploring various techniques to address these challenges, such as attention mechanisms, GANs, and transfer learning. These advancements are likely to lead to even more powerful and versatile CNNs, capable of tackling increasingly complex problems and driving innovation across various domains.

7.5.1 THE CONVOLUTION LAYER

Convolutional layer is a fundamental component of CNNs, specifically designed for analyzing grid-like data, such as images or time-series data. Convolution operation is performed by this layer. In order to generate feature maps, small trainable filters, also called as kernels, move across the input data, multiplying and adding elements at each location. As the network gets deeper, it learns more sophisticated representations like structures, objects, and semantic information. Each filter is trained to identify particular patterns or features, including edges, textures, or gradients. Filters have adjustable sizes (e.g., 3 × 3, 5 × 5), and their number determines the depth of the output feature map, with more filters allowing the network to capture a greater variety of features [3].

The performance of the convolution operation is defined by various hyperparameters, including the following:

1. **Stride:** Determines the step size of the filter as it moves across the input, influencing the spatial dimensions of the output. A stride of 1 results in a dense feature map, while larger strides downsample the data.
2. **Padding:** Decides how to handle the edges of the input. Common strategies include the following:
   o **Valid Padding:** No padding, resulting in reduced output size
   o **Same Padding:** Adds padding so the output size matches the input size, preserving spatial dimensions
3. **Activation Function:** After the convolution, a nonlinear function like ReLU is applied to introduce nonlinearity, enabling the network to learn complex patterns and relationships.

The design of convolutional layers ensures efficiency and robustness through two key principles:

- **Parameter Sharing:** A single filter is applied across the entire input, reducing the number of trainable parameters and making the network computationally efficient.
- **Local Connectivity:** Filters operate on localized regions of the input, making the model focus on small, meaningful regions while reducing complexity.

Translation invariance is another feature of these layers that allows them to identify patterns in the input regardless of where they are located. For example, whether an object is in the top-left corner or the center of an image, the convolutional layer can still detect it. This property is critical in tasks like image recognition and object detection, where patterns may appear at different locations.

7.5.2 POOLING LAYER

Pooling layers are a critical component of CNNs used to reduce the spatial dimensions of feature maps, making the model more computationally efficient and less prone to overfitting. Pooling layers allow the network to concentrate on important information by summarizing small areas of a feature map keeping dominating features while eliminating less important data. Common types of pooling include max pooling, which selects the maximum value in a region to emphasize strong activations, and average pooling, which computes the average value for a smoother representation. Global pooling is sometimes used to summarize entire feature maps into single values before feeding them into fully connected layers. Pooling helps reduce dimensionality, computational costs, and overfitting while ensuring robust feature generalization.

7.5.3 FULLY CONNECTED LAYER

The fully connected (FC) layer in a CNN is the final stage that connects all neurons from the previous layer to every neuron in its layer, enabling global feature integration and decision-making. It takes the convolutional and pooling layers' flattened output as a collection of features and uses weights and biases to determine how they relate to one another. Every neuron in the FC layer models complicated relationships and generates predictions by performing a linear transformation and then an activation function (such as ReLU, sigmoid, or softmax). FC layers are primarily used for classification, mapping learned features to class scores, or for regression tasks, outputting continuous values.

7.5.4 LOSS FUNCTION

The loss function in a CNN measures the difference between the network's predicted output and the actual target, guiding the model's learning process. It measures the error and provides feedback during training, helping the network update its weights using backpropagation and optimization techniques like stochastic gradient descent (SGD). The choice of a loss function is crucial and varies based on the type of task being solved, as different tasks require different methods to evaluate prediction errors effectively. For classification tasks, the cross-entropy loss is one of the most commonly used loss functions. It works by comparing the predicted probabilities of the network with the true class labels, ensuring that the model outputs higher probabilities for correct classes. Hinge loss, which is particularly useful for margin-based classifiers like support vector machines (SVMs). This loss function focuses on maximizing the margin between predicted and actual classes, enhancing the classifier's robustness. For regression tasks, where the goal is to predict continuous values, MSE and mean absolute error (MAE) are widely used, the former focusing on squared differences and the latter on absolute differences. In image segmentation tasks, where precise pixel-level predictions are required, specialized loss functions like dice loss and Intersection over Union (IoU) loss are preferred. By concentrating on their overlap, these losses are especially useful for comparing predicted segmentation masks with ground truth, guaranteeing precise border identification and segmentation. Kullback–Leibler (KL) divergence is another advanced loss function used in tasks like language modeling or probabilistic predictions, as it measures the difference between two probability distributions, helping refine models that output probabilities.

7.5.5 OPTIMIZATION ALGORITHMS

Optimization algorithms in CNNs are essential for minimizing the loss function and updating network weights during training. The most basic algorithm, SGD, updates weights iteratively based on the gradient of the loss function with respect to the weights, as shown below.

$$W = W - \eta \nabla L(W)$$

Here,

W = Weights
η = Learning rate
$\nabla L(W)$ = Gradient of the loss function with respect to W

The limitation of SGD is it can be slow and prone to oscillations. SGD with momentum addresses these issues by adding a momentum term to accelerate convergence and reduce oscillations. The update rule of SGD with momentum is as shown below:

$$v = \gamma v - \eta \nabla L(W)$$

$$W = W - v$$

Here, v is the velocity term and γ is the momentum factor.

Adaptive methods like Adagrad adjust learning rates are based on historical gradients, and the formula is as given below:

$$W = W - \frac{\eta}{\sqrt{G_t - \in}} \nabla L(W)$$

Here, G_t is the sum of squared gradients and $\in$ is a small constant.

This works well with sparse data, but it can diminish learning rates excessively, an issue resolved by RMSProp, which uses an exponentially decaying average of squared gradients.

$$W = W - \frac{\eta}{\sqrt{E[g^2]_t - \in}} \nabla L(W)$$

Here, $E[g^2]_t$ is the exponentially weighted moving average of the squared gradients.

Adam combines the strengths of momentum and RMSProp by maintaining moving averages of both gradients and squared gradients, offering fast convergence and robustness to noisy data.

$$m_t = \beta_1 m_{t-1} - (1 - \beta_1) \nabla L(W)$$

$$v_t = \beta_2 v_{t-1} - (1 - \beta_{12})(\nabla L(W))^2$$

$$W = W - \frac{\eta}{\sqrt{\widehat{v_t}} + \epsilon} \nabla L(W)$$

Here, m_t and v_t are the biased estimates of the first and second moments, respectively.

Nesterov-accelerated Adaptive Moment Estimation (Nadam) is a variant of Adam optimizer, which incorporates Nesterov momentum for further improvement of convergence speed and performance. AdaDelta, an extension of Adagrad, avoids diminishing learning rates by using a moving average of squared gradients. Selection of an algorithm depends upon dataset size, task complexity, and the gradient behavior. Large datasets or complicated architectures frequently benefit from adaptive techniques like Adam or RMSProp, which strike a balance between accuracy and efficiency, whereas simpler jobs could work well with SGD.

The code given below builds, trains, and evaluates a simple CNN using TensorFlow [4] to classify the MNIST dataset of handwritten digits. First, it imports required libraries and loads the MNIST dataset. The grayscale image data is reshaped to include a channel dimension (28 x 28 x 1) and normalized to a range of 0–1. The labels are one-hot encoded to represent the 10 classes (digits 0–9).

The CNN model is constructed using TensorFlow's Sequential API. It includes the following:

1. A convolutional layer with 32 filters of size 3 x 3, followed by ReLU activation.
2. A max-pooling layer to reduce spatial dimensions.
3. A second convolutional layer with 64 filters and ReLU activation, followed by another max-pooling layer.
4. A flattening layer to transform the 2D feature maps into a 1D vector.
5. A fully connected dense layer with 128 neurons and ReLU activation.
6. An output dense layer with 10 neurons and softmax activation for multiclass classification.

The Adam optimizer and categorical cross-entropy as the loss function are used to compile the model. Using the training data, it is trained for 50 epochs with a batch size of 32, and the test data is used for validation. Finally, the model is evaluated on the test set, and the test accuracy is printed.

```
import tensorflow as tf
from tensorflow.keras import Sequential
from tensorflow.keras.layers import Conv2D, Max-
Pooling2D, Flatten, Dense
from tensorflow.keras.datasets import mnist
from tensorflow.keras.utils import to_categorical

(train_x, train_y), (test_x, test_y) = mnist.load_
data()
```

```
train_x = train_x.reshape(-1, 28, 28,
1).astype('float32') / 255.0
test_x = test_x.reshape(-1, 28, 28, 1).astype('float32')
/ 255.0

train_y = to_categorical(train_y, 10)
test_y = to_categorical(test_y, 10)

model = Sequential([
Conv2D(32, (3, 3), activation='relu', input_shape=(28,
28, 1)),
MaxPooling2D((2,2)),
Conv2D(64, (3, 3), activation='relu'),
MaxPooling2D((2, 2)),
Flatten(),
Dense(128, activation='relu'),
Dense(10, activation='softmax')
])

model.compile(optimizer='adam', loss='categorical_cros-
sentropy', metrics=['accuracy'])

model.fit(train_x, train_y, epochs=50, batch_size=32,
validation_data=(test_x, test_y))
test_loss, test_acc = model.evaluate(test_x, test_y)
print(f'Test Accuracy: {test_acc * 100:.2f}%')
```

7.6   RECURRENT NEURAL NETWORKS

Recurrent neural networks (RNNs) are a specialized type of neural network designed for sequential data, capable of modeling temporal dependencies by maintaining a hidden state that retains information from previous steps. Unlike feedforward networks, which assume independence between inputs, RNNs process input sequences one element at a time, with shared weights across time steps, making them suitable for tasks like natural language processing, time-series analysis, and speech recognition.

The core concept of RNNs is leveraging sequential information by retaining a "memory" of past inputs. This is accomplished through recurrent connections, where a neuron's output at one time step serves as an input at the next. This recursive structure enables RNNs to handle sequences of varying lengths, offering a key advantage over neural network architectures with fixed input sizes.

RNNs are extensively applied in various domains, including the following:

1. Natural Language Processing: Applied to tasks like sentiment analysis, generating text and machine translation.
2. Speech Recognition: Converting spoken language into text.

3. Time-Series Prediction: Forecasting in financial markets, weather patterns, and other dynamic systems.
4. Music Generation: Composing melodies and harmonies.
5. Video Analysis: Understanding and predicting sequences of images.

Traditional RNNs, despite their capabilities, struggle to learn long-term dependencies due to the vanishing and exploding gradient problems. These challenges occur during backpropagation through time, where gradients can shrink or grow exponentially, making it challenging to capture relationships between temporally distant events.

To overcome these challenges, various RNN variants have been developed. Notably, LSTM networks and GRUs use gating mechanisms to capture long-term dependencies effectively, enabling the network to selectively retain or discard information across long sequences.

7.6.1   Long Short-Term Memory Networks

An LSTM is a special type of RNN designed to address the limitations of traditional RNNs, particularly the problem of vanishing gradients. This issue occurs when gradients drop to extremely low values or vanish during backpropagation from the output layers to earlier layers in standard RNNs. LSTMs achieve this through the use of additional memory cells, as well as input and output gates. Memory cells store information over long periods. These cells are the core of LSTMs and allow the network to decide which information to retain or forget. Vanishing gradients are addressed using additional additive components and forget gate activations, which helps gradients flow through the network more effectively, preventing them from diminishing too quickly.

LSTMs were proposed by Hochreiter and Schmidhuber in 1997. They address the vanishing gradient problem discussed earlier through a gating mechanism that allows for better control of information flow.

1. **Structure:**
   An LSTM unit contains three gates:
   a. Forget gate: Determines what information to discard from the memory cell.
   b. Input gate: Decides what new information to store in the memory cell.
   c. Output gate: Controls what information to output from the memory cell.
2. **Functioning:**
   - The forget gate employs a sigmoid function to produce values ranging from 0 to 1, which determines the extent to which information from the previous cell state is retained.
   - The input gate determines what new information to store in the cell state by utilizing both sigmoid and tanh functions.
   - The cell state is updated by discarding unnecessary information and incorporating new relevant information.
   - The output gate uses the updated cell state to determine the output, again employing sigmoid and tanh functions.

Examples:

1. Machine Translation: LSTMs are used in seq2seq models for translating between languages, capturing context and meaning across sentences.
2. Speech Recognition: LSTMs can process audio waveforms to transcribe speech to text, maintaining context over long audio sequences.
3. Sentiment Analysis: LSTMs can analyze text to determine sentiment, considering the entire context of a review or comment.

The following code builds and trains a simple LSTM model for a binary classification task using TensorFlow. It begins by generating dummy sequential data with train_x consisting of 1,000 samples, each having 10 time steps and 1 feature per step, and train_y containing binary labels (0 or 1) for each sample. The model is created using TensorFlow's Sequential API, starting with an LSTM layer with 50 units to process the temporal dependencies in the data, followed by a dense layer with a sigmoid activation function to output probabilities for binary classification. The model is compiled with the Adam optimizer, binary cross-entropy loss function, and accuracy as a performance metric. It is trained for 50 epochs with a batch size of 32, updating weights iteratively to minimize the loss and improve accuracy.

This is a simple LSTM network for sequential data processing, and binary classification tasks are demonstrated in this configuration. It can be expanded to operate with real-world datasets such as textual or time-series data.

```
import numpy as np
from tensorflow.keras.models import Sequential
from tensorflow.keras.layers import LSTM, Dense

train_x = np.random.random((1000, 10, 1))
train_y = np.random.randint(2, size=(1000, 1))
model = Sequential ()
model.add(LSTM(50, input_shape=(10, 1)))
model.add(Dense(1, activation='sigmoid'))
model.compile(optimizer='adam', loss='binary_crossen-
tropy', metrics=['accuracy'])
model.fit(train_x, train_y, epochs=50, batch_size=32)
```

7.6.2 GATED RECURRENT UNITS

GRUs merge the functionality of the input and forget gates in LSTMs into a single update gate, which controls the retention and addition of information. Because of this simplified design, there are fewer parameters, which facilitates easier implementation and faster training. GRUs effectively handle long-term dependencies in sequential data by dynamically regulating the flow of information, adapting to complex patterns based on the input sequence. Because of their memory efficiency and adaptability, they are frequently used for applications where sequential data modeling is essential, such as speech recognition, time-series forecasting, and natural language processing.

A GRU features two gates:

1. **Reset Gate:** Controls how much past information should be discarded.
2. **Update Gate:** Manages what information to discard and what new information to incorporate.
3. **Functionality:**
   - **Reset Gate:** Determines how new input is combined with previous memory.
   - **Update Gate:** Controls how much of the previous memory is retained.
   - **No Separate Cell State:** Information is transferred using the hidden state alone.
- **Examples:**
  1. Text Generation: GRUs can be used to generate coherent paragraphs of text, maintaining consistency in style and content.
  2. Music Generation: GRUs can learn patterns in musical sequences to compose new melodies or harmonies.
  3. Stock Price Prediction: GRUs can analyze historical stock data to forecast future prices, capturing both short-term and long-term trends.
- **Comparison:**
  - LSTMs generally have a slight edge in performance for longer sequences, but GRUs are computationally more efficient.
  - GRUs have a smaller number of parameters, which makes them easier to train and less likely to overfit on smaller datasets.
  - The decision to use LSTM or GRU typically depends on the specific task requirements and the computational resources available.

The following code demonstrates the model built using the Sequential API, with a single GRU layer comprising 32 units to process the sequential data and learn temporal dependencies. This is followed by a dense output layer with a sigmoid activation function, which outputs probabilities for binary classification.

```
import numpy as np
from tensorflow.keras.models import Sequential
from tensorflow.keras.layers import GRU, Dense

x_train = np.random.random((1000, 10, 1))
y_train = np.random.randint(2, size=(1000, 1))

model = Sequential([
GRU(32, input_shape=(10, 1)),
Dense(1, activation='sigmoid')
])
```

```
model.compile(optimizer='adam', loss='binary_crossen-
tropy', metrics=['accuracy'])
model.fit(x_train, y_train, epochs=50, batch_size=32)
```

Both LSTM and GRU have greatly enhanced the capability of RNNs to learn long-term dependencies in sequential data, making them widely used in applications such as time-series analysis and natural language processing.

REFERENCES

1. Masood S. Neural Networks and Deep Learning: A Comprehensive Overview of Modern Techniques and Applications. *Journal Environmental Sciences and Technology.* 2023 Dec 31;2(2):8–20.
2. https://github.com/rezkaaufar/pytorch-cvt
3. https://www.analyticsvidhya.com/blog/2020/10/what-is-the-convolutional-neural-network-architecture/
4. https://www.tensorflow.org/tutorials/images/cnn

8 Generative Artificial Intelligence

8.1 LARGE LANGUAGE MODELS

A large language model (LLM) is a kind of artificial intelligence (AI) algorithm that uses supervised learning techniques to process and comprehend human languages or text by applying neural network techniques with many parameters. Applications of the LLMs include chatbots, machine translation, text production, summary writing, image generation from texts, machine coding, and conversational AI. Such LLMs are Open AI's ChatGPT and Google's BERT (Bidirectional Encoder Representations from Transformers).

Numerous methods have been attempted to accomplish tasks related to natural language, but the LLM is solely built on deep learning approaches. LLMs are very effective in capturing the intricate relationships between entities in the text at hand. They can also produce the text using the syntactic and semantic structures of the specific language we want to use.

LLMs:

Model	Release Year	Parameter
GPT-1	2018	117 million
GPT-2	2019	1.5 billion
GPT-3	2020	175 billion
GPT-4	2023	1.76 trillions

Input Embeddings: Each token is embedded into a continuous vector representation. Input text is tokenized into smaller units, like words or sub-words. The input's syntactic and semantic information is captured in this embedding step.

Positional Encoding: Positional encoding is applied to the input embeddings to provide information about the token positions. This makes it possible for the model to handle the tokens while accounting for their sequential order.

Encoder: An encoder is based on a neural network technique. It determines the context and meaning of text data by analyzing the input text and generating a number of hidden states. Each encoder layer has two basic subcomponents as given below.

> ➢ Self-Attention Mechanism: By calculating attention scores, self-attention mechanism allows the model to assess the relative relevance of various tokens in the input sequence. It enables the model to take into account the relationships and dependencies among various tokens in a context-aware way.

DOI: 10.1201/9781003532170-8

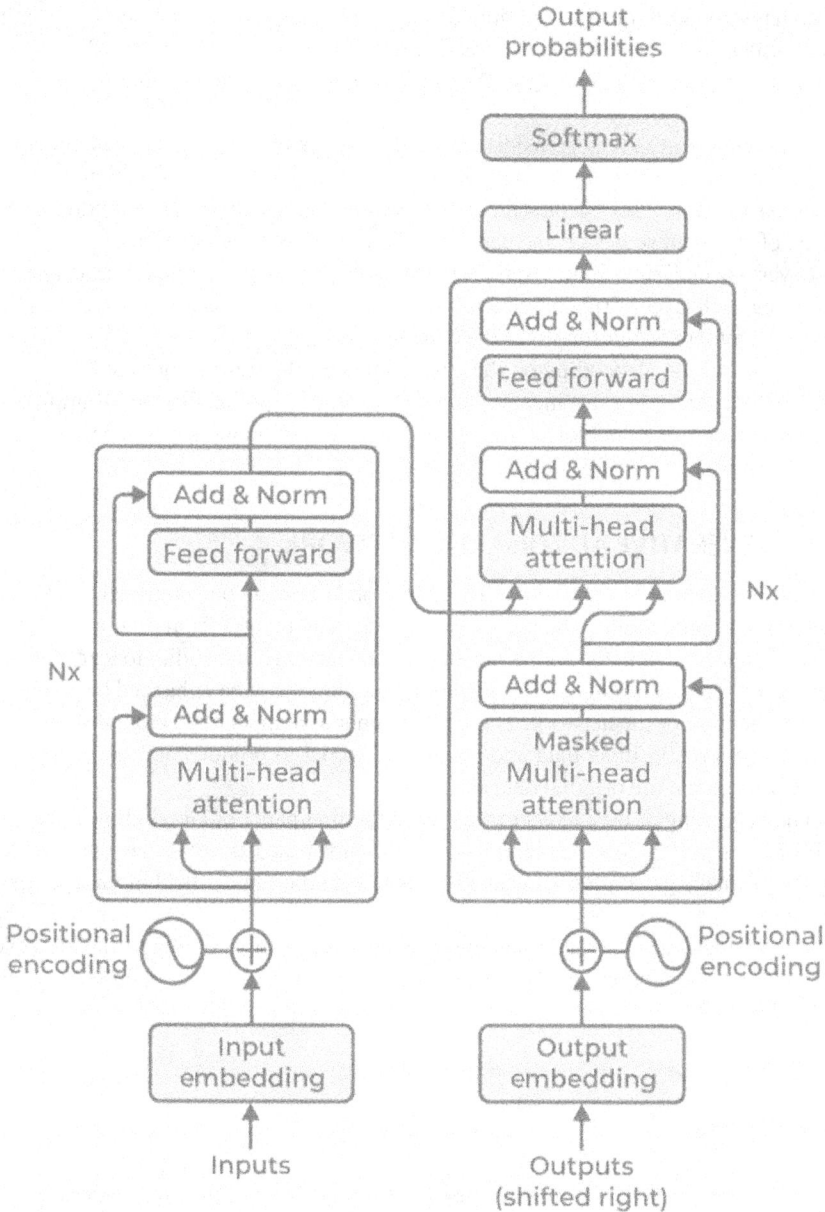

FIGURE 8.1 LLM Components.

> Feed-Forward Neural Network: Each token has to pass through an independent feed-forward neural network following the self-attention phase. FFNN comprises fully connected layers with nonlinear activation functions. This model can handle capture complex interactions between tokens.

Decoder Layers: A decoder component is sometimes added with the encoder in transformer-based models. Autoregressive generation, in which the model produces successive outputs by attending to the previously generated tokens, is made possible by the decoder layers.

Multi-Head Attention: Transformer architecture is used for multi-head attention, which involves performing self-attention concurrently while using various learned attention weights. This enables the model to simultaneously focus on multiple segments of the input sequence and capture different kinds of associations.

Layer Normalizing: In the transformer architecture, layer normalizing is applied following each layer or subcomponent. It enhances the model's capacity to generalize across many inputs and stabilizes the learning process.

Output Layers: Depending on the particular task, the transformer model's output layers may change. For instance, in language modeling, probability distribution over the subsequent token is typically generated by a linear projection followed by softmax activation.

8.2   GENERATIVE ADVERSARIAL NETWORK

Generative adversarial network (GAN) has been one of the prominent topics in research and production. The ability to generate new images from random numbers has contributed a lot in the field of unsupervised learning. The ability to learn the distribution of datasets using various different techniques can be enhanced by changing the architecture of the network. The goal of generative modeling is to independently identify patterns in input data and enable the model to produce new examples that feasibly resemble the original dataset.

The beginning of the GAN era was when the first paper of Goodfellow et al. was published in NIPS 2014. Generator–discriminator-based training has changed the course of image generation and has given a new method in the field of unsupervised learning.

The idea where some random numbers are able to produce an image that has never existed, or some random numbers generating a face that has never been seen, seems

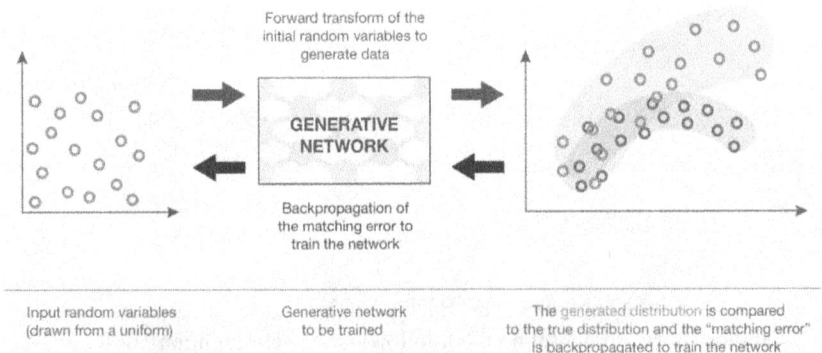

FIGURE 8.2   Generative Matching Networks.

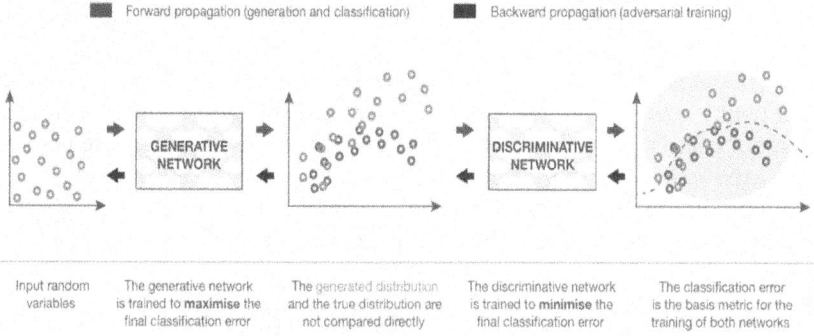

Forward propagation (generation and classification)   Backward propagation (adversarial training)

| Input random variables | The generative network is trained to **maximise** the final classification error | The generated distribution and the true distribution are not compared directly | The discriminative network is trained to **minimise** the final classification error | The classification error is the basis metric for the training of both networks |

FIGURE 8.3   Roles of Generator and Discriminator in GAN.

like a magic at first glance; however, the ability of computers aren't magic but some bunch of smart algorithms, which need a processing unit to produce such results.

The idea of generating image has been long there but has the inability to produce better results. The underlying principle before GANs was to use random numbers, with distribution as the input and vector as the output, which equals the dimension of an image from the original dataset, with a generator based on the neural network, as a function to learn the parameters. The model learns by comparing the output vector with the image vector using different methods. This in turn is learned by the neural network using the backpropagation algorithm.

Since the probability distribution of the dataset is a very complex one, the generator network is unable to learn the distribution most of times. This is a direct method of training generative networks.

Since there was a need of new methods to learn the distribution and the idea of GAN evolved, GAN is based on a min–max game, which consists of two networks—a discriminator and a generator. The duty of a generator is to generate image, where the input is a random vector generated from a predetermined distribution and the output of the generator is having the dimension as that of the image. This generator network learns using a discriminator network, whose role is to identify if an image feed into a model is a real image or not, i.e., the output of model is a number between 0 and 1, where the higher value shows greater confidence in image input from a real distribution.

GAN training has a generator and a discriminator, which are trained simultaneously to improve the output.

The generator and discriminator are trained simultaneously using backpropagation to reach a point where a discriminator is unable to identify whether the input is from the real image distribution or generated as an output from a generator network.

In an ideal case, the generator and discriminator reach the point of Nash equilibrium. At this point, the discriminator has a value of 0.5 for any input, but in practical applications, the GAN is an unstable model that is highly affected by the model architecture and the values of hyperparameters. But still the results by the GAN was convincing, producing a new method of training generator networks, which have evolved greatly and revolutionized the field of unsupervised and semi-supervised learning.

Hyperparameters are one of the major components of any network that requires proper tuning for each use case. Especially for GANs that are very unstable in training, training of the networks is done simultaneously until the images are not clear. Since GANs lack in proper evaluation metric, it is hard to evaluate them too.

As described earlier, GANs are highly unstable and it's hard to train them, so any change in architecture layers and learning rate can have adverse effects on the network.

8.3   RETRIEVAL AUGMENTATION GENERATION

It is a method that combines retrieval-based techniques with generative models to produce more accurate and contextually relevant responses, especially when dealing with vast amounts of information. The idea behind retrieval augmentation generation (RAG) is to use external knowledge sources (like a database, a set of documents, or a search engine) to fetch relevant information and then feed this information into generative models (such as GPT-3 or GPT-4) to produce a final response.

8.3.1   RAG VERSUS LLMs

1. **Knowledge Limitations:** LLMs have knowledgebase till 2021 and its was trained on available data till date only. They are not updated to the current level, so they cannot work on real data. This can lead to outdated/inaccurate information. But RAG can provide us up-to-date information.
2. In RAG, it is possible to keep sensitive data out of training to have data control and to maintain security.
3. No need of retaining on full data all time leads to cost-efficiency.
4. The source of information for regular LLMs is unknown, but RAG has a verifiable source of information, which makes it more antithetic.

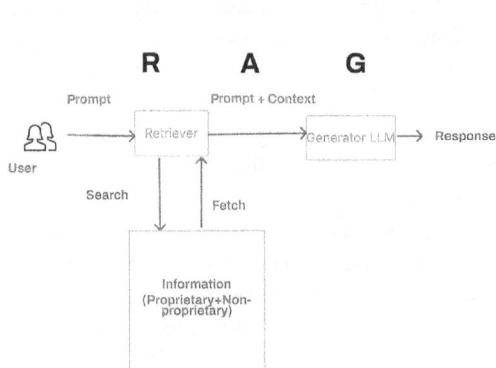

FIGURE 8.4   RAG Components.

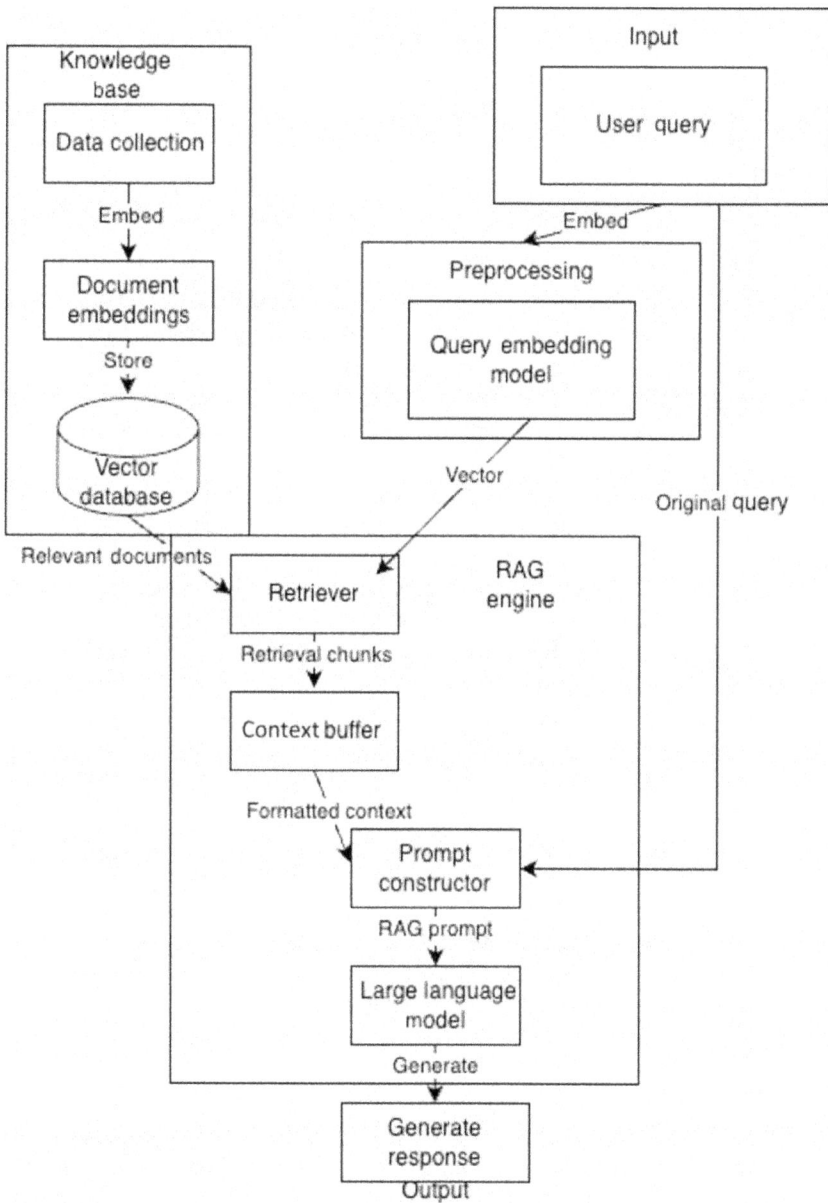

FIGURE 8.5   RAG Architecture.

In LLMs, user queries are directly forwarded, but in RAG a new component knowledge base and RAG engine are added. Knowledge base is a collection of documents. From input prompt, a query is forwarded to the retriever. Retriever retrieves relevant information from the knowledge base. Only relevant documents reach the retriever. The retriever will augment user query along with relevant documents to LLMs, which will give the final response. RAG engines perform of three roles: retrieval, augmentation, and generation. User query along with relevant augmented documents makes RAG prompt and feed to LLMs, which leads to improved output.

We will discuss each part below:

I. Knowledge Base: It consist of 3 elements.
   a. Document Collection: This is the source of information, a repository of documents containing various knowledge sources (articles, manuals, and product information).
   b. Document Embedding: Each document is processed to create document embedding (vector representations) that captures the semantic meaning of text.
   c. Vector databases: The embedding is stored in a vector database that allows for faster retrieval based on similarity searches.
      i. Input: This is the input from the user.
      ii. Prepossessing: The user query is transformed into a query embedding model, similar to how the documents were embedded.
2. RAG Engine:a. Retriever: This component searches the vector database to find relevant document embedding based on the similarity with the query vector. It retrieves the most relevant chunks of information.
   b. Context Builder: After retrieval, the selected chunks are compiled into a formatted context that helps the language model to respond accurately.
   c. Prompt Constructor: It combines the user's original query with the retrieved context, creating a RAG prompt that can be fed into a language model.
   d. Generator (LLM): The final output is a generated response that uses both the retrieved context and language model's capabilities, providing a more accurate and informative answer for the user.

8.4   TRANSFER LEARNING

A technique called transfer learning enables models to apply previously learned information to new, related tasks. A model can tackle new problems more successfully and efficiently by reusing what it has already learned rather than beginning from scratch. When there is little data available for a novel topic, this method is quite beneficial.

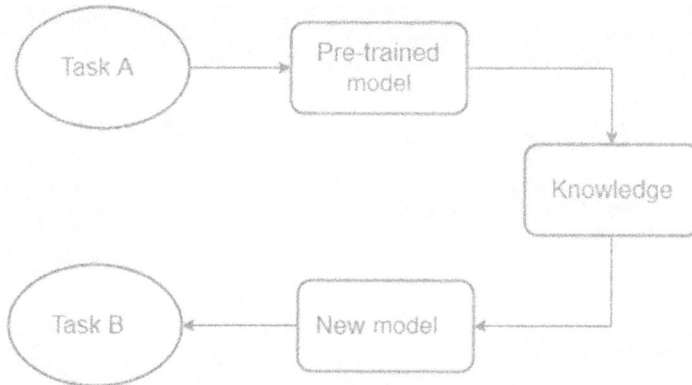

FIGURE 8.6 Transfer Learning Model.

In order to use preexisting information from a pretrained model for new tasks, transfer learning entails a systematic process:

Pretrained Model: A model that is already trained on a large dataset for a specific task is a pretrained model. This pretrained model has picked up general characteristics and patterns that apply to similar tasks.

Base Model: This pretrained model, sometimes referred to as the base model, consists of layers that have learned hierarchical representations through data processing, capturing features ranging from simple to intricate.

Transfer Layer: Find the base model's layers that contain generic data relevant to the original and new jobs. These layers, which are frequently found close to the network's top, record general, repeatable features.

Fine-tuning: Use the information from the new task to refine these chosen layers. This procedure improves accuracy and flexibility by preserving previously learned information while modifying parameters to fit the demands of the novel assignment.

Generative AI tools are very powerful tools for text, image, and video generation. They have a variety of applications and can be used in different sectors of life for different purposes, and the need for a better algorithm rises with increasing demand. Tools like ChatGPT and Gemini have created personalized virtual assistants to this community, and in the future, they will be explored more to empower the community.

9 AI in Healthcare
Diagnostics, Treatment, and Beyond

9.1 INTRODUCTION

9.1.1 OVERVIEW OF AI IN HEALTHCARE

- **Definition and Scope:** Artificial intelligence (AI) refers to a suite of technologies designed to enable machines to perform tasks that would typically require human intelligence. These technologies include machine learning (ML), which allows computers to learn from and make predictions based on data and deep learning, a subset of ML that employs neural networks to process complex data, such as images. In healthcare, AI is making its mark by transforming how patient care is delivered and how administrative processes are managed within healthcare organizations, including providers, payers, and pharmaceutical companies (Kyrimi et al. 2025).

  AI's application in healthcare is vast and growing. It ranges from enhancing diagnostic accuracy and personalizing treatment plans to optimizing administrative tasks. For instance, AI algorithms are now capable of analyzing medical imaging with a level of precision that often surpasses human radiologists, identifying malignant tumors, and guiding clinical trial design more efficiently. Despite these advances, the widespread replacement of human roles in medical processes is still a distant reality. The current focus is on leveraging AI to complement and enhance human capabilities rather than replacing them entirely (Davenport and Kalakota 2019).

- **Historical Context and Evolution:** The integration of AI into healthcare began with early systems that aimed to replicate the decision-making processes of medical experts. Initial efforts in the 20th century laid the groundwork, but significant progress was hampered by limited data and computational power. As the field evolved, the introduction of ML and, later, deep learning (De Fauw et al. 2018) technologies marked pivotal milestones. These advancements allowed for more sophisticated data analysis and pattern recognition.

  In recent years, the advent of big data and improved computational resources has catalyzed AI's role in healthcare (Talmele and Shrawankar 2022). Modern AI systems can now access and analyze extensive datasets from electronic health records, medical imaging, and genetic information. This capability enables AI to identify patterns and trends that may be invisible to human observers, leading to earlier disease detection and more

DOI: 10.1201/9781003532170-9

effective treatment strategies. For example, AI can now uncover previously unknown genetic markers linked to specific cancers, providing valuable insights for both diagnosis and research (Steiner et al. 2018).

AI also excels in predictive analytics, assessing patient risks, and forecasting treatment outcomes. Its ability to predict complications and treatment efficacy allows for more proactive and personalized care. Additionally, AI streamlines administrative functions by automating routine tasks such as scheduling, report generation, and data organization. This automation not only reduces the burden on healthcare professionals but also improves operational efficiency within healthcare systems (Shrawankar et al. 2021).

Despite these advancements, the full-scale implementation of AI in healthcare faces several barriers. Challenges such as data privacy, integration with existing systems, and the need for regulatory frameworks are critical considerations. As AI continues to evolve, its integration into healthcare promises to enhance patient care and operational efficiency while addressing these ongoing challenges (Wazalwar and Shrawankar 2021).

9.2 AI IN DIAGNOSTICS

AI has become an essential tool in medical diagnostics (Kaczmarczyk et al. 2024), transforming traditional methods by offering more precision and speed in disease detection and analysis. Its applications span across various domains, including medical imaging, pathology, and genomics. AI's ability to process large datasets and identify intricate patterns has paved the way for advancements in personalized medicine and targeted treatment strategies (Pati 2024).

Medical Imaging

- **AI in Radiology:** AI algorithms are being used to analyze medical images such as X-rays, CT scans, and MRIs. These tools can detect abnormalities, like tumors or fractures, with high accuracy, often matching or surpassing human radiologists. For instance, AI systems are used in mammography to identify early signs of breast cancer, potentially improving survival rates.
- **Case Studies:** An example of AI's impact is Google's DeepMind, which has developed systems that can accurately detect retinal diseases from eye scans. Other startups are also developing AI-based image interpretation tools to support diagnostic processes in radiology.

Pathology

- **AI in Analyzing Biopsy Samples:** AI has revolutionized the analysis of tissue samples, making it quicker and more accurate. By scanning and processing high-resolution biopsy images, AI can detect the presence of diseases like cancer, providing pathologists with valuable insights. This leads to more consistent and reliable diagnoses.
- **Innovations in Digital Pathology:** AI-powered digital pathology platforms enhance diagnostic accuracy by processing complex tissue images,

uncovering patterns that may be missed by human observation. These systems are now increasingly used in clinical practice, helping streamline the workflow for pathologists (Aggarwal et al. 2025).

Genomics

- **AI in Interpreting Genetic Data:** AI assists in decoding vast amounts of genetic information to identify variations that may cause diseases. This capability supports healthcare providers in understanding patients' genetic profiles, which is critical for developing personalized treatment plans.
- **Precision Medicine:** AI's ability to analyze genetic mutations has paved the way for precision medicine, where treatments are tailored to an individual's genetic makeup. For example, in cancer care, AI can recommend targeted drug therapies based on a patient's specific genetic alterations, resulting in more effective treatments.

9.2.1 Transforming Healthcare with AI Applications

AI is not limited to diagnostics; its applications in healthcare include robotic surgery, drug discovery, and enhancing patient outcomes.

- **Enhancing Diagnostic Accuracy:** AI systems outperform traditional methods in identifying conditions like tumors, allowing for earlier interventions.
- **Robotic Surgery:** AI-driven robotic arms enable minimally invasive surgeries, providing surgeons with greater precision and reducing patient recovery times (Knudsen et al. 2024).
- **Accelerating Drug Discovery:** AI speeds up the drug discovery process by analyzing biological data to identify new treatment targets, significantly reducing the time needed to bring new drugs to patients.

9.3   AI IN TREATMENT

AI is significantly revolutionizing treatment methods in healthcare, by contributing to drug discovery, personalized medicine, and robotic surgery. Despite the challenges in implementation, its potential for transforming medical care is vast.

9.3.1 Drug Discovery and Development

- **AI's Role in Identifying New Drugs:** AI algorithms have the ability to predict compounds that could be effective against various diseases, speeding up the drug discovery process. Traditional drug development can take years, with significant costs involved. AI reduces this timeline by analyzing vast datasets of biological information and chemical compounds to identify promising drug targets. By simulating chemical interactions, AI can efficiently screen large libraries of compounds, identifying potential candidates for further testing. For instance, pharmaceutical companies leverage AI to explore the efficacy of new molecules and compounds, leading to the discovery of innovative treatments more quickly (Abbas 2024).

- **Accelerating Clinical Trials:** AI not only expedites drug discovery but also optimizes clinical trials by identifying suitable candidates and analyzing trial data in real time. Machine learning (ML) models can sort through patient data, considering factors like genetics, medical history, and current health status to select the best participants for a trial. This targeted approach improves trial outcomes and accelerates the drug approval process, bringing new treatments to patients faster.

9.3.2 Personalized Medicine

- **Tailoring Treatments Using AI:** Personalized medicine is a groundbreaking application of AI in healthcare, focusing on customizing treatment plans based on individual patient data. By analyzing medical history, genetic profiles, lifestyle factors, and responses to past treatments, AI creates a tailored approach to care, potentially leading to more effective outcomes. In cancer care, for instance, AI can assess genetic mutations in tumors and suggest targeted drug therapies specifically designed for those mutations, enhancing treatment effectiveness (Marra and Laskin 2020).
- **Success Stories:** Notable examples include AI-driven cancer treatment recommendations where AI systems identify the most effective therapies based on a patient's unique genetic markers. Companies like Foundation Medicine and Flatiron Health are working on creating personalized cancer treatment plans, addressing the complexity of genetic variants in cancer. The integration of AI in precision medicine aims to shift from a one-size-fits-all approach to individualized care, reducing adverse reactions and improving success rates.

9.3.3 Robotic Surgery

- **Advances in Robotic-Assisted Surgeries:** AI is at the forefront of robotic-assisted surgeries, enhancing precision and control during surgical procedures. Modern robotic systems, often guided by AI, allow for minimally invasive surgeries that reduce recovery times and improve patient outcomes. These systems provide surgeons with better visualization and dexterity, allowing them to perform complex procedures with heightened accuracy (BBC News 2024).
- **Benefits and Limitations:** While robotic surgery offers numerous advantages such as minimal invasiveness, shorter recovery times, and reduced risk of human error, it also comes with limitations. High costs and the need for specialized training present challenges to widespread adoption. Additionally, technical difficulties and the need for seamless integration into clinical workflows remain hurdles to be addressed.

AI in treatment is already making strides in personalized medicine, accelerating drug discovery, and enhancing robotic surgery. Its applications have the potential to deliver more effective, tailored healthcare solutions, transforming traditional treatment models. Although challenges in implementation and integration remain, ongoing research and development promise a future where AI plays an indispensable role in patient care.

9.4 AI IN PATIENT MANAGEMENT AND MONITORING

AI's integration into patient management and monitoring is transforming healthcare delivery, making it more proactive and personalized. The use of AI-powered wearable technology and remote patient monitoring is particularly impactful in managing chronic diseases, enhancing patient outcomes, and improving accessibility to healthcare.

9.4.1 WEARABLE TECHNOLOGY

- **AI-Powered Wearables:** Modern wearable devices, such as smartwatches, fitness trackers, and health-monitoring patches, are equipped with AI algorithms that continuously track a variety of health metrics. These devices collect data on vital signs like heart rate, blood pressure, sleep patterns, oxygen levels, and physical activity. AI then processes this vast amount of data to provide personalized health insights and recommendations. For instance, smartwatches can detect irregular heart rhythms, potentially identifying atrial fibrillation in its early stages, which is crucial for timely medical intervention.
- **Examples and Outcomes**: Continuous glucose monitors (CGMs) for diabetes provide real-time tracking of blood sugar levels, helping patients make informed decisions. Wearable ECGs detect heart anomalies, allowing for timely medical intervention, ultimately improving patient outcomes.

9.4.2 REMOTE PATIENT MONITORING

- **AI's Role in Telemedicine:** Telemedicine has become increasingly important, especially in remote and underserved areas. AI enhances remote patient monitoring by facilitating virtual consultations, automating health assessments, and analyzing patient data to support decision-making. AI-driven platforms can collect data from wearable devices, smartphones, or home health monitors and provide clinicians with actionable insights. For instance, AI can process data from a patient's digital health record and wearable devices during a teleconsultation to offer a comprehensive health status analysis, guiding healthcare professionals in diagnosis and treatment planning.
- **Impact on Chronic Disease Management:** For chronic conditions like heart disease and diabetes, AI analyses patient data over time, predicting potential health issues and enabling early interventions, thereby reducing hospital admissions and improving patient quality of life.

9.5 AI IN ADMINISTRATIVE TASKS

AI streamlines healthcare administration by automating routine processes, managing patient data, and reducing operational costs.

9.5.1 WORKFLOW OPTIMIZATION

- **Automating Administrative Processes:** AI applications, such as robotic process automation (RPA), handle repetitive tasks like scheduling, billing, and record-keeping. This automation reduces the administrative burden on medical staff, allowing them to focus more on patient care. For example, RPA can manage claims processing, clinical documentation, and revenue cycle management, speeding up operations (Pahuja 2024).
- **Reducing Operational Costs:** By automating tasks, healthcare facilities can significantly cut costs and enhance efficiency. With AI handling routine activities, there's a reduction in manual errors, ultimately saving time and resources.

9.5.2 ELECTRONIC HEALTH RECORDS

- **Managing and Analyzing Patient Data:** AI improves electronic health record (EHR) systems by enabling accurate data entry, predictive analytics, and seamless patient data management. Advanced AI can analyze vast amounts of medical data, supporting clinicians in making informed decisions for better patient care. AI's role extends to detecting coding errors in claims processing, saving stakeholders time and money through efficient audits (Shah et al. 2024).

While AI's impact on administrative tasks isn't as revolutionary as in patient care, it brings significant efficiency, addressing issues like 25% of nurses' time spent on regulatory activities. Although technologies like chatbots have shown promise for tasks such as prescription refills and appointment scheduling, usability concerns remain.

9.6 ETHICAL AND PRIVACY CONSIDERATIONS

The integration of AI in healthcare brings significant ethical and privacy challenges, particularly in data security, transparency, bias, and equitable access.

9.6.1 DATA PRIVACY

- **Ensuring Patient Data Security:** With AI relying on vast amounts of sensitive health data, safeguarding patient information is crucial. Measures like data encryption, secure storage, and strict access controls are vital to prevent data breaches. Healthcare organizations must prioritize protecting this information to maintain patient trust and confidentiality.

- **Regulations and Compliance:** Regulatory frameworks like Health Insurance Portability and Accountability Act (HIPAA) in the United States and General Data Protection Regulation (GDPR) in Europe govern data privacy. These regulations enforce strict guidelines on how patient data is collected, stored, and shared, ensuring that AI applications in healthcare adhere to legal and ethical standards.

9.6.2   Bias and Fairness

- **Addressing AI Bias:** AI systems can inadvertently introduce bias, affecting healthcare outcomes. For example, predictive algorithms might show bias based on gender or race, potentially leading to inequitable care. To mitigate this, developers must ensure that AI models are trained on diverse datasets and regularly monitored to identify and address biases.
- **Ensuring Equitable Access:** AI solutions must be designed to serve all populations fairly, avoiding disparities in healthcare access. Equitable AI should consider various socioeconomic, cultural, and regional factors, ensuring that advancements in AI-driven healthcare do not widen existing gaps.

9.6.3   Transparency and Accountability

AI systems, especially deep learning algorithms used for image analysis, often operate as "black boxes," making them difficult to interpret. When patients receive diagnoses or treatment recommendations from AI, they deserve to understand the reasoning behind those decisions. However, current AI technologies may lack the ability to provide clear explanations.

- **Accountability for Mistakes:** AI systems in healthcare are not immune to errors. Establishing accountability for incorrect diagnoses or treatment recommendations made by AI is a complex issue that healthcare providers and regulators need to address. Additionally, there is a risk that AI could dehumanize healthcare, making decisions overly data-driven and potentially overlooking the nuances of empathy and human judgment.

9.6.4   Balancing AI with Human Care

As AI's role in patient care grows, it's crucial to maintain a balance between AI's efficiency and the human touch in healthcare. While AI can streamline processes and enhance diagnosis accuracy, healthcare institutions and regulatory bodies must monitor its impact and create governance mechanisms to address ethical challenges responsibly. This ongoing attention will ensure that AI's benefits are maximized while minimizing potential negative consequences (Landau et al. 2025).

9.7 CHALLENGES AND LIMITATIONS

While AI presents exciting possibilities for transforming healthcare, it also faces several challenges and limitations that must be addressed for its successful integration into the industry (Bertl et al. 2024).

9.7.1 TECHNICAL CHALLENGES

- **Limitations of Current AI Technologies:** AI technologies are still evolving, and their current limitations include data quality issues and algorithmic accuracy. Healthcare data is often fragmented, stored in different formats, and filled with inconsistencies, making it difficult for AI systems to analyze accurately. Additionally, many AI algorithms require extensive training on high-quality datasets to ensure accuracy, and without this, their effectiveness in real-world healthcare settings may be compromised. Moreover, some AI models, particularly deep learning algorithms, function as "black boxes," providing little transparency into how they arrive at specific conclusions, which can limit their use in clinical decision-making.
- **Integration with Existing Systems:** Integrating AI solutions into current healthcare systems and workflows is a significant challenge. Many healthcare facilities use legacy systems that may not be easily compatible with modern AI technologies. Moreover, a seamless integration requires healthcare professionals to adapt to new tools and processes, which often involves a steep learning curve and potential disruptions to established workflows. Customization and interoperability between AI systems and existing EHRs are crucial for smooth implementation.

9.7.2 REGULATORY AND LEGAL CHALLENGES

- **Navigating Complexity:** AI tools must navigate complex regulations to ensure patient safety, privacy, and unbiased operation. Establishing clear guidelines is vital, balancing innovation with safety requirements.
- **Liability Issues:** When AI systems make errors, defining who is responsible—the healthcare provider, AI developer, or institution—remains unclear. Proper frameworks for accountability are essential to manage risks and protect patients.

9.7.3 COST AND INFRASTRUCTURE

Implementing AI demands significant investment in IT infrastructure, data storage, and computational resources. Smaller healthcare facilities, especially in underserved areas, may struggle to afford these technologies, risking increased disparities in care access.

9.7.4 Public Perception

- **Building Trust and Acceptance:** Public perception is a critical factor in the adoption of AI in healthcare. Patients may be wary of relying on AI for their health-related decisions due to concerns about privacy, data security, and the impersonal nature of machine-driven care. Educating patients and the public about the benefits and limitations of AI can help build trust and alleviate concerns. Healthcare providers must emphasize that AI is a tool to support, not replace, human expertise, highlighting its role in enhancing, rather than detracting from, patient-centered care.

9.8 FUTURE DIRECTIONS

AI's future in healthcare is filled with promise, with several innovations and trends shaping the next decade.

9.8.1 Emerging Trends

- **Innovations on the Horizon:** Upcoming advancements in AI will revolutionize healthcare (Parthasarathy 2024), such as mental health applications that provide personalized therapy and AI-driven gene editing for targeted treatments. Additionally, real-time diagnostics, continuous patient monitoring, and AI-powered virtual assistants will support patients in managing their health independently.
- **Predictions for AI's Impact:** AI is expected to drive a shift toward personalized medicine, allowing treatments tailored to each patient's genetic makeup and lifestyle. As AI's capabilities in image analysis, speech, and text recognition continue to grow, it will become integral to clinical tasks, improving healthcare outcomes and reducing costs. However, AI will augment, rather than replace, clinicians—freeing them to focus on empathy, patient communication, and holistic care.

9.8.2 Research and Development

- **Ongoing Research Efforts:** Research initiatives are rapidly advancing AI technologies, focusing on areas like precision medicine, drug discovery, and disease prediction. AI-powered drug discovery is expected to uncover novel treatment pathways for complex diseases such as cancer and Alzheimer's, significantly accelerating the process.
- **Collaboration between Tech Companies and Healthcare Providers:** Partnerships between tech companies and healthcare institutions are vital for developing new AI solutions. These collaborations will help ensure AI tools are tailored to real-world healthcare needs, drive innovation, and facilitate the integration of AI into everyday clinical practice (Alowais et al. 2023).

AI's role in healthcare's future will hinge not only on technological capabilities but also on overcoming adoption challenges. This includes gaining regulatory approval, integrating AI with EHRs, and ensuring standardization. Widespread adoption will likely take longer than technological maturity, with the limited use of AI in clinical settings within the next 5 years and more extensive implementation within 10.

While AI will become more sophisticated, it won't replace human clinicians. Instead, it will support them, handling tasks like data analysis, diagnostics, and patient communication. In turn, healthcare professionals will focus on unique human skills, such as empathy and decision-making.

9.8.3 SEAMLESS AI INTEGRATION

The ultimate goal is seamless AI integration into healthcare, creating a future where AI systems act as partners in care. As AI continues to advance, it will redefine patient–provider relationships, enabling more efficient, effective, and personalized healthcare experiences.

9.9 CASE STUDIES

CASE STUDY REMOTE SURGERY USING AI AND ROBOTICS

Background: In 2024, a notable remote surgery was performed on a 57-year-old woman with a complex abdominal condition. The procedure was conducted by a surgical team located over 1,200 kilometers away from the patient (Panahi 2024).

TECHNOLOGY USED:

1. **da Vinci Surgical System:** Advanced robotic platform enabling minimally invasive surgery.
2. **AI-Powered Navigation:** Provided real-time guidance and feedback during the procedure.
3. **High-Speed Connectivity:** Enabled secure, real-time control and video streaming.

Procedure: The surgery, involving complex laparoscopic techniques, was successfully completed with the robotic system controlled remotely. AI-enhanced navigation improved precision and outcomes.

OUTCOME:

- **Success:** The patient experienced minimal complications and a faster recovery.
- **Feedback:** Surgeons praised the AI and robotic system for their accuracy and efficiency.

LESSONS LEARNED:

1. **Access to Care:** Remote surgery can provide specialized care to underserved areas.
2. **Challenges:** Issues included communication latency and cybersecurity needs.
3. **Future Implications:** This case highlights the potential for expanding remote surgical capabilities globally.

SUCCESSFUL IMPLEMENTATIONS

1. IBM Watson for Oncology

- **Application:** IBM Watson for Oncology uses AI to assist oncologists in diagnosing and treating cancer. It analyses patient data, medical literature, and clinical trial results to recommend personalized treatment options (Somashekhar et al. 2018).
- **Outcome:** Successfully deployed in several hospitals, it has shown promise in providing evidence-based treatment recommendations and aiding in decision-making.
- **Lessons Learned:** The system demonstrated the potential of AI to support complex medical decisions, but challenges included integrating Watson into existing workflows and adapting it to various cancer types.

2. Google's DeepMind Health

- **Application:** DeepMind's AI technology is used for diagnosing eye diseases by analyzing retinal scans. It can detect conditions like diabetic retinopathy and age-related macular degeneration with high accuracy.
- **Outcome:** Implemented in the UK's National Health Service (NHS), it has improved diagnostic accuracy and reduced the time required for analysis.
- **Lessons Learned:** The project highlighted the importance of high-quality data and collaboration with healthcare providers. However, issues like data privacy and system integration were noted.

3. PathAI

- **Application:** PathAI leverages AI to enhance the accuracy of pathological diagnoses by analyzing medical images. It assists pathologists in identifying cancerous tissues in biopsy samples.
- **Outcome:** The technology has been successfully used in several pathology labs, leading to improved diagnostic accuracy and efficiency.
- **Lessons Learned:** PathAI's success underscores the value of AI in augmenting human expertise. Challenges included ensuring algorithm transparency and overcoming initial resistance from pathologists.

LESSONS LEARNED

- **Integration with Existing Systems:** Successful AI applications often require seamless integration with existing healthcare systems and workflows. Addressing interoperability issues and ensuring that AI tools complement rather than disrupt current practices is crucial.
- **Data Quality and Privacy:** High-quality data is essential for AI effectiveness. Maintaining data privacy and addressing ethical concerns about patient information are vital to the success and acceptance of AI applications.
- **User Training and Adoption:** Training healthcare professionals to effectively use AI tools and addressing their concerns about new technologies can facilitate smoother adoption and maximize the benefits of AI.
- **Continuous Evaluation:** Ongoing evaluation and iteration are necessary to refine AI systems based on real-world feedback and performance, ensuring that they continue to meet clinical needs effectively.
- Contains supplementary charts and graphs that visually summarize and support the key findings and data presented.

9.10   CONCLUSION

SUMMARY OF KEY POINTS

- **Impact of AI:** AI is transforming healthcare through improved diagnostics, personalized treatment plans, and enhanced patient management. Key areas of impact include faster and more accurate diagnoses, predictive analytics for disease management, and advancements in virtual and mental health support.
- **Challenges and Considerations:** Despite its potential, AI faces challenges such as data privacy concerns, algorithmic bias, and the need for effective integration with existing systems. Addressing these issues is crucial for ensuring equitable and effective AI use in healthcare.

IMPLICATIONS FOR THE FUTURE

- **Shaping the Future:** AI is set to revolutionize healthcare by augmenting the capabilities of healthcare professionals, leading to more precise diagnoses, tailored treatments, and preventive measures. As

AI technology evolves, its role in healthcare will expand, offering new opportunities for improving patient outcomes and efficiency.

- **Responsible Implementation:** Ensuring the responsible use of AI involves developing robust cybersecurity measures, establishing clear guidelines for AI algorithms, and fostering collaboration between healthcare organizations, researchers, and regulatory bodies. Continuous investment in R&D and addressing limitations such as bias and data quality will be essential.
- **Public Perception and Trust:** Building public trust in AI is vital. While patients are open to using AI for health purposes, they still value human interaction in complex cases. Effective communication and education about AI's benefits and limitations will help integrate these technologies smoothly into healthcare practice.

Overall, the future of AI in healthcare promises significant advancements in patient care, efficiency, and access to personalized treatment (Aparna 2024). By overcoming current challenges and fostering collaboration, AI has the potential to greatly enhance the healthcare landscape.

REFERENCES

Abbas, Ahmed. (2024). *The Role of AI in Drug Discovery*. Chemistry Europe. https://chemistry-europe.onlinelibrary.wiley.com/doi/10.1002/cbic.202300816

Aggarwal, Arpit, Bharadwaj, Satvika, Corredor, Germán, Pathak, Tilak, Badve, Sunil, & Madabhushi, Anant. (2025). Artificial intelligence in digital pathology — time for a reality check. *The Nature Reviews of Clinical Oncology*. https://link.springer.com/article/10.1038/s41571-025-00991-6

Alowais, S. A., Alghamdi, S. S., Alsuhebany, N., Alqahtani, T., Alshaya, A. I., Almohareb, S. N., Aldairem, A., Alrashed, M., Bin Saleh, K., Badreldin, H. A., Al Yami, M. S., Al Harbi, S., & Albekairy, A. M. (2023). Revolutionizing healthcare: The role of artificial intelligence in clinical practice. *BMC Medical Education*, *23*, Article 689. https://bmc-mededuc.biomedcentral.com/articles/10.1186/s12909-023-04698-z

Aparna, M. (2024). Role of AI in healthcare. *Proceedings of the 5th International Conference on Data Science, Machine Learning and Applications*, *2*. https://link.springer.com/chapter/10.1007/978-981-97-8043-3_153

BBC News. (2024, February 18). Surgeons perform world's first remote surgery using 5G technology. *BBC News - Surgeons Perform World's First Remote Surgery Using 5G Technology*.

Bertl, Markus, et al. (2024). Challenges for AI in healthcare systems. *Bridging the Gap between AI and Reality*, 165–186. https://link.springer.com/chapter/10.1007/978-3-031-73741-1_11

Davenport, T., & Kalakota, R. (2019). The potential for artificial intelligence in healthcare. *Future Healthcare Journal*, *6*(2), 94–98. https://doi.org/10.7861/futurehosp.6-2-94

De Fauw, J., et al. (2018). Clinically applicable deep learning for diagnosis and referral in retinal disease. *Nature Medicine*, *24*(9), 1342–1350. https://www.nature.com/articles/s41591-018-0107-6

Kaczmarczyk, Robert, Wilhelm, Theresa Isabelle, Martin, Ron, & Roos, Jonas. (2024). Evaluating multimodal AI in medical diagnostics. *npj Digital Medicine*, 7, Article 205. https://link.springer.com/content/pdf/10.1038/s41746-024-01208-3.pdf

Knudsen, J. Everett, et al. (2024). Clinical applications of artifcial intelligence in robotic surgery. *Journal of Robotic Surgery*. https://doi.org/10.1038/s41746-024-01208-3

Kyrimi, Evangelia, et al. (2025). Explainable AI: definition and attributes of a good explanation for health AI. *AI and Ethics*. https://doi.org/10.1007/s43681-025-00668-x

Landau, Marina, Kroumpouzos, George, & Goldust, Mohamad. (2025). Balancing AI and human interaction in aesthetic dermatology. *The Archives of Dermatological Research*, 317, Article 426. https://link.springer.com/article/10.1007/s00403-025-03997-3

Marra, Marco, & Laskin, Janessa. (2020). Personalized onco-genomics: Using whole genome analysis to guide treatment decisions in cancer care. *Nature Cancer*, 1(7), 722–734. https://doi.org/10.1038/s43018-020-0074-0

Pahuja, K. (2024, January 11). AI in healthcare: Beyond automation to transformation. *Forbes*. https://www.forbes.com/councils/forbesbusinesscouncil/2024/09/16/ai-in-healthcare-beyond-automation-to-transformation/

Panahi, Omaid. (2024). AI in surgical robotics: Case studies. *Austin Journal of Clinical Case Reports*. https://www.researchgate.net/publication/385498766_AI_in_Surgical_Robotics_Case_Studies

Parthasarathy, R. (2024, June 21). 6 ways AI is reshaping healthcare diagnostics & treatment. *Fusemachines*. https://hitconsultant.net/2024/06/21/6-ways-ai-is-reshaping-healthcare-diagnostics-treatment/

Pati, R. (2024, July 3). *AI Revolutionizing Healthcare: From Diagnosis to Treatment and Beyond.* https://dypsst.dpu.edu.in/blogs/ai-revolutionizing-healthcare

Shah, Nigam H., Halamka, John D., Saria, Suchi, Pencina, Michael, & Tazbaz, Troy. (2024). A nationwide network of health AI assurance laboratories. *JAMA*, 331, 337–338. https://doi.org/10.1001/jama.2023.23822

Shrawankar, U., Malik, L., & Arora, S. (Eds.). (2021). *Cloud Computing Technologies for Smart Agriculture and Healthcare* (1st ed.). Chapman and Hall/CRC. https://doi.org/10.1201/9781003203926

Somashekhar, S. P., Kumarc, C. R., Rauthan, A., & Arun, K. R. (2018). Application of IBM Watson for Oncology in Indian tertiary cancer center: A double-blinded validation study. *JCO Clinical Cancer Informatics*, 2, 1–9. https://ascopubs.org/doi/full/10.1200/CCI.17.00055

Steiner, D. F., et al. (2018). Impact of deep learning assistance on the histopathologic review of lymph nodes for metastatic breast cancer. *The American Journal of Surgical Pathology*, 42(12), 1636–1646. https://journals.lww.com/ajsp/Abstract/2018/12000/Impact_of_Deep_Learning_Assistance_on_the.6.aspx

Talmele, Girish, & Shrawankar, Urmila. (2022). Real-time cyber-physical system for healthcare monitoring in COVID-19. *International Journal of Web-Based Learning and Teaching Technologies (IJWLTT)*, 17(5), 1–10. https://doi.org/10.4018/IJWLTT.297622

Wazalwar, S. S., & Shrawankar, U. (2021). Distributed education system for deaf and dumb children and educator: A today's need. In: Singh Mer, K. K., Semwal, V. B., Bijalwan, V., & Crespo, R. G. (Eds.). *Proceedings of Integrated Intelligence Enable Networks and Computing. Algorithms for Intelligent Systems.* Springer, Singapore. https://doi.org/10.1007/978-981-33-6307-6_35

10 Agriculture Developments Using ML and AI

10.1 INTRODUCTION

Artificial intelligence (AI) (Liu 2020) is the study of tools and technologies used to solve tasks that require human intelligence, including tasks such as natural language understanding, processing, generation, visual perception, and decision-making. Machine learning (ML) and deep learning (DL) are the two most widely used AI approaches. With breakthrough technologies, AI has transformed every aspect of life, including agriculture (Alaba et al. 2024). With more than 50% workforce employed in agriculture, a low expert to farmer ratio requires necessary AI interventions like automatic diagnosis and recommendation of proper advisories. The major hurdles in agricultural production are decision-making related to crop production, disease and pest infestation, weather forecasting, yield prediction, advisory systems for enhanced crop productivity, etc. (Olson and Anderson 2021). Agricultural productivity is mostly influenced by temperature, soil fertility, water availability, water quality, etc. For predicting these parameters accurately, improved AI techniques are being applied. While the technological explosion has made farming little easier, small and marginal farmers still face many obstacles. Unlike other technologies, AI has the potential to reach out to individual farmers much more easily and improve the life of farmers. The consideration of two life cycles, namely, agriculture and farmers, has a gigantic scope to intervene and enormously improve the same (Olson and Anderson 2021).

Agriculture life cycle starts from land preparation for the crop followed by seed sowing, irrigation, weeding, fertilizer application, pest and disease management, harvesting, post-harvest processing, storage, and marketing. Various AI techniques have the potential to affect and improve all the phases of the life cycle, some of which are already available and some still need to be worked on. In an ideal smart ecosystem, a farmer would be guided by an artificially intelligent assistant that would suggest the most appropriate date and method to prepare the land based on the geographic information system (GIS) and remote sensing data of that region. Using a block chain and recommender system-enabled supply chain, farmers would collect quality seeds to sow after land preparation. Scheduled weeding would be handled by low-cost smart weeding and fertigation (fertilization and irrigation) systems. The identification of pest and disease with their suitable management practices may be handled by AI-enabled mobile applications. The yield prediction may be done through drone-based smart application, and the predicted yield will help in selecting the appropriate market and buyer.

DOI: 10.1201/9781003532170-10

10.2   SOME IMPORTANT METHODOLOGIES

10.2.1   Soil Management

Soil management is a fundamental aspect of agricultural practices, directly influencing crop productivity, nutrient availability, and overall sustainability. The integration of AI and ML technologies into soil management strategies has emerged as a promising avenue for optimizing agricultural processes and ensuring long-term soil health. This section explores the literature and research findings pertaining to the application of AI and ML in soil management (Pattnaik et al. 2023).

10.2.2   Precision Soil Mapping

AI and ML algorithms have demonstrated their use in precision soil mapping, providing detailed insights into soil composition, nutrient levels, and moisture content. By analyzing vast datasets derived from various sources such as remote sensing and soil sensors, models were developed that can generate high-resolution soil maps (Ahila Priyadharshini et al. 2019). These maps enable farmers to make informed decisions about nutrient application, irrigation, and crop selection based on the specific needs of different soil zones within a field.

10.2.3   Nutrient Management

Optimizing nutrient management is critical for maximizing crop yields while minimizing environmental impact. AI-powered models, as seen in the work can analyze soil data alongside historical crop performance to recommend precise fertilizer applications. ML algorithms can adapt to changing conditions, allowing for dynamic adjustments in nutrient prescriptions based on real-time data, weather patterns, and crop development stages.

10.2.4   Soil Health Monitoring

Maintaining soil health (Mamatha et al. 2024) is essential for sustainable agriculture. AI and ML contribute to soil health monitoring by analyzing indicators such as microbial activity, organic matter content, and soil structure. The use of AI in interpreting soil health data to identify trends and potential issues, aiding in the development of proactive soil management strategies (Azizi et al. 2020).

10.2.5   Erosion Prediction and Control

Soil erosion poses a significant threat to agricultural productivity and environmental stability. AI models, exemplified in studies by utilizing machine learning to predict erosion risk based on factors such as topography, land use, and weather conditions. This information empowers farmers to implement targeted erosion control measures, preserving soil structure and preventing loss of fertile topsoil.

10.2.6 DECISION SUPPORT SYSTEMS

Integrated decision support systems, combining AI and ML, offer comprehensive solutions for soil management. These systems, showcased in their search by incorporating data on soil, weather, and crop conditions to provide actionable insights. Farmers can leverage these recommendations for optimal land use planning, cover cropping strategies, and erosion control practices.

10.2.7 CHALLENGES AND OPPORTUNITIES

While the application of AI and ML in soil management presents numerous benefits, challenges also exist. Ensuring the accessibility of these technologies to small-scale farmers, addressing data security concerns, and refining models for diverse agroecosystems are key challenges discussed in works. Overcoming these challenges requires collaborative efforts between researchers, policy-makers, and technology developers.

10.2.8 AI AND ML APPLICATIONS IN AGRICULTURE

In the present scenario, AI and ML techniques are being exponentially applied in the various areas of the agricultural domain. These areas can be categorized into the following groups: soil and water management, crop health management, crop phenotyping, recommender-based systems for crops, semantic web- and ontology-driven expert systems for crops, and Geo-AI. The applications of AI-, ML-, and DL-based techniques in these areas are discussed in the following sections.

Soil and Irrigation Management: (Azizi et al. 2020) Soil and irrigation are the most viable components of agriculture, as they are the determinant factors for the optimum crop yield. In order to obtain enhanced crop yield and to maintain the soil properties, appropriate knowledge about the soil resources is required (Alkhudaydi and Zhou 2019). Irrigation scheduling becomes crucial when water resources are scarce. Therefore, soil- and irrigation-related issues should be managed properly and cautiously to ensure a potential yield in crops. In this regard, AI- and ML-based techniques have shown potential ability to resolve soil- and irrigation-related issues in crops. A range of ML models such as regression-based models, support vector machines (or regressors), artificial neural networks, and random forest algorithm are being used. Many researchers have used remote-sensing data with ML techniques for determining soil health parameters (Archana and Saranya 2020).

Crop Health Management: Every year a significant amount of yield is damaged due to the attack of disease-causing pathogens and insect–pest infestation. In order to manage the spread of diseases and insect pests, proper management practices should be applied at the earliest. Therefore, there is the requirement of an automatic disease and pest identification system. In this regard, image-based diagnosis of diseases and pests have become the de facto standard of automatic stress identification. This kind of automated detection methodology uses sophisticated DL-based AI techniques that reduce the intervention of human experts. There have been several attempts to diagnose the diseases and insects–pests in crops using DL techniques.

The application of AI in the food sector is becoming progressively significant owing to its capability to assist in minimizing food wastage, improving production hygiene, enhancing the cleaning process of machines, and managing disease and pest control; therefore, there are numerous instances of employing AI and ML in the agri-food industry (Shrawankar et al. 2021). Automated frameworks can collect a huge amount of data in a matter of a few seconds on a single food item and analyze it rapidly. Even though agriculture practice is broad, AI finds its application in some major areas of the agriculture sector, such as supply chain management, soil, crop, diseases, and pest management. Some of the proposed models using AI techniques with their limitations are as follows. (a) For soil management: fuzzy logic-based SRC-DSS (Soil Risk Characterization Decision Support System) for soil classification; MOM (management-oriented modeling) for minimization of nitrate leaching; and artificial neural network (ANN) to estimate soil enzyme activity and soil structure classification (Pattnaik et al. 2023). (b) For crop management: CALEX to formulate scheduling guidelines, PROLOG to remove redundant tools from the farm, ANN to detect nutrition disorders in crops, and ANN to predict rice yield accurately. (c) For disease management: computer vision system (CVS) to detect multiple diseases at high speed; fuzzy logic-based database, which is accurate in test environments; ANN-GIS, which has got an accuracy of 90%; and the expert system using rule-base in disease detection for faster detection and treatment of disease. (d) For weed control: invasive weed optimization (IWO), big data-based ANN-GA, and support vector machines. All these methods did not consider all the parameters; they are all application-specific toward a particular crop or environmental parameter. There is a need to design AI frameworks using multiple parameters and that can be used for multiple crops. There has been a critical pattern to ruminate about the utilization of massive data procedures and strategies to agribusiness as a significant opportunity for utilization of the information and communication technologypack, for financing, and for achieving added significance inside the agriculture sector. Applications of massive data in agriculture are not sternly regarding primary cultivation but also assume a significant part in enhancing the effectiveness of the whole supply chain, thus reducing food security worries.

Big Data Analytics: Big data analysis (Mark 2019) is outlined as a system in which cutting-edge analytic methods operate on huge datasets. Therefore, it is a combination of two technical entities with a massive amount of datasets, and a collection of analytical tool categories including data mining, statistics, AI, predictive analytics, and natural language processing (NLP), forming an important component of business intelligence (Shrawankar and Dhule 2021). Lately, big data turns out to be a subject of broad and current interest equally in academic research and industry. It characterizes enormous and unstructured data generated by a large number of sources. Several of the most prevalent data processing techniques employ big data techniques. Big data is depicted by the subsequent attributes. Big data is being used in numerous fields such as big service business industries like Amazon to learn customer behavior and needs more precisely to tailor product prices accordingly, enhance operational productivity, and cut down personal costs. Even social networking sites such as Facebook, Twitter, and other networking sites utilize big data analytics to study your social behavior, interests, and social connections and then endorse specific products. In an intelligent transportation system, big data techniques can handle the enormous quantity of diverse and complex data generated over the period to provide safe and superior facilities aimed at drivers and passengers in the transportation system. In the agriculture field, big data shows a huge potential for solving many challenges of farming and consequently boosting the agriculture production quality and quantity. Big data analytics can be used to determine soil quality, diseases and pest interruption, and water requirement, and predict harvesting time for crops.

10.2.9 CHALLENGES AND LIMITATIONS

Despite the promising potential of AI in agriculture (Dharmaraj and Vijayanand 2018), the practical application of AI-based techniques faces several challenges. Understanding and addressing these challenges are crucial for the successful implementation and widespread adoption of AI technologies in the agriculture sector.

Limited Access to Technology:

One of the primary challenges is the limited access to AI technology, particularly among small-scale and resource-constrained farmers. The high costs associated with acquiring and implementing AI solutions, including hardware, software, and data connectivity, create a digital divide. Bridging this gap and ensuring equitable access to AI tools are essential for maximizing the benefits across diverse agricultural landscapes (Mishra and Mishra 2023).

Data Quality and Availability:

AI algorithms heavily rely on high-quality and extensive datasets for training and decision-making. In agriculture, the availability of accurate and diverse datasets can be a challenge. Issues such as inconsistent data quality, limited historical records, and variability in data formats pose obstacles to the development of robust AI models. Collaborative efforts to collect, curate, and share agricultural data are essential for enhancing the effectiveness of AI applications.

Interoperability and Standardization:

The agricultural sector comprises a variety of equipment, sensors, and software solutions from different vendors. Ensuring interoperability and standardization of AI-based technologies is a significant challenge. The lack of standardized data formats and communication protocols hinders seamless integration of AI tools into existing farming practices. Developing industry-wide standards can promote compatibility and facilitate a more cohesive AI ecosystem.

User Acceptance and Education:

Farmers and agricultural stakeholders may face resistance to adopting AI technologies due to a lack of understanding or familiarity. The complexity of AI systems and the need for specialized knowledge may deter users from embracing these tools. Effective education and training programs are essential to demystify AI, empower users with the necessary skills, and build confidence in the practical benefits of AI applications in agriculture.

Data Privacy and Security Concerns:

Agriculture involves sensitive data related to crop performance, soil conditions, and farm management practices. Concerns about data privacy and security are significant barriers to the widespread adoption of AI. Farmers may be hesitant to share their data due to fears of misuse or unauthorized access. Implementing robust data protection measures, clear privacy policies, and secure data-sharing frameworks is crucial for addressing these concerns.

Tailoring Solutions to Local Contexts:

AI applications need to be tailored to the specific needs and contexts of diverse agricultural systems. Solutions developed for one region or crop type may not be directly applicable elsewhere. Understanding the local intricacies, cultural practices, and environmental conditions is vital for designing AI applications that align with the unique challenges faced by farmers in different geographic areas (Sarkar et al. 2022).

Ethical Considerations and Bias:

As AI algorithms learn from historical data, there is a risk of perpetuating biases present in that data. In agriculture, this could lead to biased recommendations or decisions, impacting resource distribution and outcomes. Addressing ethical considerations and ensuring fairness in AI applications are crucial to building trust and fostering responsible AI adoption in agriculture (Bhat and Huang 2021).

Scalability and Adaptability:

Implementing AI solutions that are scalable and adaptable to changing agricultural practices and technologies is a challenge. The rapid evolution of both AI technologies and agricultural methods requires flexible solutions that can accommodate new data sources, sensors, and innovations. Scalability ensures that AI applications remain relevant and effective as the agricultural landscape evolves.

10.2.10   FUTURE TRENDS AND OPPORTUNITIES

The future of agricultural robots holds exciting possibilities. Ongoing research aims to overcome current challenges, improve robot adaptability, and introduce new functionalities. Collaborative efforts between researchers, engineers, and farmers are crucial for refining and expanding the capabilities of agricultural robots, ultimately contributing to a more sustainable and technologically advanced agriculture sector.

10.3   CONCLUSION

The application of AI and ML can provide viable solutions to major problems in agriculture, such as soil health management, irrigation scheduling, crop health management, disease/pest identification, and crop phenomics. The use of AI and ML techniques in the agriculture domain and the survey of different AI-related technologies discussed in this chapter will help in deducing a generic framework toward precision agriculture that will improve the overall crop productivity. AI is a powerful tool in the field of agriculture for accurate weather prediction, disease/pest forewarning, and assisting the stakeholders in accurate and real-time prediction of various related parameters to obtain maximum yield at minimum cost. AI tools will transform the agriculture industry with better agricultural practices, which in turn will benefit the farmers and aid in improving the economy of the country.

REFERENCES

Ahila Priyadharshini, R., S. Arivazhagan, M. Arun, and A. Mirnalini. "Maize Leaf Disease Classification Using Deep Convolutional Neural Networks." *Neural Computing and Applications* 31, no. 12 (2019): 8887–8895, https://doi.org/10.1007/s00542-018-4277-2.
Alaba, Fadele Ayotunde, Abayomi Jegede, Usman Sani, and Emmanuel Gbenga Dada. "Artificial Intelligence of Things (AIoT) Solutions for Sustainable Agriculture and Food Security." In *Artificial Intelligence of Things for Achieving Sustainable Development Goals*, pp. 123–142. Cham: Springer Nature Switzerland, 2024.
Alkhudaydi, T. and J. Zhou. "SpikeletFCN: Counting Spikelets from Infield Wheat Crop Images Using Fully Convolutional Networks." *Proceedings of the International Conference on Artificial Intelligence and Soft Computing*, pp. 3–13, 2019.
Archana, K., and K. G. Saranya. "Crop Yield Prediction, Forecasting, and Fertilizer Recommendation Using Voting-Based Ensemble Classifier." *International Journal of Computer Science and Engineering* 7, no. 5 (2020): 1–4.
Azizi, A., Y. A. Gilandeh, T. Mesri-Gundoshmian, A. A. Saleh-Bigdeli, and H. A. Moghaddam. "Classification of Soil Aggregates: A Novel Approach Based on Deep Learning." *Soil & Tillage Research* 199 (2020): 104586, https://doi.org/10.1016/j.still.2020.104586.
Bhat, S. A., and N. F. Huang. "Big Data and AI Revolution in Precision Agriculture: Survey and Challenges." *IEEE Access* 9 (2021): 110209–110222, https://doi.org/10.1109/ACCESS.2021.3107585.
Dharmaraj, V., and C. Vijayanand. "Artificial Intelligence (AI) in Agriculture." *International Journal of Current Microbiology and Applied Sciences* 7, no. 12 (2018): 2122–2128.
Liu, Simon Y. "Artificial Intelligence (AI) in Agriculture." *IT Professional* 22, no. 3 (2020): 14–15.
Mamatha, Bommireddy, Chandana Mudigiri, Guguloth Ramesh, Pakala Saidulu, Nayaki Meenakshi, and Chuncha Laxmi Prasanna. "Enhancing Soil Health and Fertility Management for Sustainable Agriculture: A Review." *Asian Journal of Soil Science and Plant Nutrition* 10, no. 3 (2024): 182–190.
Mark, Ryan. "Ethics of Using AI and Big Data in Agriculture: The Case of a Large Agriculture Multinational." *The ORBIT Journal* 2, no. 2 (2019): 1–27.

Mishra, H., and D. Mishra. "Artificial Intelligence and Machine Learning in Agriculture: Transforming Farming Systems." *Research Trends in Agricultural Science* 1 (2023): 1–16.

Olson, Daniel, and James Anderson. "Review on Unmanned Aerial Vehicles, Remote Sensors, Imagery Processing, and Their Applications in Agriculture." *Agronomy Journal* 113, no. 2 (2021): 971–992.

Pattnaik, Binaya Kumar, Chandan Sahu, Shuvasish Choudhury, Subhas Chandra Santra, and Debojyoti Moulick. "Importance of Soil Management in Sustainable Agriculture." In *Climate-Resilient Agriculture, Vol. 1: Crop Responses and Agroecological Perspectives*, pp. 487–511. Cham: Springer International Publishing, 2023.

Sarkar, Md Ridoy, et al. "A Comprehensive Study on the Emerging Effect of Artificial Intelligence in Agriculture Automation." In *2022 IEEE 18th International Colloquium on Signal Processing & Applications (CSPA)*. IEEE, 2022, https://doi.org/10.1109/CSPA53579.2022.9769992.

Shrawankar, Urmila, and Chetan Dhule. "Virtualization Technology for Cloud-Based Services." In *Cloud Computing Technologies for Smart Agriculture and Healthcare*, pp. 3–17. Chapman and Hall/CRC, 2021.

Shrawankar, Urmila, Latesh Malik, and Sandhya Arora, eds. *Cloud Computing Technologies for Smart Agriculture and Healthcare*. CRC Press, 2021.

11 AI Transforming Education

Personalized Learning and Intelligent Tutoring Systems

11.1 INTRODUCTION

The landscape of global education is constantly evolving, and one of the keys turning points is the introduction of artificial intelligence (AI), which has begun to reshape traditional teaching methods (Yang and Park 2021). Historically, educators have been at the center of instructional practices, but AI is now stepping in to assist and transform these conventional roles (Edwards and Roy 2023). This chapter explores the diverse applications of AI in education, highlighting innovative approaches that have the potential to revolutionize both teaching and learning (Sinha and Bose 2022).

The importance of AI in modern education cannot be overstated. Advanced AI technologies provide educators with new tools to engage students, personalize instruction, and reduce the workload associated with assessments (Garcia and Lee 2021). By leveraging data, AI can offer personalized learning experiences tailored to the unique needs of individual students, moving away from the one-size-fits-all model traditionally used in classrooms (Kumar and Sharma 2020). This shift allows students to progress at their own pace, following their personal interests and learning styles (Huang and Li 2020). Additionally, the COVID-19 pandemic has accelerated the digital transformation of education, emphasizing the need for flexible and adaptive learning models that AI can provide (Jensen and Chen 2021).

This work seeks to examine the various roles AI plays in educational environments, from early childhood education to higher education institutions (Singh and Chatterji 2020). Specifically, the study aims for the following:

- Analyze how AI-powered personalized learning tools impact student engagement and academic achievement (Anderson and Thompson 2021).
- Investigate the effectiveness of AI-supported intelligent tutoring systems in offering individualized feedback and assistance (Patel and Smith 2019).
- Explore AI's role in managing administrative tasks and assessments to reduce the workload on educators (Wilkinson and Crossley 2022).
- Assess the ethical challenges and considerations related to AI integration in school systems (Vincent and Roberts 2020).
- Examine AI's ability to address the educational needs of learners with diverse abilities (Shaikh et al. 2023).

DOI: 10.1201/9781003532170-11

11.1.1 AI IN EDUCATION

The integration of AI in education has been an area of academic interest for several decades. Early developments transitioned from basic programmed instruction to advanced ML algorithms capable of adapting to specific learning needs (Zhang and Maguire 2021). As education systems expanded, research shifted toward automating repetitive tasks in computer-assisted learning, focusing on streamlining routine processes (Ullman and King 2021). Initial studies explored the benefits of computer-assisted instruction for automating monotonous tasks, such as rote learning (Solomon and Naik 2020). More recent research, however, has concentrated on adaptive learning technologies, intelligent tutoring systems, and data-driven educational tools (Lahiri and Bose 2022). These advancements have allowed for a more personalized learning experience, tailoring study paths to match individual students' responses and prior knowledge (Kapoor and Kulshrestha 2020). The evolution of AI in education demonstrates its potential to enhance accessibility to learning resources and create immersive learning experiences that engage students deeply, driving AI toward significant educational breakthroughs (Chen and Wang 2019).

To address the specific educational needs of learners with disabilities, such as those who are deaf or dumb, the development of specialized educational systems is crucial. The importance of such systems, like the *Distributed Education System for Deaf & Dumb Children and Educators*, has been explored as a way to enhance access to education for all learners (Wazalwar and Shrawankar 2020). Additionally, speech user interfaces, which integrate AI to improve accessibility, have shown promise in helping diverse student groups communicate and learn more effectively (Shrawankar and Thakare 2010).

11.1.2 AI TECHNOLOGIES: PROGRESS AND APPLICATION

The history of AI's application in education is marked by continuous technological advancements, evolving from rule-based expert systems in the 1980s to modern tools powered by deep learning and natural language processing (NLP) (Diaz and Clark 2022). For example, AI-driven intelligent tutoring systems no longer rely solely on numerical inputs but now provide adaptive feedback to help students navigate complex problem-solving scenarios (Majid and Jafri 2021). Additionally, AI integrated with virtual and augmented reality technologies is establishing new, immersive learning environments (Fisher and Green 2021). Platforms like zSpace, which utilize virtual reality, offer students hands-on learning experiences that could revolutionize traditional education (Darrin and Smith 2021). While these technologies hold great promise for individualized learning, they also raise potential concerns, such as the risk of job displacement due to automation, societal homogenization, and environmental impacts if not implemented carefully (Bennett and Marshall 2021).

11.1.3 APPLICATION IN EDUCATIONAL ENVIRONMENTS

The education sector has seen a recent influx of AI applications, revolutionizing the use of innovative technology for tasks like online testing, grading, and personalized learning (Garcia and Lee 2021). AI-powered adaptive learning systems, such as those used by platforms like Khan Academy and Coursera, adjust content and assessments to match the learner's pace and level of proficiency (Singh and De Souza 2023). These systems have demonstrated success across various subjects, including mathematics, science, economics, and even philosophy (Sinha and Bose 2022). Additionally, AI has proven effective in predictive analytics, identifying students at risk of dropping out and highlighting areas where they face the most difficulties, allowing for timely interventions (Jensen and Chen 2021). Despite these advancements, it is essential to closely examine these learning gaps to ensure meaningful support is provided to struggling students (Inam and Khan 2023). Research has also shown the importance of developing accessible educational systems for learners with special needs, such as those who are deaf or dumb. The *Distributed Education System for Deaf & Dumb Children and Educators* is an example of an innovative approach to meeting these needs (Wazalwar and Shrawankar 2020). Furthermore, speech user interfaces have proven to be beneficial in facilitating more inclusive learning experiences for diverse student populations (Shrawankar and Thakare 2010).

11.1.4   BOOSTING LEARNING WITH AI-DRIVEN ANALYTICS

AI-driven analytics can significantly enhance the learning experience by providing educators with detailed insights into student behavior and performance (Baker and Greene 2020). With the integration of AI in various learning management systems (LMS), educators can monitor student engagement and share performance data with the entire class (Carson and Jenkins 2020). By analyzing time-lapse data that tracks student progress over extended periods, educators can identify performance patterns, pinpoint areas where students are struggling, and predict when and which students require intervention (Zhao and Lin 2020). These AI-powered tools help create a more adaptable educational environment by providing the data needed to plan targeted interventions for diverse learning needs (Singh and Chatterji 2020).

11.1.5   AI IN LANGUAGE LEARNING

AI has significantly transformed how students learn and practice new languages by integrating intelligent tutoring systems with technologies like NLP (Lahiri and Bose 2022). These AI-driven tools provide interactive language practice through chatbots, consistent feedback, and personalized assessments, adapting to the unique needs of each learner (Singh and De Souza 2023). By offering a highly customizable learning experience, AI enhances traditional language learning methods with accessible and engaging drills, making it easier for students to grasp new concepts quickly and effectively (Zhang and Maguire 2021).

11.1.6   ETHICAL AND EQUITY CONSIDERATIONS IN AI EDUCATION

As AI becomes more embedded in educational systems, its ethical and equity implications are gaining attention. Concerns regarding the fairness of AI algorithms, especially in areas like student evaluation and admissions, highlight the need for transparent systems that do not perpetuate historical biases (Vincent and Roberts 2020). This study stresses the importance of establishing clear ethical guidelines to govern AI's role in education (Diaz and Clark 2022).

The current study also explores the impact of AI on the teaching profession, where gaps in understanding exist regarding how AI might alter the professional responsibilities of teachers (Shaikh et al. 2023). The research addresses concern about whether AI could undermine the traditional role of educators (Prasad and Saini 2021). While much literature focuses on AI's effect on students, there is a significant lack of research into how AI reshapes teachers' roles and the necessary professional development to integrate AI effectively into classrooms (Edwards and Roy 2023).

11.1.7 CULTURAL AND CONTEXTUAL ADAPTABILITY OF AI TOOLS

Another critical area for further research is the cultural adaptability of AI tools in education. The effectiveness of AI applications varies across different cultural settings, and it is essential to design tools that accommodate diverse perspectives (Solomon and Naik 2020). Ensuring that AI educational technologies are inclusive and globally accessible is vital to their success (Thakur and Hamilton 2022).

11.1.8 EFFECTIVENESS AND LONGEVITY IN THE FIELD

Long-term research is needed to assess the sustainability and impact of AI in education over extended periods (Zhao and Lin 2020). While short-term studies have shown positive outcomes, there is limited data on the long-term effects of AI on student motivation, learning abilities, and overall success (Bennett and Marshall 2021). Understanding how continuous use of AI affects these factors is crucial for determining its lasting influence (Adams and Brown 2022).

11.1.9 SCALABILITY AND ACCESSIBILITY

The scalability of AI solutions in education presents mixed results. While many AI tools have demonstrated scalability on a large scale, challenges remain in making them accessible to institutions with limited resources (Bennett and Marshall 2021). Scalability is key to AI's success, but it requires adaptable models that do not depend solely on high-capacity infrastructure (Adams and Brown 2022).

11.1.10 INTEGRATING OTHER TECHNOLOGIES

AI's integration with other emerging technologies, such as blockchain for tamper-proof academic records and Internet of Things (IoT) devices for enriched learning environments, opens new possibilities for educational experiences (Carson and Jenkins 2020). This convergence of technologies has the potential to create more immersive and comprehensive educational opportunities. However, more research is needed into the best ways to do this and the implications for data security and privacy (Zhao and Lin 2020).

11.1.11   AI Adoption for Education across the Globe

AI adoption in education varies widely depending on the educational systems and policies of different countries. Some nations have advanced rapidly in exploring and implementing AI, while others are just starting to recognize its potential (Singh and Chatterji 2020). Comparative research helps identify successful strategies that facilitate the effective integration of AI into diverse educational systems (Patel and Smith 2019). Moreover, specialized educational systems, such as the *Distributed Education System for Deaf & Dumb Children and Educators*, have been developed to address the unique learning needs of children with disabilities (Wazalwar and Shrawankar 2020). Additionally, advancements like speech user interfaces in computer-based education systems offer significant improvements in accessibility for diverse student populations (Shrawankar and Thakare 2010).

11.1.12   Culture in AI Design and Deployment

Cultural factors significantly influence AI's design and deployment in education. Emerging research highlights that culturally responsive AI systems can better adapt to the cultural and linguistic diversity of learners (Solomon and Naik 2020). This approach ensures that AI tools provide inclusive educational support, respecting local customs and learner contexts (Shaikh et al. 2023).

11.1.13   AI's Ethical and Societal Dimensions

The ethical and societal implications of AI in education are crucial, particularly in terms of equity and fairness. Issues such as unequal access to AI tools and the potential reinforcement of existing biases necessitate continuous research and policy interventions to ensure AI's equitable impact on educational processes (Vincent and Roberts 2020).

11.1.14   Future Directions and Policy Considerations

Comprehensive policy frameworks are needed to guide AI's integration into educational systems. These frameworks should address data protection, standards for ethical AI usage, equitable access to AI-driven education, and sustainability measures to safeguard the interests of all stakeholders (Diaz and Clark 2022).

11.1.15   Advanced AI Applications in Education

Advanced AI applications can transform curriculum development and instructional design by analyzing large volumes of educational content and student performance data. This enables educators to create dynamic, adaptive curricula that incorporate real-time student feedback and improve learning outcomes (Anderson and Thompson 2021).

11.1.16   AI for Enhancing Teacher Professional Development

Advanced AI applications can transform curriculum development and instructional design by analyzing large volumes of educational content and student performance data. This enables educators to create dynamic, adaptive curricula that incorporate real-time student feedback and improve learning outcomes (Anderson and Thompson 2021).

11.1.17 AI IN EDUCATIONAL ADMINISTRATION

AI is increasingly used in educational administration, from student enrolment and resource allocation to scheduling (Wilkinson and Crossley 2022). Automating these processes allows educational institutions to streamline operations, freeing up teachers to focus on student engagement (Davis and Patel 2019).

11.1.18 USE OF DATA ANALYTICS BY EDUCATIONAL ADMINISTRATORS

AI-driven data analytics enable educational administrators to make informed decisions by analyzing vast datasets (Baker and Greene 2020). This facilitates policy advice, optimization of teaching programs, and identification of effective practices through data-driven insights (Zhao and Lin 2020).

11.1.19 AI SOLUTIONS IN EDUCATION'S SUSTAINABILITY

As AI becomes more integrated into education, its environmental impact must be considered. Research into sustainable AI models aims to mitigate the energy consumption of AI algorithms and data centers, ensuring that AI use aligns with broader environmental sustainability goals (Solomon and Naik 2020).

11.1.20 FINANCIAL AND INFRASTRUCTURAL SUSTAINABILITY

Sustainable AI integration in education must be both financially viable and adaptable to various educational models (Bennett and Marshall 2021). Studies emphasize the importance of considering the total cost of AI implementation, including maintenance and scalability, to ensure long-term sustainability (Adams and Brown 2022).

11.1.21 INTERDISCIPLINARY APPROACHES TO AI IN EDUCATION

AI in education opens new opportunities for interdisciplinary learning, enabling educators to design experiences that integrate critical thinking and creativity across subjects like STEAM (Science, Technology, Engineering, Arts, and Mathematics) (Singh and Chatterji 2020).

The interdisciplinary nature of AI in education involves collaboration among fields like computer science, education, psychology, and sociology. Such collaborations ensure that AI solutions are pedagogically informed and culturally sensitive (Wilkinson and Crossley 2022).

11.1.22 AI FOR STUDENTS WITH DISABILITIES

AI technologies offer new ways to support students with disabilities through personalized learning experiences tailored to their needs (Shaikh et al. 2023). Assistive technologies, such as AI-driven speech-to-text conversion and reading aids, promote equal access to educational resources (Solomon and Naik 2020).

11.1.23 ETHICAL AI IN EDUCATION

The rise of AI in education necessitates the creation of ethical and legal frameworks to prevent misuse and ensure that AI serves educational purposes ethically (Vincent and Roberts 2020).

11.1.24 AI AND POLICY DEVELOPMENT IN A DEVELOPING WORLD

In developing countries, cost-effective AI solutions like chatbots and automated test proctors provide affordable opportunities to enhance skills relevant for higher education and employment (Patel and Smith 2019). Innovations in AI must consider both educational value and affordability (Adams and Brown 2022).

11.2 EVOLUTION OF AI IN EDUCATION

The integration of AI in education marks a shift from the traditional one-size-fits-all approach to more adaptive, personalized learning environments. Historically, education systems have relied on standardized teaching methods where all students follow the same curriculum and pace, often ignoring each student's individual learning needs and preferences (Singh and Chatterji 2020). Lack of personalization and flexibility have been key factors in the adoption of AI technologies in the educational environment (Kapoor and Kulshrestha 2020).

11.2.1 EARLY APPLICATION POSSIBILITIES OF AI IN EDUCATIONAL TECHNOLOGIES

Early applications of AI in education focused mainly on the development of intelligent instructional systems (ITS) (Patel and Smith 2019). These systems were designed to mimic the role of a human tutor and provide students with personalized instruction and immediate feedback based on their performance (Huang and Li 2020). Unlike traditional teaching methods, ITS used AI algorithms to analyze student responses and adapt the learning material in real time, ensuring that each student received individualized support tailored to their learning pace and style (Davis and Patel 2019).

In addition, AI-powered automated grading systems emerged that streamlined the process of evaluating educators (Garcia and Lee 2021). Using NLP and ML techniques, these systems provided faster and more consistent task feedback, allowing educators to focus on more complex learning tasks (Gomez and Wang 2022). This is an important milestone in reducing the administrative burden on teachers and providing timely feedback to students (Fisher and Green 2021).

11.2.2 KEY MILESTONES AND PROGRESS

Over the years, AI has continued to develop, playing an increasingly important role in education. Several key advancements have been made in this field. One such milestone is the development of adaptive learning systems. These systems, such as Newton, use AI to analyze large amounts of data generated from student interactions with educational content, allowing for the creation of customized learning paths based on an individual's strengths, weaknesses, and preferences (Kapoor and Kulshrestha 2020). AI-powered systems can predict student performance and provide tailored interventions before students fall behind (Davis and Patel 2019).

Another significant development is the use of big data and learning analytics. By collecting and analyzing data on student behavior, AI systems allow educators to gain a deeper understanding of how students learn, informing teaching strategies (Baker and Greene 2020). The increasing importance of data-driven decision-making in modern education is largely driven by AI technologies. These changes have led to more focused teaching practices and have provided a more student-centered approach to learning (Jensen and Chen 2021).

The incorporation of AI into virtual and blended learning environments has also transformed education. As the world shifts to online learning, AI-driven platforms play a crucial role in managing complex data and personalizing student experiences (Xu and Nguyen 2023). AI can adjust content delivery, monitor student participation, and predict the risk of dropout, playing an essential role in ensuring student success on online learning platforms (Young and Sullivan 2019).

11.2.3 THE IMPACT OF AI ON TRADITIONAL LEARNING ENVIRONMENTS

The impact of AI on traditional education is significant. AI not only improves the efficiency of administrative tasks such as assessment but also enhances the quality of learning through personalized learning systems (Anderson and Thompson 2021). Unlike the rigid structure of conventional classrooms, AI-powered learning environments offer flexibility, allowing students to learn at their own pace and receive tailored support when needed (Lahiri and Bose 2022).

Furthermore, AI has changed the role of educators from simply providing knowledge to facilitating personalized learning experiences (Majid and Jafri 2021). Teachers can now access real-time data about student performance, allowing them to intervene at the right time and address each student's specific needs (Garcia and Lee 2021). This shift toward individualized education has significantly improved student engagement and learning outcomes (Huang and Li 2020).

Despite its numerous benefits, AI integration has also raised concerns, particularly regarding data protection and accessibility (Diaz and Clark 2022). Ensuring that AI technology remains fair and inclusive remains a crucial challenge, as students from underprivileged backgrounds may lack the necessary resources to benefit from these advancements (Bennett and Marshall 2021).

In conclusion, the evolution of AI in education represents a paradigm shift from standardized teaching to a more individualized, data-driven approach. As AI continues to advance, it is poised to further transform the educational landscape, making learning more accessible, efficient, and tailored to the needs of each student (Sharma and Graham 2022).

11.3 PERSONALIZED LEARNING THROUGH AI

Personalized learning represents a shift from traditional, standardized learning methods to a more flexible, student-centered approach. It recognizes that each student has unique strengths, challenges, learning preferences, and needs. In traditional classrooms, a one-size-fits-all model often fails to engage students—either because the material is too difficult or because it is too easy. Personalized learning closes this gap by tailoring the educational experience to individual learners, making the process more relevant, engaging, and efficient.

This approach is based on meeting the needs of students so that they can develop at their own pace. The adaptability of personalized learning helps students overcome certain learning gaps and capitalize on their strengths. It shifts the focus from a rigid curriculum to dynamic learning pathways, ensuring that content is not only delivered but also understood, retained, and applied. It empowers students to take control of their learning journey, fostering a greater sense of belonging, self-efficacy, and motivation.

- **Key AI Technologies in Personalized Learning:** AI plays a critical role in enabling personalized learning, making it more efficient and scalable. AI technologies involved in personalized learning include the following:
- **Machine Learning:** ML analyses large amounts of educational material to identify patterns in student behavior and performance. It then uses this insight to dynamically adjust learning paths and recommend resources tailored to student needs (Anderson and Thompson 2021, 150–165).
- **Natural Language Processing:** NLP allows AI systems to interact with students using natural language, making the learning experience more interactive and responsive. This is especially useful for tutoring systems or chatbots that help students with questions (Diaz and Clark 2022, 223–237).
- **Data Acquisition:** Data acquisition technology helps analyze large datasets to obtain significant insights, such as identifying overall student struggles or outlier performance. These insights drive a personalized learning path (Baker and Greene 2020, 34–49).
- **Predictive Modelling:** AI-based predictive models analyze past student performance to predict future learning outcomes. By identifying students who may be at risk of falling behind, educators can provide targeted support interventions before learning problems become serious (Jensen and Chen 2021, 1–20).

These technologies work together to create a robust framework for personalized learning that improves adaptability and effectiveness.

- **Benefits of AI in Personalized Learning**
  - **Adapting Learning Paths Based on Student Needs:** AI-powered systems can create customized learning paths that adapt to each student's abilities, preferences, and learning pace. These systems can adjust course content on the fly; provide additional resources, exercises, or simpler

explanations when students get stuck; and move on to more complex topics as students progress (Kapoor and Kulshrestha 2020, 524–541).

- **Increasing Engagement and Motivation:** AI-powered personalized learning increases engagement by tailoring learning materials to students' interests and preferred learning styles. This prevents students from losing focus because the material is too easy or too difficult. By presenting interactive and customized content, AI can keep students motivated and encourage them to actively participate in learning (Majid and Jafri 2021, 417–433).
- **Improving Results through Adaptive Assessment:** AI facilitates adaptive assessment that evolves based on student performance. Instead of providing standardized tests, AI systems dynamically adjust the difficulty of questions to match students' current understanding. This helps identify specific areas of weakness while maintaining engagement and ensuring that the assessment is neither too overwhelming nor too easy (Gomez and Wang 2022, 400–418).
- **Instant Feedback for Continuous Improvement:** AI can provide instant feedback on assessments, assignments, and tasks, giving students instant insight into their performance. Instead of waiting for a teacher to grade, students can receive detailed feedback immediately after completing an assignment. It helps them understand mistakes, correct them quickly, and strengthen their understanding of basic concepts (Garcia and Lee 2021, 567–582).
- **Challenges of AI-Driven Personalized Learning**

While AI offers many benefits for personalized learning, it also poses significant challenges:

- **Privacy Concerns:** AI systems rely on the collection and analysis of large amounts of student data, raising concerns about data privacy and security. Protecting sensitive student information and ensuring compliance with privacy regulations such as GDPR or FERPA are critical to building trust in AI-powered education technology (Vincent and Roberts 2020, 144–162).
- **Technological Limitations:** Not all educational institutions have the necessary infrastructure or technical expertise to effectively implement AI-based personalized learning systems. Furthermore, the accuracy of AI predictions and recommendations depends on the quality and variety of data used to train the model. Insufficient or biased data can lead to erroneous conclusions (Thakur and Hamilton 2022, 150–167).
- **Teacher and Student Acceptance of AI-Driven Personalization:** Integrating AI into the classroom may face resistance from teachers and students. Teachers may fear that AI will undermine their role, while students may be hesitant to trust or rely on AI-driven systems for learning. Overcoming this challenge requires fostering a deeper understanding of how AI complements the role of educators and enhances the learning experience without replacing human interaction (Shaikh et al. 2023, 56–66).

- **Bias in AI Models:** AI systems are only as good as the data they are trained on. If learning materials contain inherent biases, such as socioeconomic, gender, or racial biases, AI systems may inadvertently incorporate these biases into their recommendations or evaluations. Ensuring diversity in data collection and training models to avoid bias is critical to fair and equitable personalized training (Singh and Chatterji 2020, 214–247).
- **AI's Role in Predictive Modeling and Learning Path Adaptation**
  - AI supports predictive modeling, which can predict likely learning outcomes based on past student performance. By analyzing historical data, AI can identify students who are at risk of lagging behind and recommend interventions before significant learning shortcomings develop. This proactive approach ensures that students receive timely support, preventing further academic difficulties (Baker and Greene 2020, 34–49). The expected model can also help teachers customize their teaching strategies to meet the needs of individual students without taking them to the data. For example, AI can generate performance boards, gather students' progress, and highlight areas to be improved. Teachers can use these insights for fine teaching and provide additional resources or personal assistance to students who need additional assistance (Kapoor and Kulshrestha 2020, 524–541).
- **The Role of AI in Creating Customized Learning Paths**
  - AI-managed platforms allow the creation of a personal learning path based on the current level of student skills. Unlike traditional education systems, which follow a rigid, linear progression, AI-enabled platforms constantly adjust content and assessments to match a student's learning pace. For example, language-learning platforms like Duolingo use AI to analyze student progress and adapt lessons accordingly (Majid and Jafri 2021, 417–433). This ensures that students continue to learn material that is appropriately challenging while avoiding content that is too simple or too advanced.
  - By constantly adapting the learning experience, AI keeps students in their zone of proximal development (ZPD), the zone where learning is most effective because the task exceeds their current abilities but can still be accomplished with instruction. This improves both the learning experience and knowledge retention (Singh and Chatterji 2020, 214–247).
- **Artificial Intelligence Adaptive Feedback and Instant Evaluation**
  - Another important contribution of AI to personalized learning is real-time assessment and adaptive feedback. Instead of waiting for periodic teacher evaluations, AI systems can provide immediate feedback on assignments, tests, or interactive tasks. This instant feedback helps students understand their mistakes in real time, correct them, and improve their understanding of key concepts (Garcia and Lee 2021, 567–582). Instant feedback is especially useful in STEM subjects, where learning is often based on foundational knowledge that needs to be reinforced before moving on to more complex topics.

- AI-powered adaptive feedback also enables a more iterative learning process. If a student struggles with a certain topic, AI can provide additional resources or remedial exercises to prevent abandonment. This ensures that students continuously improve and all areas of weakness are treated immediately, reducing the risk of falling behind (Gomez and Wang 2022, 400–418).

11.3.1 CHALLENGES AND LIMITATIONS

Some users noted that while AI tools are useful, they can also be challenging to use. This indicates that the design and implementation of these tools may need further improvement to enhance communication and usability (Vincent and Roberts 2020, 144–162).

11.3.2 INCREASED ENGAGEMENT

Participants frequently mentioned that AI tools increased their interest in subjects. This suggests that when AI is effectively integrated into learning, it can boost students' motivation and effort (Majid and Jafri 2021, 417–433). The findings show that AI can positively influence educational outcomes and engagement, particularly with intelligent tutoring systems (ITSs). However, there are notable differences in how effective these tools are, and the challenges highlighted indicate a need for further refinement to meet diverse educational needs.

The strong link between engagement and improved learning emphasizes the importance of designing educational AI tools that actively engage users. Overall, the feedback themes not only highlight the potential benefits of AI in enhancing learning experiences but also point out the existing challenges and limitations that participants encounter (Singh and Chatterji 2020, 214–247).

11.4 CONCLUSION

The analysis of participant feedback highlights both the benefits and challenges of AI in education. While AI has the potential to significantly improve learning experiences and increase student engagement, there is a need for better design and implementation of these tools. Personalized learning through AI can help tailor educational experiences to individual students, improving their performance and motivation. For example, adaptive learning platforms adjust the difficulty of tasks based on a student's performance, while ITSs provide immediate, personalized feedback similar to a human tutor (Garcia and Lee 2021, 567–582).

AI's integration into education is transformative, bringing both challenges and opportunities. By addressing technical, ethical, and infrastructural issues, educators and institutions can harness AI to create personalized, engaging, and effective learning environments. While the road to successful AI implementation is complex, these proposed solutions provide a way forward, enabling a more adaptive and inclusive educational future (Gomez and Wang 2022, 400–418).

Overall, while the feedback shows that AI can enhance learning and engagement, there are still challenges to address. Future improvements should focus on making AI tools easier to use, more adaptable, and more accurate to fully realize their potential in education.

REFERENCES

Adams, R. J., and H. Brown. 2022. "Challenges of Implementing AI in Low-Resource Educational Settings." *Global Education Review* 29 (1): 88–104.

Anderson, J. M., and L. R. Thompson. 2021. "The Impact of Artificial Intelligence on Personalized Learning and Student Engagement." *Journal of Educational Technology* 45(2): 150–165.

Baker, S., and H. Greene. 2020. "Predictive Analytics in Education: Trends and Insights." *Educational Data Science* 3 (1): 34–49.

Bennett, S., and D. Marshall. 2021. "The Role of AI in Mitigating the Digital Divide in Education." *Journal of Educational Policy* 36 (2): 237–254.

Carson, T., and A. Jenkins. 2020. "Artificial Intelligence and the Future of Education Systems." *Journal of Innovation in Education* 8 (3): 175–191.

Chen, M., and J. Wang. 2019. "Virtual Reality in Education: A Tool for Learning in the Experience Age." *International Journal of Information and Educational Technology* 9 (8): 545–550.

Darrin, C., and M. Smith. 2021. "Augmented Reality in Education: A New Technology for Teaching and Learning." *New Horizons in Education* 63 (1): 22–37.

Davis, L. E., and N. Patel. 2019. "AI-Driven Personalized Learning Paths and Their Impact on High School Students' Academic Performance." *Educational Technology Research and Development* 67 (3): 749–771.

Diaz, V., and M. Clark. 2022. "Ethical Considerations in the Use of AI for Education: A Review of Challenges." *AI & Ethics* 4 (3): 223–237.

Edwards, A., and P. Roy. 2023. "Ethical Implications of AI in Education: A Critical Review." *Ethics and Information Technology* 25 (2): 123–139.

Fisher, M., and S. T. Green. 2021. "Virtual Reality in the Classroom: Assessing the Impact on Student Cognitive and Affective Outcomes." *IR in Education Journal* 4 (1): 60–75.

Garcia, E., and R. Lee. 2021. "Automated Grading Systems and Feedback: A Study of Effectiveness and Student Satisfaction." *Assessment & Evaluation in Higher Education* 40 (4): 567–582.

Gomez, E., and Y. Wang. 2022. "Automated Teacher Systems: How AI Is Changing the Landscape of Student Assessment." *Assessment in Education: Principles, Policy & Practice* 29 (4): 400–418.

Huang, X., and M. Li. 2020. "The Impact of Intelligent Tutoring Systems on Student Engagement and Learning Outcomes." *Journal of Artificial Intelligence Learning Environments* 2 (3): 528–539.

Inam, A., and B. Khan. 2023. "Analyzing the Digital Learning Divide: Social Inequalities and Structural Barriers to Accessing Information Communication Technology in Classroom Teaching in Intermediate (K to 12) Settings in Pakistan." *Journal of Positive School Psychology* 7 (5): 2458–2478.

Jensen, R., and L. Chen. 2021. "Practical Predictive Models for Identifying Higher Education Students at Risk of Dropping Out." *Journal of Educational Data Mining* 12 (1): 1–20.

Kapoor, A., and I. Kulshrestha. 2020. "Adaptive Learning Platforms in Higher Education: Enhancing Student Engagement and Performance." *Journal of Learning Media* 8 (5): 524–541.

Kumar, A., and P. Sharma. 2020. "Overcoming the Digital Divide with AI-Driven Educational Platforms." *Education and Information Technologies* 25 (6): 4071–4095.

Lahiri, S., and N. Bose. 2022. "Exploring the Benefits of AI-Based Language Learning Apps on ESL Students' Outcomes." *Language Learning & Technology* 26 (1): 134–150.

Majid, I., and K. Jafri. 2021. "AI in the Classroom: Personalized Learning through Machine Learning Algorithms." *Journal of Educational Research & Development* 2 (3): 417–433.

Patel, R., and M. Smith. 2019. "Intelligent Tutoring Systems: Personalizing Instruction in Real Time." *Education AI Research* 3 (4): 41–60.

Prasad, K., and H. Saini. 2021. "Social and Ethical Considerations for AI Tutors in K-12 Education." *AI & Ethics* 4 (1): 55–58.

Shaikh, P., L. Graham, and A. A. Lashari. 2023. "A Perspective on Empowerment of Education through AI for Disadvantaged Teachers: Inclusive Education in Pakistan." *Journal of Positive School Psychology* 7 (5): 56–66.

Sharma, P., and L. Graham. 2022. "Understanding the Role of AI in Personalized Education: A Perspective on Policy and Practice." *Educational Policy* 36 (3): 570–590.

Shrawankar, Urmila, V. M. Thakare. 2010, 15–17 December. "Speech User Interface for Computer Based Education System." ICSIP2010, Chennai, India, Scopus Indexed.

Singh, G., and M. Chatterji. 2020. "AI in Education: A Systematic Literature Review of Trends and Challenges." *International Journal of Educational Technology* 29 (3): 214–247.

Singh, P., and A. De Souza. 2023. "Exploring the Role of Augmented Reality in Enhancing Interactive Learning Experiences in the Classroom." *Innovative Teaching* 3 (4): 210–225.

Sinha, L., and M. Bose. 2022. "AI in Educational Technology: Review and Future Directions." *Educational Technology Research & Development* 47 (6): 735–758.

Solomon, A., and H. Naik. 2020. "Artificial Intelligence in Education: Bridging the Skills Gap." *Fratern* 122: 170–178.

Thakur, L., and E. Hamilton. 2022. "Machine Learning in Education Settings: Opportunities and Threats to Student Learning." *Journal of Applied Educational Research* 10 (1): 150–167.

Ullman, B., and T. King. 2021. "Adaptive Study Models and Student Support Systems: A Road Map for the Future of Learning with AI." *Educational Research: Theory & Practice* 23 (1): 140–155.

Vincent, J., and N. Roberts. 2020. "Ethical Implications of Using Artificial Intelligence in Schools." *Review of Research in Education* 47 (3): 144–162.

Wazalwar, Sampada, Urmnila Shrawankar. 2020, September. "Distributed Education System for Deaf & Dumb Children and Educator: A Today's Need." IIENC2020: Integrated Intelligence Enable Networks and Computing, Gopeshwar, UK, India, https://doi.org/10.1007/978-981-33-6307-6_35.

Wilkinson, D., and S. Crossley. 2022. "Leveraging Artificial Intelligence for Accessibility in Higher Education." *Special Needs Education* 17 (6): 419–430.

Xu, D., and C. Nguyen. 2023. "Investigating the Impact of AI on the Flipped Classroom Model: A Case Study in Higher Education." *Computers in Education* 14 (3): 1036–1028.

Yang, H., and S. Park. 2021. "A Review of AI in Higher Education Learning: A Review and Future Directions." *Innovative Learning Technologies* 3 (2): 112–127.

Young, J., and N. Sullivan. 2019. "Integrating AI into Online Learning: Potentials and Limitations." *Online Education Journal* 5 (1): 95–110.

Zhang, M., and G. Maguire. 2021. "AI Tutors in the Education Sector: Automatic Question Generation and Student Feedback." *Educational AI Journal* 9 (1): 91–105.

Zhao, Y., and H. Lin. 2020. "From Data to Decisions: The Role of Analytics in Educational Leadership." *Educational Administration Quarterly* 59 (1): 45–73.

12 Technological Uses of AI and ML for Helping Elderly and Special Needs People

12.1 INTRODUCTION

The use of artificial intelligence (AI) and machine learning (ML) is revolutionizing healthcare by creating innovative solutions that assist the elderly and individuals with special needs. As populations age and the number of people with disabilities increases, technology offers valuable tools to ensure independence, improved health outcomes, and enhanced quality of life. This chapter explores the many ways AI and ML are transforming care for these individuals by enabling predictive analytics, personalized healthcare, and assistive technologies.

With the integration of AI and ML, assistive technologies are becoming more intelligent, offering customized support that adapts to the needs of users. These systems have the potential to significantly reduce the burden on caregivers and medical professionals by providing automated assistance for tasks ranging from monitoring vital signs to improving mobility and even offering emotional companionship (Simon and Aliferis, 2024).

AI is one of the emerging trends in today's technological landscape. AI has given huge contributions to industries and medical healthcare systems, but there is another important area, that is, for a revolution and qualitative changes from the introduction of AI: it is the improvement of the lives of people with physical disabilities and elderly people with needs.

Despite the fact that the life of people with disabilities has always been a little more difficult and not a normal life in the context of understanding the specifics of each individual, AI provides a sure shot guarantee of new opportunities for these people by providing solutions that can help them perform everyday tasks with more ease and independently. The contribution of AI in the life of the elderly and specially visualized, physically impaired, and needy people will be of great support to them, and this will make their lives easy, swift, and comfortable.

Our assignment has explored various technological uses of AI and ML that are designed to assist the elderly and needy people with special needs. It highlights the solutions to the problems faced by them.

DOI: 10.1201/9781003532170-12

12.2   AI AND ML OVERVIEW

- AI encompasses a broad field that includes creating machines capable of performing tasks that require human intelligence, such as recognizing speech, making decisions, and solving complex problems. AI is employed in natural language processing (NLP), computer vision, and robotics (Simon and Aliferis, 2024).
- ML is a subset of AI focused on the ability of machines to learn from data without being explicitly programmed. ML is used to develop models that can predict outcomes and improve assistive technologies by learning user preferences and behaviors (Rus et al., 2024).
- In healthcare, AI and ML help in predicting diseases, automating patient monitoring, and offering decision support to caregivers (Chauhan et al., 2023). These technologies are increasingly being embedded in smart homes, wearable devices, and robotics to assist elderly and special needs individuals (Frauendorf and de Souza, 2023).

12.3   ASSISTIVE TECHNOLOGIES FOR THE ELDERLY

The elderly population faces numerous challenges related to mobility, cognitive decline, and social isolation. AI and ML have enabled the creation of assistive devices that help in managing these issues effectively.

- **Wearable Devices:** AI-driven wearables like smartwatches and health monitors track essential health metrics such as heart rate, blood pressure, and oxygen levels. These devices often come equipped with fall detection algorithms that can send alerts to caregivers or emergency services when necessary.
  - Example: Apple Watch and Fitbit use AI to monitor users' health data and send real-time alerts in case of irregularities.
- **Smart Homes:** AI is transforming homes into smart environments where elderly individuals can live independently. Voice-controlled assistants like Amazon Alexa and Google Home help control appliances, set reminders for medications, and even order groceries.
  - **Automated Lighting:** Smart lighting systems adjust based on movement and time, providing safety during the night.
  - **Voice Commands:** AI-powered voice assistants allow the elderly to control devices and access information without manual intervention.
- **Robotics:** Robots designed for elderly care are becoming more advanced with AI integration. Robots like Honda's ASIMO assist with daily tasks such as mobility, medication reminders, and even companionship (Rincon and Marco-Detchart, 2024).
  - **Emotional Support Robots:** Robots like PARO, a robotic seal, provide comfort to elderly individuals suffering from dementia by responding to touch and voice.

12.4 SUPPORTING INDIVIDUALS WITH SPECIAL NEEDS

People with physical, sensory, or cognitive impairments face unique challenges that AI and ML are helping mitigate. These technologies offer ways to improve communication, mobility, and learning (Park et al., 2025).

- **Speech Recognition:** For individuals with speech impairments, AI-powered speech recognition systems can interpret limited vocal patterns and convert them into understandable text or speech. Tools like Google's Speech-to-Text API are helping people with speech disabilities communicate more effectively.
  - o Example: AI-based augmentative and alternative communication (AAC) devices assist individuals with conditions such as autism or cerebral palsy.
    - – **Computer Vision for the Visually Impaired:** AI enables visually impaired individuals to navigate their environment more easily. Applications like Seeing AI by Microsoft use ML to describe objects and people, and even read text aloud in real time.
  - o Example: OrCam MyEye is a wearable AI device that helps visually impaired users read text, recognize faces, and identify objects using real-time image processing (Mansoor et al., 2022).
    - – **AI in Prosthetics:** AI-driven prosthetics use ML algorithms to adapt to the user's specific movement patterns, offering a more natural range of motion. These prosthetics improve dexterity and mobility for individuals with limb loss.
  - o Example: Open Bionics creates AI-powered prosthetics that adjust to muscle signals, giving users greater control over their artificial limbs (Gill et al., 2025).

12.5 PERSONALIZED HEALTHCARE FOR THE ELDERLY

AI and ML are playing a significant role in creating personalized healthcare plans tailored to the individual needs of elderly patients. These technologies analyze vast amounts of data to predict health risks, recommend treatments, and monitor progress.

- **Predictive Analytics:** By analyzing historical health data, AI models can predict the likelihood of health issues such as Alzheimer's disease, heart disease, or stroke. This allows for earlier interventions and more effective care management.
  - Example: ML models analyze genomic data to determine risks for genetic disorders in elderly patients, enabling personalized treatments.
- **Telemedicine:** AI-powered telemedicine platforms provide elderly patients with remote access to healthcare professionals. These systems can also analyze medical images and patient data to offer real-time diagnostic support.
  - Example: Platforms like Babylon Health use AI to assist doctors in diagnosing conditions through video consultations, reducing the need for in-person visits.

12.6 COGNITIVE SUPPORT SYSTEMS

As elderly individuals age, cognitive functions such as memory, attention, and problem-solving often decline. AI and ML are being used to develop systems that help slow cognitive deterioration and maintain mental agility.

- **Memory Enhancement Apps:** AI-based applications offer memory training exercises that are personalized to the user's abilities. These apps help in strengthening cognitive functions and slowing the onset of memory-related diseases like dementia.
  - Example: Apps like Lumosity use AI to create personalized training programs that adapt based on the user's performance.
- **Virtual Companions:** AI-powered chatbots and virtual assistants provide emotional support by engaging in conversations with elderly users. These systems help reduce social isolation and promote mental well-being.
  - Example: ElliQ is a virtual companion designed for the elderly that encourages interaction and helps keep them mentally active.

12.7 CHALLENGES IN AI AND ML ADOPTION FOR ELDERLY AND INDIVIDUALS WITH SPECIAL NEEDS

Despite the numerous advantages, there are several challenges in adopting AI and ML for assisting the elderly and individuals with special needs.

- **Ethical Concerns:** Privacy is a significant issue, especially when it comes to handling sensitive healthcare data. AI systems must be designed to protect user data and respect privacy while providing accurate and reliable support.
- **Affordability:** Advanced AI-driven assistive technologies can be expensive, limiting access to those who cannot afford them. There is a need for more affordable solutions that can be scaled for broader use.
- **Technological Literacy:** Many elderly individuals have difficulty using modern technologies. There is a need for user-friendly interfaces and proper education on how to use AI-based systems effectively.

12.8 CASE STUDIES

Several companies and research institutions have developed AI-driven solutions to assist the elderly and individuals with special needs. These case studies demonstrate how technology is improving lives.

- **OrCam MyEye:** This AI-powered device helps the visually impaired by reading texts aloud, recognizing faces, and identifying objects. The device has been successfully used by thousands of individuals to regain a sense of independence.
- **ElliQ:** Designed to help elderly individuals combat loneliness, Elliq uses AI to engage in conversations, remind users of daily tasks, and connect them with family members.

Following are the case studies that we will discuss for the aforementioned individuals.

1. Sign language recognition and translation (Microsoft AI)
2. AI/ML system for visually impaired people
3. AI-based fall detection systems for the safety of the elders
4. AI/ML in wheelchair navigation and control

CASE STUDY 1   SIGN LANGUAGE RECOGNITION AND TRANSLATION (MICROSOFT AI)

Deaf and mute individuals more often than not find it difficult to convey themselves to non-American Sign Language (ASL) speakers. Under Microsoft's "AI for Good" initiative, an advanced AI system was introduced to identify (ASL through the use of computer vision (Srivastava et al., 2024).

The system uses ML models, particularly convolutional neural networks (CNNs), along with cameras to capture and interpret hand and body movements. These movements are then translated into text or speech in real time, facilitating smoother communication, especially in places like hospitals, customer service centers, and workspaces.

This aims to reduce the problems faced in a conversation with deaf and mute people.

Problems Faced by Sign Language Users:

Limited Communication with Non-Signers:

- Difficulty communicating with individuals who do not know sign language, leading to misunderstandings and exclusion (Sharma et al., 2024).

Lack of Accessibility in Public Spaces:

- Many public services, such as hospitals, government offices, and transportation systems, lack adequate provisions for sign language interpretation (Wazalwar and Shrawankar, 2017).

Social Isolation:

- Difficulty engaging in casual or spontaneous conversations with non-signers can lead to feelings of social isolation.

Technological Limitations:

- Many communication technologies (like voice-based systems) do not accommodate sign language users effectively (Harshini et al., 2024).

Working:

1. Detection of Gestures Using Computer Vision:
   - The AI leverages computer vision methods to capture movements of the hands and body using a camera, such as those found on smartphones or webcams.
   - Pre-trained deep learning models, mainly CNNs, are utilized to detect specific gestures in the video stream. These models have been trained on extensive datasets featuring diverse sign language gestures.
2. Extracting Features:
   - The system processes the video stream on a per-frame basis. It extracts critical data points such as hand shapes, orientations, movements, and facial expressions, which are crucial in sign languages like ASL.
   - Microsoft employs skeleton tracking (a technology similar to what was used in Kinect) to capture body and hand movements in 3D space for higher accuracy.
3. Recognizing Gestures:
   - Each video frame is analyzed by a gesture recognition algorithm, which may be a CNN or a recurrent neural network (RNN), to identify dynamic gestures.
   - These models are trained on sign language datasets and can detect both single gestures and sequences of signs that combine to form sentences.
4. Converting to Text or Speech:
   - After detecting a gesture, the system maps it to the corresponding text (either a word or a sentence) in the spoken language. For more dynamic sign languages, an NLP module converts the sequence of signs into grammatically correct sentences (Shrawankar and Thakare, 2013).
   - A text-to-speech engine then translates these recognized signs into spoken language, facilitating real-time communication.
5. Two-Way Communication:
   - Microsoft's AI system is equipped with speech-to-text capabilities, enabling non-sign language users to speak, with their words translated into animated sign language for deaf or mute individuals. This is achieved by integrating automatic speech recognition (ASR) with an avatar-based system that animates sign language.

How It Is Helping People:

- Microsoft's AI promotes smooth conversations between sign language users and non-sign language users in real time, making it particularly useful in situations where interpreters are unavailable.

- In workplaces, the system helps deaf or mute employees engage in meetings, presentations, and team activities, providing them with an equal opportunity to participate.
- For students with hearing impairments, it offers a way to better inter-act with teachers and classmates who don't know sign language. Additionally, it can serve as a tool for people who wish to learn sign language.
- In healthcare, the system allows patients who are deaf or mute to communicate directly with medical professionals, improving care without requiring a live interpreter.
- In everyday scenarios like shopping, transport, or banking, this AI-driven solution can break down communication barriers for deaf and mute communities.

Limitations:

- There are hundreds of sign languages globally (e.g., ASL, BSL, and Indian Sign Language). While Microsoft's system supports some, like ASL, many are not yet fully integrated.
- Differences in regional dialects and variations in signs can result in recognition inaccuracies.
- Sign languages have unique grammatical structures that differ from spoken languages. The AI may struggle to preserve context and nuances in translations, affecting grammatical accuracy.
- Fingerspelling, where each letter is signed individually, is particularly challenging for the AI, especially when users sign quickly.
- To develop highly accurate models, substantial datasets are required for each sign language. However, acquiring these datasets is diffi-cult, particularly for regional sign languages, limiting the system's scalability.
- Many datasets lack natural conversational flow, including transitions between signs and region-specific colloquial gestures.
- People vary in their signing style due to factors such as speed, per-sonal preference, or physical limitations (e.g., arthritis). The AI some-times fails to adapt to these personal differences, lowering translation quality.

CASE STUDY 2   AI/ML SYSTEM FOR
VISUALLY IMPAIRED PEOPLE

This report examines the diverse challenges encountered by visually impaired individuals in areas such as accessibility, employment, education, and social interactions. It highlights the role of AI in supporting those with visual impairments. The report briefly outlines the criteria for vision testing, discusses how researchers utilize deep learning models for diagnosing and classifying eye diseases, and explores the creation of AI-driven wearable devices designed to assist people with visual disabilities (Boussihmed et al., 2024).

PROBLEMS FACED BY VISUALLY IMPAIRED INDIVIDUALS:

- **Mobility Challenges:**
  - Difficulty recognizing oncoming traffic and changes in traffic signals.
  - Impaired ability to navigate their surroundings, especially in unfamiliar environments (Kim, 2024).
- **Access to Visual Information:**
  - Difficulty accessing visually presented information, which can hinder day-to-day activities and learning.
- **Educational Challenges:**
  - Significant effort required to learn Braille and develop reading and writing skills.
  - Limited access to educational materials in accessible formats.
- **Misconceptions:**
  - A common misconception is that all visually impaired individuals are completely blind, but rather it's a spectrum (Bhatlawande et al., 2023).

AI SOLUTIONS:

1. **Navigation Assistance:** AI-powered applications like Aira and Be My Eyes provide real-time visual assistance through video calls, connecting users with sighted volunteers or professionals. GPS-based systems further enhance navigation by offering verbal directions and identifying obstacles in unfamiliar environments (Safiya and Pandian, 2024).
2. **Object Recognition:** ML models are employed in apps such as Seeing AI and Microsoft's Soundscape to recognize and describe objects, text, and scenes. This technology enables users to better understand and interact with their surroundings.
3. **Text Recognition:** Optical character recognition (OCR) technologies, exemplified by apps like KNFB Reader, allow visually impaired individuals to access printed materials. These apps convert text into speech and can recognize different fonts and handwriting, broadening access to written content.
4. **Wearable Devices:** Smart glasses and other wearable technologies, such as OrCam MyEye, provide real-time audio feedback to assist visually impaired users. These devices can recognize faces, read text, and identify products, enhancing user engagement with their environment.

5. **Social Interaction and Communication:** AI-driven platforms, including virtual assistants, facilitate communication for visually impaired individuals by providing information and reminders through voice commands.

WORKING OF SMART GLASSES FOR VISUALLY IMPAIRED INDIVIDUALS

Smart glasses for visually impaired users leverage various technologies to enhance daily living and navigation. Here's an overview of their functionality:

1. **Camera and Sensors:** Equipped with a camera and additional sensors, the glasses capture live video of the surroundings.
2. **Real-Time Video Streaming:** The video is streamed to a remote operator or AI system for analysis.
3. **Object and Scene Recognition:** Using computer vision, the system identifies objects, people, and text, providing audio feedback.
4. **Audio Feedback:** Visual information is converted into auditory cues through speakers or earbuds.
5. **Navigation Assistance:** Integrated GPS provides verbal directions and alerts users to nearby obstacles.
6. **User Interaction:** Users can interact via voice commands or buttons for specific information or assistance.
7. **Connectivity with Other Devices:** Many smart glasses can connect to smartphones or other devices to enhance their functionality, allowing users to access additional apps and services, such as calls or voice assistants, for more independence in daily tasks.

LIMITATIONS:

- **Limited Field of View and Object Detection:** Smart glasses often have a restricted field of view, limiting their ability to detect objects outside of their focus range.
- **Performance in Challenging Lighting Conditions:** Smart glasses rely heavily on cameras and sensors to detect and interpret objects or text. In low light or very bright environments, their accuracy can be compromised.
- **Reliance on Stable Internet Connectivity:** Many smart glasses that use cloud-based AI systems for image recognition, navigation, or text reading require stable Internet connectivity to process data and provide real-time feedback.
- **Incomplete Scene Understanding:** Smart glasses generally excel at identifying individual objects but struggle with providing a holistic understanding of complex scenes. For instance, while the glasses may

recognize a table, they might not communicate its exact position or the surrounding obstacles.

- **Battery Life and Device Weight:** Smart glasses, especially those that provide real-time visual and audio feedback, consume significant power. Many models have a limited battery life, which can restrict their usage throughout the day.

CASE STUDY 3   AI-BASED FALL DETECTION SYSTEMS FOR THE SAFETY OF THE ELDERS

Falls among the elderly pose serious health issues, leading to worst injury and treatment costs. Early detection and intervention of such a fall can effectively mitigate this fall risk. The purpose of this case study is to assess the efficacy of AI- and ML-based fall detection systems in improving the safety and quality of life for elderly people. According to the World Health Organization (WHO), falls are estimated to be the second leading cause of accidental or unintentional injury deaths worldwide (Periša et al., 2022).

PROBLEMS FACED BY ELDERLY INDIVIDUALS DUE TO FALL:

- Physical Injuries: Falls produce different fractures, head injuries, internal soft tissue damages, and internal bleeding.
- Psychological Effects: They may lose confidence, become isolated and withdrawn, anxious, and even experience depression due to the fear of falling again.
- Long-Term Health Issues: Falls often lead to reduced mobility, increased dependency, and chronic pain.

AI/ML INNOVATIVE SOLUTIONS:

1. **Wearable Devices for Fall Detection:**
    Wearable devices, equipped with sensors like accelerometers and gyroscopes, worn by aged people can track the time-varying movement of the elderly in real time. Algorithms based on ML process their sensor data and detect a fall in the individuals. Previous case studies have stated that the usage of wearable devices can help achieve high accuracy in fall detection.
2. **Smart Flooring Systems:**
    A smart flooring system integrates sensors and IoT technologies to detect falls. This can be installed in common areas of an assisted living facility or at home. It is a non-intrusive method for detecting falls. The data collected by the sensors is analyzed by ML algorithms to recognize the fall events and alert caregivers.

BENEFITS:

- **Timely Alerts:** Both systems offer timely alerts to caregivers, which enhances the fall response time.
- **High Accuracy:** Advanced use of ML algorithms ensures high accuracy in fall detection.
- **Improved Safety:** These systems augment the safety and quality of the life of geriatrics by minimizing extreme injuries from falls.

CHALLENGES/LIMITATIONS:

- **Cost:** The upfront cost of these systems is quite high.
- **Maintenance:** Continuous checking requires regular maintenance and update for maximum performance.
- **Privacy:** Continuous monitoring raises the issue of privacy, which should, therefore, be addressed.

AI- and ML-based fall detection systems will place important advances in the safety and quality of elderly people's lives. High accuracy level, along with time alerts, would greatly minimize the possibility of severe injuries from falls.

CASE STUDY 4   AI/ML IN WHEELCHAIR NAVIGATION AND CONTROL

AI-powered wheelchair navigation represents a fusion of cutting-edge technology and human-centered design, focusing on improving the quality of life for individuals with mobility challenges. These wheelchairs use AI to assist users in navigating their environment autonomously, making independent mobility more accessible.

By combining sensors, cameras, and intuitive controls like voice commands or touch interfaces, these wheelchairs allow users to safely and confidently explore their surroundings.

PROBLEMS FACED BY HANDICAPPED INDIVIDUALS:

People with disabilities, particularly those with mobility challenges, which include elderly individuals in a wheelchair, disabled people, or people suffering from sedentary syndromes, face many difficulties in daily life, such as the following:

- **Limited Mobility:**
  - Moving around independently is difficult, especially in public spaces or rough terrain.

- **Accessibility Issues:**
  - Buildings, streets, and transportation systems are often not designed to be easily navigable for wheelchair users.
- **Dependence on Others:**
  - Many people with mobility issues rely on family members or caregivers to assist them with daily tasks like moving around or accessing specific locations.
- **Navigational Challenges:**
  - For those who have difficulty with sight or hearing in addition to mobility issues, navigating through unfamiliar or busy environments can be overwhelming.
- **Physical Strain:**
  - Manually operating traditional wheelchairs can be exhausting, especially over long distances or rough surfaces.

HOW IT HELPS HANDICAPPED AND ELDERLY PEOPLE

- **Freedom to Move:** These smart wheelchairs can drive themselves, allowing users to go where they want without needing help from others. This means more independence and the chance to explore new places.
- **Safety First:** With special sensors, these wheelchairs can see obstacles in their path, like furniture or bumps in the ground. They can steer around these obstacles, helping keep users safe from accidents.
- **Learning to Help:** The more a user interacts with the wheelchair, the better it understands their preferences. It can learn which routes they like best or how fast they prefer to go, making every journey smoother.
- **Alerting Users:** These smart systems can warn users about dangers, like steps or curbs, helping them navigate tricky spots safely.
- **Connecting to Home:** Some wheelchairs can connect to smart home devices, allowing users to control lights, sdoors, and other things in their homes right from their wheelchair.

BENEFITS:

- **Better Mobility:** AI-powered wheelchairs can help people with limited physical abilities move around more easily by improving navigation and control.
- **Improved Safety:** These systems can detect obstacles and avoid collisions, reducing the risk of accidents and keeping users safer.
- **Cost-Effective in the Long Run:** AI wheelchairs may eventually be cheaper because they allow users to control the chair more independently, reducing the need for help from caregivers.
- **Personalized:** The wheelchair's settings can be adjusted to meet each user's specific needs.
- **Increased Accessibility:** AI-powered wheelchairs can handle different terrains, giving users more freedom to move around in public spaces and improving their quality of life.

FUTURE PROSPECTS AND POTENTIAL

The future of AI and ML in assisting the elderly and special needs individuals is promising. Emerging technologies such as 5G, edge computing, and brain–computer interfaces (BCIs) will enable more sophisticated assistive devices.

- **AI-Powered Rehabilitation:** AI systems will continue to advance in assisting with physical therapy and rehabilitation. These systems will adapt to the patient's progress and create personalized recovery plans.
  - Example: AI-powered robotic exoskeletons are being developed to assist individuals with mobility impairments in walking and regaining strength.
- **Smart Clothing:** Integrating AI into wearable textiles will enable real-time monitoring of health parameters and provide continuous feedback to healthcare providers.
  - Example: AI-powered smart textiles can monitor heart rates, detect falls, and even track movements to alert caregivers in case of emergencies.

The future potential of AI/ML projects in assisting elderly and special needs people is highly promising. These technologies offer innovative solutions to improve independence, safety, and quality of life. As advancements continue, AI-powered tools like sign language translation systems, smart glasses, fall detection devices, and autonomous wheelchairs will likely become more accurate, accessible, and integrated into daily life.

However, challenges such as high costs, privacy concerns, and technical limitations need to be addressed. Continued research and development will be crucial to overcoming these hurdles, ensuring that these technologies can serve a broader audience effectively. With further improvements, AI and ML will revolutionize caregiving, healthcare, and mobility for individuals with disabilities and the elderly, fostering greater inclusion and autonomy.

12.9   CONCLUSION

AI and ML are transforming healthcare for the elderly and special needs populations by offering intelligent, automated, and personalized solutions. These technologies enable independence, improve health outcomes, and provide emotional support. Despite challenges related to privacy, cost, and technological literacy, the future of AI and ML in this field is bright. By continuing to innovate and address these barriers, AI will play an ever-increasing role in shaping the future of healthcare for vulnerable populations.

REFERENCES

Bhatlawande, Shripad, Neel Gokhale, Dewang V. Mehta, Parag Gaikwad, Swati Shilaskar, and Jyoti Madake. "Electronic Travel Aid for Crosswalk Detection for Visually Challenged People." In *Intelligent Systems and Applications: Select Proceedings of ICISA 2022*, pp. 249–259. Singapore: Springer Nature, 2023.

Boussihmed, Ahmed, Khalid El Makkaoui, Ibrahim Ouahbi, Yassine Maleh, and Abdelaziz Chetouani. "A TinyML Model for Sidewalk Obstacle Detection: Aiding the Blind and Visually Impaired People." *Multimedia Tools and Applications* (2024): 1–28.

Chauhan, Ritu, Abhiyush Satyam, Eiad Yafi, and Megat F. Zuhairi. "Predict the Elderly Fall Using IoT and AI Technology." In *International Conference on Cyber Security, Privacy in Communication Networks*, pp. 101–113. Singapore: Springer Nature, 2023.

Frauendorf, José Luiz, and Érika Almeida de Souza. *The Architectural and Technological Revolution of 5G*. Springer, 2023.

Gill, Sukhpal Singh, Muhammed Golec, Jianmin Hu, Minxian Xu, Junhui Du, Huaming Wu, Guneet Kaur Walia et al. "Edge AI: A Taxonomy, Systematic Review and Future Directions." *Cluster Computing* 28, no. 1 (2025): 1–53.

Harshini, P. J., Mohammed Atheequr Rahman, James Allen Raj, and P. Durgadevi. "Sign Language Recognition System for Seamless Human-AI Interaction." In *International Research Conference on Computing Technologies for Sustainable Development*, pp. 124–144. Cham, Switzerland: Springer Nature, 2024.

Kim, In-Ju. "Recent Advancements in Indoor Electronic Travel Aids for the Blind or Visually Impaired: A Comprehensive Review of Technologies and Implementations." *Universal Access in the Information Society* (2024): 1–21.

Mansoor, C. M. M., Sarat Kumar Chettri, and H. M. M. Naleer. "A Remote Health Monitoring System for the Elderly Based on Emerging Technologies." In *International Conference on Emerging Global Trends in Engineering and Technology*, pp. 513–524. Singapore: Springer Nature, 2022.

Park, Jong Wan, Chang Woo Ko, Diane Youngmi Lee, and Jae Chul Kim. "Prediction of Late-Onset Depression in the Elderly Korean Population Using Machine Learning Algorithms." *Scientific Reports* 15, no. 1 (2025): 1196.

Periša, Marko, Ivan Cvitić, Petra Zorić, and Ivan Grgurević. "Concept, Architecture, and Performance Testing of a Smart Home Environment for the Visually Impaired Persons." In *EAI International Conference on Management of Manufacturing Systems*, pp. 3–14. Cham: Springer International Publishing, 2022.

Rincon, J. A., and C. Marco-Detchart. "Robotic Precision Fitness: Accurate Pose Training for Elderly Rehabilitation." In *International Conference on Intelligent Data Engineering and Automated Learning*, pp. 410–419. Cham, Switzerland: Springer Nature, 2024.

Rus, Cosmin, Monica Leba, and Remus Sibisanu. "SOS-My Grandparents: Using the Concepts of IoT, AI and ML for the Detection of Falls in the Elderly." In *World Conference on Information Systems and Technologies*, pp. 164–173. Cham, Switzerland: Springer Nature, 2024.

Safiya, K. M., and R. Pandian. "A Real-Time Image Captioning Framework Using Computer Vision to Help the Visually Impaired." *Multimedia Tools and Applications* 83, no. 20 (2024): 59413–59438.

Sharma, Vaidehi, Abhay Kumar Gupta, Abhishek Sharma, and Sandeep Saini. "A Unified Approach for Continuous Sign Language Recognition and Translation." *International Journal of Data Science and Analytics* (2024): 1–15.

Shrawankar, Urmila, and Vilas Thakare. "A Hybrid Method for Automatic Speech Recognition Performance Improvement in Real World Noisy Environment." *Journal of Computer Science* 9, no. 1 (2013): 94.

Simon, G. J., and C. Aliferis, eds. *Artificial Intelligence and Machine Learning in Health Care and Medical Sciences: Best Practices and Pitfalls* [Internet]. Cham (CH): Springer, 2024. PMID: 39836790.

Srivastava, Sharvani, Sudhakar Singh, Pooja, and Shiv Prakash. "Continuous Sign Language Recognition System Using Deep Learning with MediaPipe Holistic." *Wireless Personal Communications* 137, no. 3 (2024): 1455–1468.

Wazalwar, Sampada S., and Urmila Shrawankar. "Interpretation of Sign Language into English Using NLP Techniques." *Journal of Information and Optimization Sciences* 38, no. 6 (2017): 895–910.

Index

281

For Product Safety Concerns and Information please contact our EU
representative GPSR@taylorandfrancis.com
Taylor & Francis Verlag GmbH, Kaufingerstraße 24, 80331 München, Germany

* 9 7 8 1 0 3 2 8 7 3 4 6 6 *